D0496999

Away From Home

Away From Home

Canadian Writers in
Exotic Places

KILDARE DOBBS

DENEAU

DENEAU PUBLISHERS & COMPANY LTD.
760 BATHURST STREET
TORONTO, ONTARIO
M5S 2R6

©Kildare Dobbs
This Selection

Typeset by Jay Tee Graphics
and
Printed and bound
in Canada

First Printing 1985
First Paper Edition 1988

Canadian Cataloguing in Publication Data
Dobbs, Kildare, 1923
Away from Home
Bibliography: p.
Includes index.
ISBN 0-88879-119-4 (cloth)
ISBN 0-88879-128-3 (paper)

1. Voyages and travels — Addresses, essays, lectures.
2. Canadian prose literature.

PS 8367.   T72A96 1985   C818' .08 C85-099369-5
PR9197. 7. A96 1985

*This book has been
published with the assistance
of the Canada Council and
The Ontario Arts Council
under their block grant
programs.*

No part of this book may be reproduced, stored in a retrieval
system or transmitted in any form or by any means,
electronic, mechanical, photocopying, recording, or
otherwise, except for purpose of review,
without permission of the publisher.

TO LUCINDA AND SARAH

Le monde entier est toujours là
Blaise Cendrars

CONTENTS

PREFACE

Travel-writing as a literary *genre* needs no defence. It is an ancient form which has produced a number of classics from Marco Polo's *Travels* to Wilfred Thesiger's *Arabian Sands*. In our own time even the debased kind that appears in travel brochures and newspapers may sometimes rise above itself. Authors of fiction have found it an alternative vehicle for imaginative writing, and social scientists a medium of popular communication.

An anthology, however, may need some words of explanation, if not apology. Aside from the editor's literary bias — a matter of nature and hence largely unconscious — there are principles of choice that should be avowed.

The present volume is a selection of travel-writing by English-speaking Canadians from the 1840s to the present day. Ideally, perhaps, it should be accompanied by a similar volume of French-Canadian work. But it seems to me that Canadians of both languages would find that kind of venture too close to official biculturalism to generate any fun. The second cardinal point is that the travels recorded here are all away from home, mostly in exotic places.

The selection aspires to inclusiveness, that is, it tries to give an idea of the range and variety of Canadian travel-writing and of Canadian travellers and writers. If the volume falls short in this aspect, readers are reminded that it is in many ways a pioneering work, a first attempt of its kind. For the Canadian travel-writing of the past there is no body of scholarly criticism or notice, hardly an acknowledgement of its existence. As for the present, there is a flood of material in newspapers and magazines which no conscious person could possibly read in its entirety. So that within the aspiration to inclusiveness the

1

editor has had to work to the maxim, "If you can't be just, be arbitrary."

In pioneering times Canadians were too busy exploring our own vast territory to think much about travel beyond our borders. Later they began to look outward. The 19th century bard Alexander Gillis tells us, "I was to the United States twice. I do not say so for the sake of a boast." By the 1890s, as we learn from Sara Jeannette Duncan, travel stories were read aloud in women's sewing circles.

Sea-going Maritimers were the first in our tradition to range freely about the world. That is why the anthology begins with a Halifax man, Captain Sir Edward Belcher R.N. as he takes part in hydrographic surveys of Pacific islands. His report is followed by an excerpt from Sir George Simpson's epic dash round the world overland as he crosses Siberia. The Little Emperor of the Hudson's Bay Company's immense territories may well have been the greatest land traveller in history.

After the hearts of oak and the fur traders come soldiers, gentlewomen, diplomats, archaeologists, missionaries, professional writers and so on down to the present age of hippy drifters and mass tourism with its consumer-oriented journalism. Many, though not all types of travellers, are represented here. If the soldiers and missionaries are absent it is because of the editor's low threshold of boredom.

The object of travel-writing has always been to amuse and entertain while it instructs. As a general rule it is hard to take seriously any book or essay that lacks wit or jokes.

Most of the selections are self-contained articles or passages from travel books. A few passages of fiction have been included where they are plainly based on factual experience and express the author's point of view. The Lowry excerpt is an example. With a single exception, immigrant authors are not represented by pieces about their original homelands. Alienation is an essential part of the experience of travelling. It is the vision of estrangement that creates the world afresh. Bharati Mukherjee in Calcutta — the exception — is in her first home, yet she is doubly alienated, from India and the West.

Some readers may be disappointed by omissions, a favourite writer or cherished essay left out. It is true that some good writers have been omitted. In justice, the book should be judged by what it includes, not by what it rejects.

In general, even as tourists, Canadians are lively and adventurous travellers. (One does not count the snowbirds who have made Florida an extraterritorial province of Canada.) This anthology seeks to show that, as travel-writers, Canadians can also exemplify the virtues of style, insight and originality.

It may also help to show that a national literature need not be restricted to navel-gazing and the elusive search for identity. For it is a commonplace that every voyage is an exploration and every journey a discovery of the true self. Perhaps this is as true of imaginary travels, of vicarious experience, as it is of the real thing.

Fiji
by Sir Edward Belcher

Finding that the king was afraid to visit the ship, in consequence of my failure in visiting the town of Rewa, I determined on sacrificing a few hours and paying him a visit; as, until he was propitiated, there was no chance of obtaining the necessary supplies of hogs and vegetables. I therefore started, taking with me Lieut. Monypenny.

The distance to the town of Rewa from the anchorage is about six miles, and two to the mouth of the river, studded with unpleasant sand banks, over which there is about three feet at low water, and on which the capricious rollers at times suddenly bestow a ducking. After entering the river, the channel at low water becomes tortuous, and the drain generally bears out, although the main-banks are about four hundred yards asunder. The canoes are generally forced up by poles, similar to punting on the Thames.

The town of Rewa is situated about half a mile from the bank of the river, on the right bank of a creek, which shoots off abruptly from the main stream, the width of the creek at that point not exceeding one hundred yards.

The houses, which overlook the creek in some places, are firmly constructed with posts, which do not rise more than seven feet from the earth. On these arise very lofty pitched roofs, varying from twenty-five to thirty feet in height, and in some instances thatched to the thickness of two feet. The doors are small, excepting in the state-house, and resemble windows or ports; those in elevated mounds with ditches remind one strongly of block-houses. In the state-house the resemblance is rendered still closer by the presence of two ship guns, as if prepared for war; certainly not very appropriate chamber companions.

The establishment of the king is situated upon a bend of the creek, the houses of his queens occupying the water-side, and his own being in an open area, in which also is the house of his principal queen, the tomb of his father and brothers, and the "fighting Bourri," or temple. This latter is a small building about twelve feet square, erected upon a mound of about ten feet elevation. The thatched roof is very steep, probably thirty feet, across the summit of which is a pole projecting about three feet at each end, studded with brilliant white porcellanic shells. (Ovula ovum.)

Their canoes are similar to most of those belonging to the low islands, very long and narrow, furnished with outriggers, and a convenient house on a platform.

The house of the king (or more properly chief of Rewa, he being subordinate to the king at Obalau) is one of the most filthy in the town. Its dimensions are about sixty feet in length by thirty wide. Two-thirds of it is well clothed with mats and kept clean; the remainder may be considered the cooking and eating hall, &c.

Three immense iron caldrons, probably intended for a whale-ship, together with other earthen vessels for boiling, occupy the cooking square. The king and favourite queen were seated upon a range of mats immediately contiguous to the fire, and on entering invited us to do the same. Shortly after, a roasted hog and vegetables were introduced, and we were invited to partake. As they had neither knives, forks, nor plates, I followed their motions, rather than the chiefs should take fresh offence, and our journey prove fruitless.

The carving of this hog was most adroitly performed by the "carver general," a professor, with a piece of slit bamboo, which by-the-bye was first cut into shape with a steel knife; therefore I suspect etiquette demands that the bamboo should be preferred. The king's barber, taster &c (or I suppose "the barber royal" to be his proper style), selects the king's portion, peels his taro, or yarn, and presents it, without any humiliating forms, in a clean leaf. This person is never permitted, under penalty of instant death, to touch his own food with his hands; and he may be seen tearing his meat like a dog from the floor with his teeth, whilst it is there held by a stick. Before the king commences eating, all present clap their hands about four times. If he drinks, finishes, or sneezes, the same is repeated. The principal queen and about ten other queens were present.

As I found that friendship was established, and the king signified his intention to visit the ship on the following Monday, I gladly took my leave.

As some mischievous persons had been busy inducing the chiefs to withhold supplies to the ship, to suit their own purposes, I visited the brother of the king, Garingaria, reported to be in the list of malcontents, and most active in the pig embargo. His house I found very superior to that of the king; very large, neat, and well arranged, but nevertheless that of a perfect savage. This Garingaria is reported as the most determined cannibal of this group. He has his friends as well as enemies, and although savage, is less deceitful than those around him. I would much rather be his prisoner than that of the king or any of his immediate retinue. He distinctly denied any participation in the plot and I instantly saw by his countenance that he spoke the truth. He immediately sent down a present of three pigs.

The king of Rewa is a very strong-built, muscular man, standing about six feet two inches; Phillips, or Thokanauto, five feet ten inches; Garingaria probably six feet four inches. The prisoner taken away in the Peacock, said to be a very fine man, we did not see. The present king, who is considered a very weak-minded man, and despised by his brothers, succeeded his father, who, according to custom, was murdered to make room for him. It is not improbable that his death will shortly enable one of the remaining brothers to succeed him. Indeed, Phillips said in his presence, "I shall be king in four years." I found there were plenty of spies to interpret falsely the few English sentences which escaped me.

As the moment approached for the king's visit, his courage failed, and as it suited my purpose to re-visit Rewa, I went up to tell him my opinion. I found myself so perplexed by the falsehoods and misrepresentations, by which he had been misled, that I left him in disgust, but not without adopting secure measures for our supplies.

On the day following, yams in profusion arrived, but few pigs; and having purchased sufficient for our crew, I declined further barter until the arrival of more pigs.

On the 13th, the *Starling* returned, bringing three pintles, belonging to the *Peacock*, Captain Wilkes, of the *Vincennes*, having in the handsomest manner despatched one of his boats to that vessel, thinking her size better adapted; at the same time offering those of the *Vincennes*, should they not answer. At this critical moment, our carpenter and armourer became ill. Fortunately, an engineer by trade happened to call upon me for assistance to recover property alleged to be piratically taken from him, and as he would be compelled to await the arrival of the parties, he consented to give his assistance in fitting and reducing the metal work, which he executed admirably; and by the evening of the 15th, we were in a condition to complete our voyage.

On the evening of the 15th, the tender of the *Vincennes* hove in sight, and Captain Wilkes himself very shortly came on board. Under any circumstances this was a satisfaction I had long hoped for, but in these remote regions, and entirely shut out from civilized beings, it became, independent of the feelings due to his promptitude in relieving our difficulties, a matter of sincere satisfaction. Unfortunately I had only that morning despatched the *Starling* to fix the position of Banga, one of the new islands not placed on the chart, and had promised to join him on Monday. Having, however, been nearly eighteen hours together, we were enabled to talk over matters of much interest to both expeditions, and as they would go over part of our ground, their observations made in the same positions would become doubly interesting.

Our observatory and tents being embarked, and rudder in order, after dinner we parted; and by the aid of the moon the *Sulphur* was again moving through the waters with her accustomed freedom.

The United States Expedition, under the command of Commodore Wilkes, had very recently returned from the Antarctic regions, via New South Wales, bringing us later English news than we had previously seen. They had visited the Tonga group, and had been about six weeks examining the Feejees, of which they intended to complete the chart. When I state that four large islands occurred in our passage alone, which are not placed on the charts, and that many unnoticed exist in the whole group, which is most erroneously set forth in the charts, the value of their labours may be easily appreciated.

Owing to threats held out that vengeance would be taken for the capture of the chief by the *Peacock*, I did not conceive it right to risk the chance of aggression, by permitting our parties to pursue their examinations where our force could not act; consequently, beyond the island of Nukulau and the beach-line little was obtained.

The anchorage of Nukulau is safe, as well as convenient. Two safe and easy passages lead to it, and with the assistance of the chart, vessels can enter at all times without a pilot. The eastern channel, by which the *Sulphur* entered, is also safe, if assisted by the chart and a boat ahead. The best anchorage is in twelve fathoms, with the outer island barely shut in with Nukulau, about two cables length from the shore, in a muddy bottom. The strongest breezes blow from south to south-west. Water can be had at Nukulau, or by sending up the river. The *Sulphur* watered at the island.

At present there are so many doubts about the proper name of the main island, that I retain "Ambow,"* this being the name understood by the chiefs and natives, and it has stood sufficiently long on the charts for preference.

It is traversed by very extensive rivers, and the chiefs assert that in the rainy season the fresh water prevails one mile beyond the breakers. It is also asserted that no one has yet reached the source of this river, and that numerous other similar streams exist. The Americans made the attempt, and I am informed penetrated six miles beyond any previous white person. I am not aware of anything to repay the labour, which probably would entail sickness on the exploring party. The mountains are lofty, and exhibit deep ravines between the ranges, which alone would account for powerful streams. They are generally shallow, and not adapted for navigation.

A code of regulations has been drawn up and signed by mark, for the chiefs of Rewa (not of Ba-ou), but as they neither read, write, nor understand the laws they have enacted (possibly Phillips may be an exception), they will prove a dead letter.

Their implements of war are clubs, spears, bows, and arrows; but the club appears to be that generally in use. Probably the spear may be used on the first charge, but in conversation they never say that "a man was speared"; it is invariably "clubbed." These clubs are very neatly made, of a strong hard wood, resembling live oak in grain, and ornamented with coloured sennit, made from cocoa-nut fibre. They generally carry with them short clubs, similar to "life preservers," which are the club root of a peculiar tree affording a knob about the size of an orange, the stem, or handle, seldom exceeding three-quarters of an inch in diameter. These are either carved or smoothly polished. It is a very formidable weapon, and probably, excepting in actions where numbers are engaged, their most fatal instrument of death. They readily part with any of their arms or ornaments for whale teeth, which are at all times irresistible articles in traffic.

The costume of the men is similar to that of the Tonga group, or most of the Pacific Islands, viz., a simple maro round the waist. The chiefs who possess European finery, seldom exhibit it, excepting Phillips (Thokanauto), who generally made his appearance in white trousers, shirt, waistcoat, and surtout. Indeed, I would not permit him to visit the ship in any other costume. This chief speaks English, French, and Spanish, is clever and intelligent, and has made one or two voyages in an American trader to Tahiti, and the neighbouring islands. It is probable that he will shortly have the chief power at Rewa, as he broadly hinted in the presence of his brother. It is to be hoped that he will attain it by a more civilized process than the customary mode.

The king or principal chief of Ambow, "Old Snuff," as he is termed, resides at Bauo, or Bow, about thirty miles up the river, and near to the river which empties itself northerly at Obalauo. His son, "Young Snuff," is described as an active, intelligent young man, much prepossessed in favour of our countrymen.

Indeed, the abstraction of the Rewa chief by the Americans has irritated the natives amazingly, and will probably injure their mercantile interests. The story told here is that this chief resented some indignity offered him by an American trader on some former visit, and on the return of some of the crew in another vessel, they were "clubbed." It is stated that he was kept chained in her main top, but escaped, and swam ashore. However, on the arrival of the American squadron, the *Peacock* was despatched to demand this chief. His capture was achieved as before stated. This was the version given by the missionaries. Doubtless we shall hear the facts in a more authenticated form, when the narrative of the exploring voyage comes out.

Both men and women take great pride in dressing their hair. Although it is long enough sometimes to reach to the waist, it nevertheless has a strong disposition to curl or frizzle, and the main object appears to be to render each individual hair independent, presenting an uniform mob, similar to the wigs of our bishops. In one instance I measured the distance from the skin to the outer edge of the hair, which was six inches. In some cases of the first class queens, the external shape was beautifully even and round, generally coloured by powder, of a very light lead colour. The men in many instances have their hair party-coloured; sometimes black, red, blue, and lead, or dirty white, on the same scalp. In several instances I noticed a single red long lock cultivated from the side of a thick frizzled black mob. These colours are obtained from different barks, the whitish or lead colour from the ashes of the bark of the bread-fruit tree. Those who cannot maintain a barber frequently cover the hair with tapa, which gives it the appearance of a turban.

This style of dress, with their thick black beards, and tapa thrown over the shoulder, gives them a Turkish aspect. They are inordinately fond of paint. Vermilion is equal to gold; but failing this, they besmear themselves with a thick coating of lampblack, and oil or varnish, and vary it by scoring off until the skin shews, or by coloured ashes. Their chief object in dress is to render themselves as unlike human beings as possible; the more terrific, the more admired. They have nearly the same abhorrence of a white skin as we have of a black one.

The women wear an ornamented belt, about four inches deep, with six inches fringe, called a leekee. They are very neatly worked, and are becoming. The queen of Rewa had no other covering. Her hair, however, was very neatly dressed, and as perfect as if she had come from under the hands of a French frisseur.

I am afraid that the missionaries will find these people far beyond their powers. They have no chiefs of sufficient importance to carry into effect any important change, and possibly if any one attempted it otherwise than by example, his head might pay the forfeit. They are too self-willed and independent to be driven, and at the present moment far too ferocious to submit to any restraint.

I put the question to Phillips, who answered immediately to the point. "They have no objection to the residence of the missionaries, and would feed them; and would not molest any one voluntarily embracing their religion. But they dislike their spying into their houses. By-and-bye, when they see more of them, and understand them, the people may come round."

"But," I observed, "the chiefs should set the example, as the kings of all the other islands have done."

"What did they give them for helping them?"

I replied, "Nothing; they were induced by the superior advantages which the Christian religion offered."

As he could not be made to comprehend this part of the subject, and appeared restless, I changed the topic.

With a light air from the eastward, we pursued our course for the island of Banga, and about four a.m. observed the *Starling* at anchor. Lieut. Kellett came on board at daylight, but as nothing offered of sufficient interest to detain the ship, I merely landed to secure the position, and complete the survey which had been commenced by the *Starling*.

The anchorage is safe and convenient, and probably, had I been aware of its existence, would have been selected in preference to Nukulau for our astronomical position, as being more detached from a large population. Not long since it possessed its full portion of inhabitants; but on the death of their king, who was tributary to the king of Rewa, the chiefs determined to throw off the yoke, and become independent.

Such a pretext for war was not overlooked, and a band of warriors immediately issued forth to reduce them to submission, or in plainer terms, to rob them of all they possessed. This was found difficult by reason of their fastnesses, the towns being situated in many cases on the very summit of the mountains, elevated one thousand four hundred feet above the sea.

Finding they were not sufficiently strong, reinforcements were demanded, which were sent under the command of Garingaria, or raised by him under a contract that he might exterminate them. His brother, Thokanauto (or Phillips), who is upheld as the white man's friend (but only so long as he can get anything from him), was foremost in destroying the villagers by fire, and committing other brutal acts. The expedition resulted in victory to the besiegers, the death of the principal chief, and several hundreds of the population. The son of the chief was spared to govern, under the usual subjection.

The sequel will hardly be credited, yet it is beyond doubt: cannibalism to a frightful degree still prevails amongst this people, and, as it would seem, almost as one of their highest enjoyments. The victims of this ferocious slaughter were regularly prepared, being baked, packed, and distributed in portions to the various towns which furnished warriors, according to their exploits; and they were feasted on with a degree of savage barbarity nearly incredible! They imagine that they increase in bravery, by eating their valorous enemy.

This Garingaria is a noted cannibal, and it is asserted that he killed one of his wives and ate her. This he denied, and accounted for her death (which took place violently by his order) on other grounds. He did not attempt a denial of his acts at Banga, nor did Phillips. These occurrences are of late date. I am told they threw one or more of the heads (which they do not eat) into the missionary's compound.

The population of the Feejees are very tall, far above the height of any other nation I have seen. Of five men assembled in my tent, none was under six feet two inches. It was rather an awkward subject to tax Garingaria with in his own house, and solely attended by his own dependent, our interpreter; but he took it very quietly, and observed that he cared not for human flesh, unless it was that of his enemy, and taken in battle. When he used this expression, I could not help thinking that his lips were sympathetically in motion, and that I had better not make myself too hostile. I therefore bid him good evening.

From *Narrative of a Voyage Round the World, 1836-1842* (1843) by Capt. Sir Edward Belcher R.N., 1799-1877. Born in Halifax, N.S., Belcher was a Canadian Capt. Bligh, efficient but cruel. More than once charged with abusing his men, he was accused by his wife merely of giving her venereal disease. Despite these and other setbacks Belcher became a knight and an admiral.

*I think, although Ambow on charts, that it should be written Ambauo. Bauo being the residence of the principal or king.

SIBERIA
by Sir George Simpson

On the twentieth of August we reached Kansk, standing on a river of the same name, and containing a population of three thousand souls. At the ferry we were met by the mayor, the commissary, the hatman of Cossacks, and other officers. It was the most interesting place that we had seen to the west of Irkutsk, occupying a beautiful valley surrounded by green hills, and possessing a woollen manufactory besides some salt works. Still we remained only a couple of hours, being unwilling to lose time, more particularly as the improvement of the roads, in consequence of the undulating character of the surface, was enabling us to gallop over hill and dale at the rate of twelve versts.

The villages were very numerous, not only on the road but as far back on either side as we could see; and the people all looked healthy, comfortable and happy. In any place, where the post house was out of repair, our police officer used to pounce on the best house for our use; and as the owners would neither make any demand nor accept any remuneration, we were generally obliged to compromise the matter by forcing a small gift on the host's wife or daughter. The dwelling in which we breakfasted to-day, was that of a person who had been sent to Siberia against his will. Finding that there was only one way of mending his condition, he worked hard and behaved well. He had now a comfortably furnished house and a well cultivated farm, while a stout wife and plenty of servants bustled about the premises. His son had just arrived from Petersburg to visit his exiled father, and had the pleasure of seeing him amid all the comforts of life, reaping an abundant harvest, with one hundred and forty persons in his pay.

In fact, for the reforming of the criminal, in addition to the punishment of the crime, Siberia is undoubtedly the best penitentiary in the world. When not bad enough for the mines, each exile is provided with a lot of ground, a house, a horse, two cows, and agricultural implements, and also, for the first year, with provisions. For three years he pays no taxes whatever — and for the next ten only half of the full amount. To bring fear as well as hope to operate in his favour, he clearly understands that his very first slip will send him from his home and his family to toil, as an outcast, in the mines. Thus does the government bestow an almost parental care on all the less atrocious criminals.

In the afternoon, after passing through a new settlement of exiles called Borodino, we came in sight of the Siansky Mountains, celebrated for their singularly rich mines of gold and silver.

Next day we entered Krasnoyarsk, the capital of the province of Yenissei. We were, as usual, received with great civility by the municipal authorities, who came to meet us at the ferry on the Yenissei, and provided us with an excellent house. I called on the governor, a civilian of the name of Kapilloff, who very politely pressed me to dine with him the next day, being the anniversary of the emperor's accession to the throne. I declined the honour, however, through my anxiety to get forward, and begged for horses to continue our journey as soon as ever our carriages should have undergone a few necessary repairs. I called also on the chief magistrate of police, who was very attentive, placing his carriage and four horses at my disposal: whilst with him, I happened to sneeze, when, according to etiquette, he bowed to me and wished me good health.

We strolled through the town, finding little to interest us excepting the tomb of Von Resanoff, erected in 1831 by the Russian American Company. There was the usual number of public buildings, all of wood, such as churches, hospitals and barracks. Among the exiles in the place there was one of high rank, Lieutenant General Davidoff, banished for participating in some attempt or other at revolution. He was very comfortably, nay happily, settled with his whole family about him, sons-in-law, brother-in-law, and so on, and appeared to enjoy all the luxuries and elegancies of polished life. So far as the eye could judge, General Davidoff was no more an exile than Governor Kapilloff himself.

For our own immediate purpose of racing against time, we could hardly have come more inopportunely to Krasnoyarsk. Everybody was idler than his neighbour, on the occasion of the consecration of a new church by the Bishop of Tomsk, situated rather ornamentally, I thought, than usefully, on the face of a hill at the distance of a verst and a half from the nearest house. At the conclusion of the ceremony, the chairman of the building committee gave a grand entertainment to the bishop, the governor, and all the higher functionaries generally, the whole party, I understood, displaying as much zeal as if St. Nicholas's wet day had brought them together; and, in imitation of so good an example, the lower orders speedily filled the streets, and kept them filled, too, for the most of the night, with drunken males and females. I had heard that the men of Krasnoyarsk, on account of their size and strength, were frequently drafted into the Imperial Guards; but whether it was that I was out of humour by reason of the delay, or that they showed themselves under disadvantageous circumstances, I saw nothing particular to admire in them.

The town stands on the Yenissei in a level plain, embosomed in hills, being said to derive its name from some neighbouring cliffs of red earth. It may be considered as the centre of the district, where the mania for gold washing which broke out about fifteen years ago, has been carried to its greatest height, a mania which has brought not only agriculture, but even commerce into comparative neglect and disrepute. Of the population, amounting to about six thousand, the great majority are more or less infected with the malady. As an instance of the speculative character of this occupation, one individual, who embarked in the business about three years ago, obtained no returns at all till this season, when he has been richly repaid for his outlay of a million and a half of roubles, by one hundred and fifty poods of gold, worth thirty-seven thousand roubles each, or rather more than five millions and a half in all. Such a lucky hit as this serves, of course, to give a fresh impulse to the spirit of gambling, which animates both foreigners and natives alike. A Prussian botanist and physician, entirely wrapped up in the love of his favourite sciences, had actually started on a pilgrimage to Kamschatka for the sole purpose of examining the vegetation. When, however, he got as far as the golden district of Yenissei, he paused and pondered for a time in the fair town of Krasnoyarsk, till at length, as the bad luck of physic and botany would have it, he was chained to the spot in the double capacity of husband and gold washer.

Speaking of marriage, a young lady's charms are here estimated by the weight not of herself, but of her gold. A pood is a very good girl and, according to Cocker, who appears to get the better of Cupid here as well as elsewhere, two or three poods are clearly twice or thrice as good a wife.

At present the mines and washeries are very unfavourable to the settlement and cultivation of Siberia, by calling away the labourers from more steady occupations to the precarious pursuit of the precious metals. Already has the effect been seriously felt in Krasnoyarsk, where a pood of meat has risen, in ten years, from a rouble and a half to twenty roubles, and where fowls, such as we bought at Nishney Udinsk for a quarter of a rouble a piece, cost three roubles a pair. When, however, these mining and washing operations shall have been reduced to a more regular system, they will afford an extensive market for the produce of the surrounding country, and thus, in the end, become the firmest support of the very agriculture which they now embarrass.

The province of Yenissei alone has this year yielded five hundred poods of gold. The most valuable washeries are those on the Tonguska, which falls into the river that gives name to the district, a considerable way to the north of Krasnoyarsk. The richest washing tract in Eastern Siberia is said to be the triangle bounded by the Angara to the east, the Yenissei to the west, and Chinese Tartary to the south.

Expecting that we should start during the night, I laid myself down in the evening, as I had done ever since leaving Irkutsk, at the bottom of the carriage. In the morning, however, I found that I had slept without being rocked, for there we were still in Krasnoyarsk; and, notwithstanding my reiterated applications for horses, we were detained till ten in the morning, in a place, of which hardly a single inhabitant, what between washeries and holidays, seemed capable of attending to any ordinary business. Almost everything, in fact, had gone wrong, since we entered the province of Yenissei; and even our policeman was generally so far behind, that we had to wait for him at the stations.

We passed through a beautiful country for pasturage, well wooded and well settled. Soon after leaving the town, we overtook the principal chief of the Burats on his way to visit the Emperor Nicholas.

In face and general appearance, he resembled an Indian of North America; he was, however, a man of education and address, and wore a handsome uniform. This potentate was attended by an interpreter.

In each town and village, by the by, along the great thoroughfare, there is an ostrog with a sentry at the door. These wooden forts are used for locking up the convicts, while passing onward to their respective destinations. The convicts travel in parties of two or three hundred each, very lightly chained together, and escorted by soldiers; and, in order still further to prevent escape, sentinels are stationed at every three or four miles on the road. Under all these circumstances, attempts at desertion are very rare and scarcely ever succeed.

At Kesalskaya, which we reached at one next morning, we found the postmaster drunk and stupid. He not only would give us no horses himself, but endeavoured also to deter others from giving us any assistance. Not contented with negative churlishness, the fellow insisted on removing the candle, which by law should be kept burning all night in every post-house. A scuffle ensued between my ever ready fellow-traveler and the worthy functionary, in which the former was likely to come off second best; but, feeling that, at least on this occasion, he had done nothing to merit a drubbing, I rescued him, candle and all, from the rascal's fury. In the course of an hour we obtained cattle from some of the villagers and took our departure.

Sixty versts of very bad roads brought us, at two in the afternoon, to Atchinsk, where we were provided by the authorities with a house, in which we took breakfast and dinner in one. Our landlady was a jolly, good-humoured, handsome dame, whose husband was washing away for gold at the distance of a hundred versts. Under this agreeable and communicative lady's tuition I should have picked up the Russ in no time.

The population of this town is about two thousand, while that of the surrounding villages is five times the amount. All this is the work of the last twenty years; and the rapid growth of the neighbourhood, almost rivaling the mushroom-like settlements of the United States, show how successfully the government is proceeding in the colonization of Siberia. Many of the inhabitants, and even some of the principal merchants, are Jews. Though the soil in the vicinity is said to be very rich, yet here, as well as at Krasnoyarsk, the monotonous labours of the husbandman have been, in a great measure, superseded by the more attractive occupation of hunting up the precious metals.

Atchinsk stands on the Tchulim, a tributary of the Oby, which is here so tortuous in its course, that a circuit of six hundred versts, according to my information, may be avoided by a portage of twenty-five. It is the most westerly town, at least on this route, in this tiresome province; and, at the distance of seventeen versts beyond it, there stands a pillar to mark the boundary not only between Yenissei and Tomsk, but also between Eastern and Western Siberia. The traveler, however, has but little reason for congratulating himself upon the change. The farther that one advances to the westward, the more rapidly do the roads, the post-houses and the houses degenerate. The same regulations, it is true, apply to the whole country, so that the entire difference lies not in the theory but in the practice. These regulations, drawn up by Catherine the Second in her own hand-writing, are a lasting memorial of the sagacity and vigilance of that illustrious sovereign.

About a hundred versts from Atchinsk, there are said to be some remains, in the shape of dilapidated tombs, of a race that had apparently made greater advances in civilization than any of the modern aborigine of Siberia. There is also a steppe of about two hundred versts distance on which the neighbouring Tartars have, from time immemorial, been accustomed to congregate, for the purpose of enjoying all kinds of athletic sports. On such occasions they stake their women, horses and other valuables; and, though the authorities often receive complaints of foul play from the losers, yet, for obvious reasons, they seldom interfere between the gamblers.

In the course of the day, a distance of three versts occupied several hours. The road was execrable and the night dismal and dark. We repeatedly got off the right track; and when, at length, to our joy we reached a post-house at midnight, we found neither fire nor light while the inmates, a man, two women and a child, were all fast asleep on the same shakedown.

Next day everything seemed to become worse and worse — the road abominable, the stages long, the country dreary, the stations comfortless, the delays constant and the postmasters uncivil. Besides being poor and miserable in appearance, the people were said to be really bad, robberies and murders being so common as to render traveling very unsafe in some parts of the district. At our first station of to-day we were detained two hours for want of horses, while the post-house was a filthy hovel with a draggle-tailed creature of a landlady. Besides breakfasting, we killed time, as well as we could, by entering into conversation with our draggle-tailed hostess, who proved to be an amusing gossip. Her husband had been "exiled," as she said, for being saucy to his master, or more probably, we thought, to his master's goods and chattels. She was very inquisitive about ourselves, taking me at first for a Turk turned Russian, next guessing that I was a German, and lastly hitting on my country. Under this lively lady's roof we witnessed an instance of the strictness with which some of the traveling regulations were observed. The courier with the mail had lost his podoroshnoya at his last station; and though, in most countries, the bags would have been a sufficient passport, yet the luckless fellow was here detained, till a certificate of his having once had a podoroshnoya could be procured.

In the course of the day we passed a number of small carts on four wheels, each drawn by two horses and loaded with twenty poods of tea, on its long and weary way to Russia. Autumn had commenced in right earnest; and the fall of the leaf was rapid. We had still before us, on this the fifth of our English September, fully three-fourths of the distance from Irkutsk to Petersburg; so that, if things did not mend we had a fair chance of being overtaken by the early and sudden winter of this climate.

At the Kia, another tributary of the Oby, we spent three hours in crossing; and cold, wet, sleepy, and unwell as I was, I thought this the most miserable portion of my whole journey. After crossing, we came to the ruins of Kyskal, a village of four hundred and fifty houses, which was consumed by fire on the morning of the preceding Easter Sunday. Several lives had been lost; and many more would have been so, if the flames had burst forth a few hours earlier, when most of the inhabitants, according to time-hallowed custom, were helplessly drunk. We had great difficulty in obtaining shelter, till a young and pretty woman induced her drowsy husband to admit the starving and shivering strangers; and we were not sorry to be detained in this snuggery, for want of horses, till daylight.

Our next two days were as uncomfortable as possible, weather and roads bad, nothing to eat but black bread and sour milk, and most vexatious delays at every station. On the second of these miserable marches, when we were within four miles of Tomsk, our Russian's ricketty vehicle — a drag in every sense of the word — again broke down; and, as the peasants, from some scruple or other, would neither be coaxed nor bullied into taking it on, the owner was obliged to embark with us, amid some superstitious forebodings on our part as to the probable consequences. On reaching Tomsk, where there proved to be no post-house, we repaired to the proper magistrate, who, after examining our podoroshnoya and finding all right, proceeded to billet us on some of the citizens. Our lot fell on a dismal house in the suburbs, of which the proprietor had gone to Tobolsk, leaving his young wife, a buxom enough damsel, in the charge of an ancient duenna; and, in spite of the vigilance of her guardian, the fair mistress of the mansion peeped into the room, merely to ascertain, of course, whether Englishmen looked like other people.

The absence of my Russian fellow traveler's wardrobe, by preventing us from calling on the governor before the morrow, added upwards of half a day to the wrong side of that gentleman's account — a very vexatious entry in our traveling ledger at this advanced season of the year.

Between the events of the day, and a severe cold caught at the passage of the Kia, I went to bed in not very good humour, though this was the first time for fourteen nights that I had doffed my clothes or slept out of the carriage. I had no great reason, however, to congratulate myself on the change, for I scarcely closed an eye. I felt feverish; I missed my accustomed jolting; and, what was worse than everything else, the good lady of the house, who was sleeping in an adjacent gallery, perhaps to enjoy the fresh air, or perhaps to watch the premises, kept sending forth, during the whole night, coughs, sneezes, and sighs, with various other noisy tokens of her whereabouts. I was glad to rise early, and perambulate the town, visiting the markets, where I found the butchers, like their brethren in England, dressed in blue frocks. Was the coincidence, I asked myself, the result of accident, or of imitation, or of some innate congeniality between the colour of the coat and the unctuousness of the occupation?

Tomsk stands on the Tom, and is a handsome and flourishing town with wide streets. Though many of the buildings are of brick, yet nineteen-twentieths of the houses are merely log huts. On either side of the roads, which, in rainy weather, are so many rivers of mud, there are boarded paths for the accommodation of pedestrians. The population varies considerably in amount, according to the season, being about eighteen thousand in summer, and twenty-four thousand in winter. The fluctuation is occasioned chiefly by the prevailing mania of the country; and as the birds of passage must contain far more than an average proportion of adults, the extent of the washing speculations, as compared with the other employments of the inhabitants, may be easily estimated. This fashionable pursuit is a perfect lottery, in which a hundred become poorer for one that is made rich, while, with respect to the lower classes, even the most fortunate labourers seldom derive any other benefit from their earnings than a winter of idleness, vagabondism, and dissipation. Indeed, the washeries themselves, during the very season of work, have too often become dens of drunkenness and riot; so that the different governors have been obliged, personally, to visit the establishments lying in their respective provinces, in order to curb the turbulent and profligate conduct of the adventurers.

I found here various races of people collected together, Russians, Tartars, Jews, Poles, &c., while, in proof of the spirit of toleration, Catholicism, Judaism and Mohammedanism had each its own place of worship as freely and openly as the national establishment itself.

After breakfast, we paid our respects to the governor, a frank, plain, good-humoured old soldier, who gave us, at my request, a Cossack to precede us as far as Omsk, the new capital of Western Siberia. General Tartarenoff talked much about our country and particularly about the difficulty of acquiring our language, repeating to us over and over again with great glee his whole stock of English, a few words picked up from the free-and-easy vocabulary of a common sailor at Nemel.

I met with a greater number of petty annoyances at Tomsk than at any other place in Siberia. Our Tartar driver was so quarrelsome as to require to be taken before a magistrate; horses could hardly be got for love or money; and, on crossing the river at our departure, the Charon had a grand dispute with us in consequence of our resisting his attempts at imposition. Then our fare was poor and unwholesome, though our dinner did boast of three courses. First there came soup made of grits, cabbage and water; secondly, bread and salted cucumbers; thirdly, fresh cucumbers and pickled mushrooms, with bread and tea. In the kitchen, our servants had the first two courses the same as ourselves in the parlour, while, in lieu of the third course they were regaled with plenty of nice sour milk. We had no reason however, to complain of our hostess, for such was the ordinary diet of the middle classes.

To resume my journal, on leaving the city we crossed the Tom, which was here about half a mile wide, leaving our Russian behind us in order to have the repairs of his carriage completed; and, though the roads were good, yet we could not make much progress in the absence of that gentleman, who acted in the capacity of interpreter. We passed several settlements of the aborigines, as also one of their burying grounds, in which each tomb was enclosed within a small square of logs. These Tartars were a comely race, the men being above the ordinary stature, and the women chubby and mirthful; and such of the females, as were of mixed blood, might be said even to be beautiful.

Next day, having been overtaken by my Russian fellow traveler, about ten in the morning, we began to see more symptoms of life on the road, meeting the mail and several travelers; and, at the crossing of the Oby, we found a proof of the increasing intercourse in the existence of rival ferrymen, who, however, illustrated the proverb of the cooks and the broth, by detaining us with their squabbles. The weather had improved; along the road there was much land under cultivation.

On the ensuing day we entered the Baralinsky Steppe, a flat and fertile prairie of vast extent. Among the many agricultural settlements, that studded this boundless plain, the one which most particularly attracted my attention, was a colony of Jews absolutely turned farmers — a phenomenon the more extraordinary in a country where every one else was agog in pursuit of gold and silver. But the alteration of complexion was, perhaps, more remarkable than that of disposition. Though these tillers of the ground still retained their hereditary features, yet, in spite of the usual influence of rural labour, they had exchanged the swarthy countenance and dark locks of their race, for fair skins and light hair, which were very becoming in the women, with their heads swathed in a kind of red turban. In the course of the forenoon, we had a curious remembrance of home, in a large band of gypsies, whom we met at Elkul; in appearance and habits they were the exact counterparts of their brethren and sisters in our own country.

On this our fourteenth day from Irkutsk, we reached Ubinskoi, said to mark one-third part of the distance to Petersburg. We had just previously passed through the miserable little village of Kolyvan, giving its name to one of the most valuable of the mining districts, and communicating, by a cross road to the southward, with Barnaoul, the local depot of all the precious metals of the surrounding regions. As the weather had been dry for some time, the roads were tolerable, notwithstanding the perfectly level character of the surface.

Next day at noon we reached Kainsk, standing on the Om. Though pretending to be a town, yet it was nothing but a straggling village of miserable houses with a population, many of them Jews, of less than a thousand souls. We were still on the Baralinsky Steppe, which would, in fact carry us two hundred versts farther to the western boundary of the province of Tomsk. In this immense plain there are several extensive lakes. One of them, from which our yesterday's station of Ubinskoi takes its name, empties itself into the Om; but of the others, which all lie off the road, some are salt and, of course, have no outlet.

As we arrived at noon on Sunday, the good folks at the town were just coming out of church, while their less scrupulous brethren and sisters of the adjacent villages were celebrating the day, as usual, by getting drunk — or rather by continuing drunk, for the Saturday had been the festival of John the Baptist. As a curious instance of the influence of custom not merely on private individuals but also on public opinion, the bottle is quite fashionable and orthodox on any and every holiday, excepting always St. Nicholas's dry turn, while the bath, on these sacred occasions, is shunned as one of the deadly sins. Knowing this, I was surprised to-day on seeing an old lady — with one foot in the grave and another out of it — openly emerge from a bathhouse, reeking all over with the evidence of her impiety; but, on inquiry, I found, that the apparent sinner, being an invalid, had made all right by procuring the requisite dispensation. What a blessing in point of comfort and cleanliness, if the priests could, and would prevail on the people to accept the bath in place of the bottle.

Being preceded both by the Cossack, whom I had obtained from Governor Tartarenoff, and by an officer of police, we did not encounter any delays at the post-houses. But, after leaving Kainsk, I began to suspect, that some extraordinary merit on our own part was one main cause of our getting forward so swimmingly, for the whole population of every village, whether by day or by night, flocked to see us, the males all uncovered and the females incessantly bowing. The secret gradually oozed out, that our friends ahead, as much perhaps for their own convenience as for our glory, had insinuated that I was an ambassador from the Emperor of China to the Czar, while the simple peasants, according to the natural growth of all marvelous stories, had of their own accord, pronounced me to be the brother of the sun and moon himself, pushing on to the capital, along with my interpreter and one of my mandarins, in order to implore the assistance of the Russians against the English. Private accommodations were prepared for us at every station; and we were decidedly the greatest men that had ever been seen to the east of the Uralian Mountains. As the roads were excellent, we enjoyed the joke, whirling along at the rate of twelve or fifteen versts an hour.

During the night, the officer of police left us at the boundary between the provinces of Tomsk and Omsk, so that we had now to depend on our Cossack alone. The farms of the villagers are not always near the villages, being sometimes as much as thirty versts distant. The peasants appear to be well off and really are a happy and contented race. With respect to the young women a custom was said to prevail, which would be more honoured in the breach than in the observance. Such of them as remain single at their mother's death, are at the disposal of their nearest male relative, whether father, or brother, or uncle, or guardian, who may sell their first favours in marriage or otherwise for his own private emolument; and, in justice to all nearest male relatives, I ought to add, that the damsels don't seem to dislike the practice.

At a house where we dined to-day on sour krout, an old man could not possibly conceive, how we, being English, could be coming from the east, assuring me that all the Englishmen who had ever visited Siberia had not only come from the west but had no other way to come. Knowing something of geography, our aged host explained to us, that, besides the Polar Sea on the north, and the Chinese frontier on the south, there was on the east a great ocean which was certainly far from England, the western door alone, as it were, being left open to admit our countrymen.

In the course of the afternoon we entered Omsk, the new metropolis of Western Siberia. It stands at the confluence of the Om and the Irtish, in the midst of a sandy plain, which presents no tree of larger size than a dwarf willow. Over this barren flat, which extends on all sides as far as the eye can reach, the biting winds blow from every quarter of the compass without impediment, driving before them in winter drifts of snow, and in summer clouds of dust, both of them equally pernicious to the eyes. The town is still in its infancy, having but lately supplanted Tobolsk; but already the public buildings are handsome, while the fortifications, where the two rivers do not afford protection, are formidable. It has been selected as the seat of the general government chiefly with a view to the gradual subjugation of the Kirghiz, who occupy a vast breadth of country all the way from this to the Caspian Sea; and the advance of Russia in this direction, besides being peculiarly important both commercially and politically, is the more an object of ambition on this account, that, along all the rest of the southern frontier of Siberia, the jealousy, if not the power, of China, forbids the acquisition of new territory. Besides a population of five or six thousand, there is a garrison of four thousand men; and, in fact, the place may be considered merely as a military post, for nearly all the inhabitants derive their subsistence from the presence of the troops. As to civil government, Omsk still depends on the ancient city of Tobolsk, which continues to be the capital of the united provinces of Tobolsk and Omsk.

We were hospitably received into the house of Count Tolstoy, a clever, cheerful, plain man. He had recently returned from St. Petersburg, whither he had escorted the Khan of Tashkand, lying in about 43° N. lat. and 70° E. long., on a visit to the Emperor. The chief in question may already be reckoned among the vassals of Russia; and, at no distant day, his territories will form an integral part of this colossal empire.

Next morning after breakfast, the governor general sent his carriage and four to convey me to his residence. Prince Gutchakoff, a middle-aged man of pleasing manners and address, received me kindly, expressing his regret that, according to arrangements already made along the whole route, he was unavoidably obliged to start that afternoon in order to inspect the southwestern boundary of his government — the most interesting section, as already mentioned, of the southern frontier of Siberia. He assured me, however, that he had done all in his power to facilitate my movements, having dispatched orders to have horses in readiness for me at every station; and he had very naturally assumed that, instead of taking the straight cut to Tiumen, any traveler would prefer making the circuit by Tobolsk, with its classical associations and historical renown.

I spent the greater part of the day in visiting the public buildings. The establishment in which I felt most interested, was the military school for the sons of soldiers. The number of pupils was two hundred and fifty, the expense of maintenance being estimated at twelve kopecks, or about five farthings, a day each. Besides reading, writing, drawing, geography, gunnery, &c., they are instructed in many of the native languages of the neighbourhood, such as Mongol and Kirghiz; and such of them as evince any peculiar aptitude in this way, are taught Persian, Arabic, and other oriental tongues. They are thus qualified to act as interpreters throughout central and southern Asia, receiving, in short, such an education as fits them at once to promote the ambition and to share in the destiny of their country. The boys acquire also several useful trades, architecture, gunmaking, working in metals, &c. They are all intended for the army, entering as privates, but rising, in cases of merit, to the rank of officers.

In the hospital, some of the patients were suffering so severely from military punishment that they were actually delirious. These wretches had probably been doomed to expire by inches to please the mistaken scruples of the law as to putting criminals to death at once — a very extraordinary mode, truly, of reconciling justice and humanity. The only important manufactory in Omsk was one recently established in order to provide the military with clothing.

The country about Omsk abounds in game of various descriptions; and to the south there are wild horses, which, though of a small breed, are fleet, compact and beautiful.

About seven in the evening of the first of September, precisely seventeen days after starting from Irkutsk, we resumed our journey by crossing the Irtish, leaving our Russian behind us till his most unfortunate carriage should be fitted with its third pair of new wheels. The banks of the river presented many villages and farms. The country on the upper Irtish is said to be one of the finest districts for agriculture in all Siberia; and it was there that the Emperor Paul was anxious to establish a colony of Scotch farmers — a project which, if carried into effect, could not have failed to set a useful example of skill, industry and economy to the settlers of this vast region. Speaking of agriculture in its widest sense, Barnaoul is said to be the only place in Siberia where apples have hitherto been known to thrive; and melons and cucumbers grow abundantly everywhere, the latter more particularly being to be seen in the gardens, in the windows, in the galleries, and even in the rooms.

The distance from Omsk to Tobolsk occupied us three nights and two days. The country was flat and uninteresting to the last degree, though more closely settled than any other part of Siberia that we had seen. There was a constant succession of Tartar, Kirghiz and Russian villages, while roads were branching off on either hand to more distant settlements. This was owing mainly to the fact that the neighbourhood — the nucleus, as it were, of Siberia — had been so long cultivated; for the soil, clay in the open country and sand in the woods, was generally poor.

Our Russian did not overtake us till we had waited six hours for him at one station; and he almost immediately detained us three hours more, by striking about ten versts off the road to visit a clergyman and his wife, who after all did not recognize him. He next fell sick and grew very fidgetty about his safety. Lastly, in order to make up for lost time at the expense of his driver and cattle, he spurred on the former with a thick pipe-stem, till one of the latter fell down dead. Such coercion appeared to me to be as unnecessary as it was cruel, for never did I see such driving out of England.

At one of the villages we saw a very remarkable dwarf. He was about forty years of age, thick-set, with a large head and barely two feet and a half high. For his inches, however, he was a person of great importance, being the wise man of the place and the grand arbiter in all disputes, whether of love or of business. We also met two parties of convicts. Each party consisted of seventy or eighty fellows, chained together in sixes or so by light handcuffs, and escorted by ten or twelve Cossacks.

After leaving Omsk, I was mortified to learn that there resided there an English lady, whom I had not seen. Her husband, a physician, called on me, but missed me; and I did not hear of his visit till after I had started. The weather was now telling plainly of the approach of winter. There was a good deal of snow, and the nights were frosty. These symptoms were anything but pleasant, inasmuch as we had not yet accomplished the half of our journey.

On the fourth of September, just as the sun was rising, we entered the fine old city of Tobolsk, the most interesting point in Siberian story, ever since the days of the chivalrous Yermac.

From *Narrative of a Journey Round the World, 1841-1842* (1847) by Sir George Simpson, 1787–1860. Born in Ross-shire, Scotland, for nearly 40 years Simpson was governor and the driving force of the Hudson's Bay Company's activities from Labrador to the Pacific and Russian Alaska. His overland sprint round the world in his sixties took 19 months. Probably ghost-written, the *Narrative* still expresses Simpson himself, his eye for pretty women, strong opinions and ability to sleep anywhere.

Peninsula & Orientliner
by Sara Jeannette Duncan

An Eastern voyage on a Peninsular and Oriental ship is a vague dream that haunts the gay, hard little parlour where what we call 'sewing circles' meet to hear books of travel read aloud, in our substitute for villages in the New World — chiefly that and little more. People who do not belong to the sewing circles, and are not fond of improving their minds with the printed abstract of other people's fun, don't think about it. Living several thousand miles from either end of this popular medium for sending English brides to India and Australian letters to China, and the nomads of the earth all over, they are not really so very much to blame — there is no particular reason why they should know — unless, indeed, some kindly magician like Mr. Black takes them as far as Egypt with a 'Yolande,' which was the case with me. The reflected pleasure lasted, I remember, only while the novel did; but the unfamiliar letters gathered and held a fascinating halo that will endure in my mind as long as the alphabet; and from that day in school girlhood until that other in Yokohama, I longed to set my foot on a ship of the 'P. and O.'

Orthodocia and I both found it something altogether new and strange in travelling, quite apart from the various queerness of the countries it took us to. You may have crossed the Atlantic in an upholstered palace, at all sorts of shifting angles, with three hundred other people, once or twice, and think, as we thought, that you know all there is to know about lay navigation, but you don't. You may even add to your experience, as we did, the great gray skies and tossing monotony of two weeks on the Pacific, during which your affections learn to cluster about a ministering angel in a queue, and yet leave the true philosophy of voyaging unimagined. But Orthodocia and I, from Yokohama to London, sailed with intense joy and satisfaction upon seven of the ships of the P. and O., so I know whereof I speak.

In Orthodocia's note-book the items round the corner of the page labelled 'P. and O.' begin, I observe, at Hong Kong; for though we took the voyage from Japan to China under the same paternal guidance, the conditions were so different from those of our — perhaps theatrical — expectations that we declined to recognise them as Peninsular and Oriental. We took it in January for one thing, and in January there are no punkahs, but a coal stove in the saloon instead. Also, I remember, when we partook of afternoon tea and plum cake and reminiscences in Captain Webber's cosy little cabin, there was a fire there, which didn't help us to realize the tropics. Orthodocia was obliged, moreover, to spend most of the five days in contending with her emotions about leaving the Mikado, for whose dominions she had found Hong Kong so slight a compensation. I know it was not until we were on board the stately *Sutlej*, with her prow turned towards the Straits of Malacca, that the prospect of Ceylon began to revive the drooping interest she took in the rest of the planet.

The first thing that happens when you embark on a P. and O. ship on the other side of the world is the discovery of somebody you had no special reason to believe you would ever see again in it. And it is one of the pleasantest things that can possibly happen, this sudden recognition, on a deck full of strangers, of the familiar head and shoulders of some planet pilgrim gone before. It is quite probable that I did not tell you, in my hurry to get to Japan, about a certain gentleman from New York — a certain portly, and jovial, and ripely-bald gentleman from New York, whom Orthodocia and I found on the deck of the *Duke of Westminster*, watch in hand, calculating in an incensed manner the precise number of minutes we had delayed his arrival in Yokohama by keeping the ship waiting for us. I should have mentioned him because he was the one bit of colour, the one exhilarating fact in all that grievous time. And there we fell upon him, there on the *Sutlej* aft of the smoking cabin, round, and rubicund, and funny, and New-Yorky as ever, rejoicing above everything in six extraordinary Chinese petticoats which some Celestial dame had so forgotten herself as to sell him in Canton.

Well, of all things! The very *last* people he would have expected!

And *did* we remember the 'grilled bones' on the *Duke of Westminster?* Didn't we? It was like the Pacific Ocean giving up Charles Lamb. And had we observed the peculiarities of pidgin English? 'John! run topside — catchee me one piecee gentleman — savey, John? Quick!'

John savied, and shortly returned with the special piece gentleman required, who turned out to be a great American author we had met at Lady C.P.R. Magnum's the evening before leaving Montreal.

'You know each other, I believe,' remarked Rubicundo, genially; 'and you're certain to have read this chap in any case. He simply infests the bookstalls — there's no getting away from him.' 'What *did* you say he'd written?' said my friend to me in a terrified whisper, and in the confusion of the moment I confounded the gentleman to be complimented with Mr. Howells, and answered, 'A Foregone Conclusion.' 'No getting away from him,' went on Rubicundo, cheerfully; 'we'll count a dozen of his last edition on this ship.'

'Yes,' fibbed Orthodocia, gracefully. 'Your "Foregone Delusion" is delightfully familiar to everybody, that is to say' — as he looked aghast — 'I mean *by reputation*. How very warm it is!'

Rubicundo choked suddenly, and went away; but the great American author was very amiable, and only gave the situation the slight emphasis of asking Orthodocia which part of England she came from. Later my friend took occasion to say to me privately that she had always been told that there was no such thing as American literature, and she didn't believe there was; and anyway, the careless manner in which I pronounced my words was getting to be really —

* * * *

'So they sailed away for a year and a day
To the Land where the Bong Tree grows,'

quoted Orthodocia one day dreamily, when the time-spaces began to melt into one another, and nobody knew and nobody cared, as we pulsed southward over rippling seas and under soft skies, how many knots they put up in the companion-way at eight bells as the ship's run, or how far we were from Singapore. It was a charmed voyage, a voyage to evoke imagination in the brains of a Philistine or a Member of Parliament. The very hold of the *Sutlej* was full of poetry in its more marketable shape of tea, and silk, and silver, and elephants' tusks, and preserved pineapples; and all the romance of the Orient was in the spicy smell that floated up from it. The *Sutlej*, moreover, was returning to England after discharging a Viceroy at Bombay on the way out, and her atmosphere was still full of the calm and conscious glory of it.

Your days of tropical voyaging begin in a great white marble bath. Then, if you want to indulge in the humbug and pretence of 'exercise' before breakfast, you pace up and down in the shade, awnings overhead and at the sides, over the broad white quarter-deck — holystoned hours before — and look away across the bulwarks to where morning in the sky melts into morning in the sea, and a wandering gull catches the light of both on its broad white wings. But it is easier to lie in a steamer-chair and fall into a state of reflection. There is just enough ozone in the air to keep your lungs gently in action, and make the languorous energy of your pulses a virtue, and philosophy is easy. You fancy yourself very close to the infinites, and you find the delusive contact pleasant. Rubicundo, in garments of pongee silk and a pith helmet, leaning over the taffrail in the middle distance, becomes invested with the tenderness and profundity of your own emotions; and you wonder if he too is dreamily playing ninepins with the eternal verities. Presently he takes out his watch and regards it absorbedly, giving you a shock which suggests certain sarcasms, leaving you better pleased with yourself than ever. It was only breakfast after all.

We pass the punkah-wallahs as we follow him at the clangour of the bell to the companion-way — four or five handsome little Bengalis with the Indian sun in their liquid brown eyes, barefooted, dressed in a single straight white garment reaching half-way down their small mahogany legs; red cotton sashes, and turbans. There are punkah-wallahs and punkah-wallahs, we discover later; and punkah-wallahs may be as unappetising as those of the *Sutlej* are stimulating, in a gentle, aesthetic way, to one's idea of breakfast. It is a peculiarity of Rubicundo's that he never can pass them without a facetious poke or two, from which the punkah-wallah poked squirms delightedly away, and of Orthodocia's that she must needs chirrup to them and cast her new-gotten Indian wealth in annas among them. It takes four of them to keep the punkah waving below, and a quartermaster is told off to see that they do it. Systematically, when the quarter-master is unaware, they attach the rope to their great toes, and agonise on one foot while they pull with the other, which goes to prove that the Aryan small boy is quite as ingenious in self-torture as any other.

It is wide, and cool, and spacious below where the long white table is laid, and the stewards are standing about looking weighed down, as stewards always do, by the solemnity of the approaching function. The walls are tiled in cool blue and white; outside the big square ports the sea sparkles and splashes in the sun — the sweet-voiced laughing southern sea, that bears us so merrily, as if she loved it. Quaint dwarfed cherry trees in full blossom, and orange trees laden with twinkling fruit the size of a marble, and tall waxy camellias from Orthodocia's dear Japan win her affections at first sight. Over head a large railed oval opening gives into the music-room, and across this run bridges of palms and ferns, cool and graceful. Orthodocia told the captain once that it was a little like breakfasting in the suburbs of Paradise, whereat he made as if he were shocked, but as he claimed the palm canopy as his own idea, I don't think he found her smile very objectionable.

At the breakfast-table one's first interest is naturally in the ship's officers, and there is always somebody who has already ingratiated himself with them and will point them out — the captain, the 'First,' the 'Second,' and 'Third,' the doctor, and the rest. 'P. and O.' officers ought to have a chapter to themselves — and I am convinced that I could find enough material for one, duly initialled, in Orthodocia's note-book — for they become a distinct species after one has experienced a few shipfuls of them. But we will never get round the world at this rate, and I must put the theme aside; only telling you that there is always, for instance, the engaged officer, with an absent look and a disposition to take his food indiscriminately; the musical officer, who sings 'White Wings' or 'Queen of My Heart' to the accompaniment of the young married lady at the captain's right; the flirting officer, who has a very pretty cabin to show, full of the trophies, hand-painted or worked in crewels, of other trips; the tall dark oldish officer, and the short fair boyish officer, and others whose accomplishments would take up altogether too much space, but who help, I fancy, to make a great many voyages pleasantly memorable. Captain Worcester, I remember, was rather particular about the niceties of uniform, so that the galaxy of the *Sutlej* were always apparelled exactly alike. The 'First' never appeared in cloth if his 'chief' wore ducks, nor did the 'Second' wear white raiment if black lustre monkey jackets were the order of the day. To the ancient mariner, if such a one happen to read this chronicle, these things will doubtless be trivialities, but to the feminine and aesthetic eye I know their importance will be manifest.

After breakfast one finds the breeziest spot on deck, and reposes oneself on the long Chinese steamer-chair of the person whose card of possession is most obscurely tacked on. Perhaps there is a fire muster to enliven the morning, and one languidly watches the Lascars taking prompt orders with splashing buckets, the officers getting the boats out, and the stewards trooping up with provision for the same. Captain Worcester made this a very serious function indeed, and the nutriment his pantrymen sent up was of the most solid and uninspiring character; but on another ship I took note of the provisions one morning, and found that the head steward intended always to live luxuriously to the last. They included two tins of preserved ginger — most inspiring diet for castaways — a box of macaroons, and a quantity of marmalade. Orthodocia, I remember, immediately conjured up a picture of the consumption of that marmalade, each unfortunate putting in a finger in turn, and began to select her fellow-passengers.

Or perhaps there is 'stations,' and all the ship's crew, the officer in buttons, the quartermasters in blue, the stewards in their smug black coats, the Lascar sailors in such finery as they have, and the African firemen in long, clean and primitive white garments, make a line round the quarter-deck, saluting as the captain and first officer pass on a round of inspection; then, at the quartermaster's whistle, disappearing to the depths from whence they came. The popular Nubian robe deserves another word: it is cut with great economy straight from the shoulders down to the calf of the leg, and there is an aperture at the neck, by which it is got into. It is almost ugly enough to be adopted by a dress reform society, and when the African who owns it is particularly big and black and solemn-visaged, it is usually made of spotted muslin. One or two patterns were quite sweet, and gave a special interest to 'stations.'

Then 'tiffin' — lunch is a solecism on the P. and O. — and fruits and ices in paper boats, and other tropical alleviations, while the long canvas flounce of the punkah swings lazily to and fro over the table, and Captain Worcester tells a second best story, for the best are not to be had from him till dinner-time. And then the afternoon wears goldenly away with ship cricket perhaps, at which Orthodocia once distinguished herself by sending the ball so vigorously high in the air that it carried Rubicundo's pipe into the yeasty deep, and gave him a sympathy, he said, for men who had seen active service, which he never had before. Or the five o'clock tea of the lady who always carries her own tea set, and has a private plum cake, which is quite the prevailing idea in fashionable Oriental travelling. One afternoon we pass within half a mile of a steam yacht which the 'First' declares to be sailed by the Sultan of Jahore. We descry a stout person in white in her stern, waving his handkerchief vigorously, and immediately invest him with spotless robes, ropes of jewels, and great condescension. The Sultan of Jahore! The one touch of romantic magic needful to make the East tangible to us, to give a world of realism to all that fantasy of opal sky and sea.

Early missionary associations came back upon one forcibly in a trip through the Indian Archipelago, and there is one especial association that comes back to everybody, and comes to stay. I mean everybody on the saloon list. I have seldom heard it expressed by any of the ship's officers, though I have seen numbers of them move off almost in a terrified way on hearing something about it from the lips of a passenger. In fact, I have reason to believe that a violent and distressing end was put to a most promising Affair between a certain 'First' and a charming young person from Australia once, when it became apparent that she was hopelessly addicted to the association that I refer to.

There is a high broken line on the horizon one morning, which we are given to understand indicates Sumatra, a mass of darker blue against the sky — only this and nothing more. Yet it is enough to make every individual on deck exclaim with one emotion, 'India's coral strand!' It's not India, and there's nothing even remotely suggestive of a coral strand about it, but 'our imaginations,' as the old lady who is aunt to a bishop piously remarks, 'were not given to us for nothing'; and the association is well started. She begins by looking thoughtfully for a long time at the geographical suggestions on our lee, and repeating slowly just as the bishop might have done:

> 'From many an ancient river,
>   From many a palmy plain,
> They call us to deliver
>   Their land from error's chain.'

Then she proposes that we should sing the entire hymn, but somebody — the 'Second,' I think — hurriedly interposes. He declares it would be madness to let the association take such complete hold on us so early in the trip. 'Wait,' he says, '"until the spicy breezes blow soft o'er Ceylon's isle."' And then he goes away, I think, and has himself put in irons. But we don't sing it; we content ourselves with saying it over from beginning to end, internally, seven times. By that time it has grown tolerably familiar, and we begin to resent the slightest inaccuracies in anybody's quotations from it. It takes entire possession of us; we hum it at intervals all day. I have seen two elderly gentlemen on terms of intimacy suddenly pause in the midst of an exciting political discussion and chant solemnly and simultaneously:

> 'The heathen, in his blindness,
>   Bows down to wood and stone.'

Then glare angrily at one another for an instant, and take chairs at remote and dissociated ends of the ship.

We fly to literature for surcease from affliction, and find that every author of 'Round the World' travels on board has quoted the hymn in full on the page we open — doubtless to ease his mind.

One can't expect Captain Worcester's stories to 'print' half so funnily as he told them. The story, for instance, of the first two Chinese Mandarins the P. and O. brought to England, and the special instructions the captain got from headquarters to look after them when they came aboard. How the captain turned in after a while, leaving the instructions with the 'First'; how the 'First' delegated them to the 'Second,' and the 'Second' in the course of time to the first available quartermaster. And how the quartermaster, with unshaken rectitude, came to the captain in a stilly hour of night with the terrifying message, 'Please, surr, they kings is come aboord, an' one of em's fell down the coal-hole!' Or of the terrible encounter of his chief once, while he was yet only a 'First,' which demanded all the nerve of a commander of a man-of-war, with two enraged and horror-stricken members of the Bombay Civil Service, who confronted that stern person in port with tumultuous inquiries for their beauteous brides that were to be — and had to be told, with what fortitude the captain could summon, that the young ladies, lingering too long among the ever-fascinating bazaars, had been left behind at Gibraltar!

Or of the occasional contumacious maiden he has had consigned to his fatherly care for Indian ports. Of one especial young woman who refused to 'turn in' at ten o'clock as beseemed her, but rather preferred the society of a callow subaltern and the seclusion of the hurricane deck. How he remonstrated in vain, and finally hit upon a luminous idea to preserve discipline, and set a quartermaster to place four lanterns round the young woman wherever she might betake herself. This was conspicuous and embarrassing, and as the quartermaster, acting under orders, pursued her from Dan in the prow to Beersheba in the stern, her haughty spirit was finally humbled, I believe. We heard much, too, of the whole bevies of extremely young persons who are often entrusted to a P. and O. captain, and succeed in making his life a burden to him. A favourite message from one lot of Captain Worcester's was that 'Amy' — aetat. nine — 'won't go to bed; please come down and slap her!'

And I must not forget the time-honoured P. and O. story, at the expense of a short-sighted young officer who longed to be a Nimrod, and whom some humourist sent to shoot scavenger crows near Yokohama, under the impression that they were a species of Japanese wild fowl. He brought down two brace of birds, and sent them with lively joy to the wife of the agent at Yokohama with a polite note, stating that they were the first-fruits of his gun. Meantime the joke was explained to him, and he sent in severe spasms of mind to recover the crows, instructing his coolie to buy two brace of ducks in the market to fulfil the promise of the note. The lady, who had been out, was delighted to receive the note on her return, and ordered the first-fruits to be brought to her in the drawing room. There was some delay in executing the order, and apparently some confusion in the back premises. Presently the first-fruits, lustily pursued and in a state of great excitement, flapped into the room. The coolie had only made the interesting improvement of buying live ones to represent his master's sport, and probably does not understand the reason of his chastisement unto this day. I believe the officer is still in the service. He must recognise his own ducks very often in the course of a year.

Singapore and Penang occurred during the course of this voyage, but as I am devoting my chapter to a faint picture of the joys of the voyage itself, I think I will not impart the more or less valuable impressions we were able to gather during the two or three hours we spent at each port. Orthodocia took her note-book each time to pick up any stray statistics that might come in our way, but the only note I see under 'Singapore' is 'Three yards Indian mull for hat, 2s. 6d.,' and Penang has something about fan-palms and pongee silk.

And the voyage of every day was like the voyage of the day before, always ending in the cool soft darkness that fell suddenly, and brought with it a myriad of strange stars. The watching great Venus slip down into the sea, and the waiting for the Southern Cross to lift its beauty up from the dark verge of the sky, and the listening to the meeting and the parting of the waters, as this majestic black creature of a ship pulsed onward into the infinity about us — that was all we did at night, yet each night seems to have a separate chronicle as one reads backwards, a chronicle that vanishes in the writing and is dumb in the telling.

From A Social Departure (1890) by Sara Jeannette Duncan, 1862-1922. Born in Brantford, Ontario, she became Canada's first professional journalist of her sex, writing for the *Globe*, the *Washington Post* and other papers. Her first book, *A Social Departure*, is based on her trip round the world in 1889. After her marriage in 1891 to Charles E. Cotes she lived in India and England, where most of her fiction was written.

ROME
by James de Mille

Dick lived among churches, palaces, and ruins. Tired at length of wandering, he attached himself to some artists, in whose studios he passed the greater part of his afternoons. He became personally acquainted with nearly every member of the fraternity, to whom he endeared himself by the excellence of his tobacco, and his great capacity for listening. Your talkative people bore artists more than any others.

"What a lovely girl! What a look she gave!"

Such was the thought that burst upon the soul of Dick, after a little visit to a little church that goes by the name of Saint Somebody. He had visited it simply because he had heard that its dimensions exactly correspond with those of each of the chief piers that support the dome of Saint Peter's. As he wished to be accurate, he had taken a tapeline, and began stretching it from the altar to the door. The astonished priests at first stood paralyzed by his sacrilegious impudence, but finally, after a consultation, they came to him and ordered him to be gone. Dick looked up with mild wonder. They indignantly repeated the order.

Dick was extremely sorry that he had given offense. Wouldn't they overlook it? He was a stranger, and did not know that they would be unwilling. However, since he had begun, he supposed they would kindly permit him to finish.

"They would kindly do no such thing," remarked one of the priests, brusquely. "Was their church a common stable or a wineshop that he should presume to molest them at their services? If he had no religion, could he not have courtesy; or, if he had no faith himself, could he not respect the faith of others?"

Dick felt abashed. The eyes of all the worshippers were on him, and it was while rolling up his tape that his eyes met the glance of a beautiful Italian girl, who was kneeling opposite. The noise had disturbed her devotions, and she had turned to see what it was. It was a thrilling glance from deep black lustrous orbs, in which there was a soft and melting languor which he could not resist. He went out dazzled, and so completely bewildered that he did not think of waiting. After he had gone a few blocks he hurried back. She had gone. However, the impression of her face remained.

He went so often to the little church that the priests noticed him; but finding that he was quiet and orderly they were not offended. One of them seemed to think that his rebuke had awakened the young foreigner to a sense of higher things; so he one day accosted him with much politeness. The priest delicately brought forward the claims of religion. Dick listened meekly. At length he asked the priest if he recollected a certain young girl with beautiful face, wonderful eyes, and marvellous appearance that was worshipping there on the day that he came to measure the church.

"Yes," said the priest, coldly.

Could he tell her name and where she lived?

"Sir," said the priest, "I had hoped that you came here from a higher motive. It will do you no good to know, and I therefore decline telling you."

Dick begged most humbly, but the priest was inexorable. At last Dick remembered having heard that an Italian was constitutionally unable to resist a bribe. He thought he might try. True, the priest was a gentleman; but perhaps an Italian gentleman was different from an English or American; so he put his hand in his pocket, and blushing violently, brought forth a gold piece of about twenty dollars value. He held it out. The priest stared at him with a look that was appalling.

"If you know —" faltered Dick — "any one   of course I don't mean yourself — far from it — but — that is —"

"Sir," cried the priest, "who are you? Are there no bounds to your impudence? Have you come to insult me because I am a priest, and therefore can not revenge myself? Away!"

The priest choked with rage. Dick walked out. Bitterly he cursed his wretched stupidity that had led him to this. His very ears tingled with shame as he saw the full extent of the insult that he had offered to a priest and a gentleman. He concluded to leave Rome at once.

But at the very moment when he had made this desperate resolve he saw someone coming. A sharp thrill went through his heart.

It was SHE! She looked at him and glanced modestly away. Dick at once walked up to her.

"Signorina," said he, not thinking what a serious thing it was to address an Italian maiden in the streets. But this one did not resent it. She looked up and smiled. "What a smile!" thought Dick.

"Signorina," he said again, and then stopped, not knowing what to say. His voice was very tremulous, and the expression of his face tender and beseeching. His eyes told all.

"Signore," said the girl, with a sweet smile. The smile encouraged Dick.

"Ehem — I have lost my way. I — I — could you tell me how I could get to the Piazza del Popolo? I think I might find my way home from there."

The girl's eyes beamed with a mischievous light.

"Oh yes, most easily. You go down that street; when you pass four side-streets you turn to the left — the left — remember, and then you keep on till you come to a large church with a fountain before it, then you turn round that, and you see the obelisk of the Piazza del Popolo."

Her voice was the sweetest that Dick had ever heard. He listened as he would listen to music, and did not hear a single word that he comprehended.

"Pardon me," said he, "but would you please to tell me again. I can not remember all. Three streets?"

The girl laughed and repeated it.

Dick sighed.

"I'm a stranger here, and am afraid that I can not find my way. I left my map at home. If I could find some one who would go with me and show me."

He looked earnestly at her, but she modestly made a movement to go.

"Are you in a great hurry?" said he.

"No Signore," replied the girl, softly.

"Could you — a — a — would you be willing — to — to — walk a little part of the way with me, and — show me a very little part of the way — only a very little?"

The girl seemed half to consent, but modestly hesitated, and a faint flush stole over her face.

"Ah do!" said Dick. He was desperate.

"It's my only chance," thought he.

The girl softly assented and walked on with him.

"I am very much obliged to you for your kindness," said Dick. "It's very hard for a stranger to find his way in Rome."

"But Signore, by this time you ought to know the whole of our city."

"What? How?"

"Why, you have been here three weeks at least."

"How do you know?" and the young man blushed to his eyes. He had been telling lies, and she knew it all the time.

"Oh I saw you once in the church, and I have seen you with that tall man. Is he your father?"

"No, only a friend."

"I saw you," and she shook her little head triumphantly, and her eyes beamed with fun and laughter.

"Anyway," thought Dick, "she ought to understand."

"And did you see me when I was in that little church with a measuring line?"

The young girl looked up at him, her large eyes reading his very soul.

"Did I look at you? Why, I was praying."

"You looked at me, and I have never forgotten it."

Another glance as though to assure herself of Dick's meaning. The next moment her eyes sank and her face flushed crimson. Dick's heart beat so fast that he could not speak for some time.

"Signore," said the young girl at last, "when you turn that corner you will see the Piazza del Popolo."

"Will you not walk as far as that corner?" said Dick.

"Ah, Signore, I am afraid I will not have time."

"Will I never see you again?" asked he, mournfully.

"I do not know, Signore. You ought to know."

A pause. Both had stopped, and Dick was looking earnestly at her, but she was looking at the ground.

"How can I know when I do not know even her name? Let me know that, so that I may think about it."

"Ah, how you try to flatter! My name is Pepita Gianti."

"And do you live far from here?"

"Yes, I live close by the Basilica di San Paola fuori le mure."

"A long distance. I was out there once."

"I saw you."

Dick exulted.

"How many times have you seen me? I have only seen you once before."

"Oh, seven or eight times."

"And will this be the last?" said Dick, beseechingly.

"Signore, if I wait any longer the gates will be shut."

"Oh, then, before you go, tell me where I can find you to-morrow. If I walk out on that road will I see you? Will you come in to-morrow? or will you stay out there and shall I go there? Which of the houses do you live in? or where can I find you? If you lived over on the Alban Hills I would walk every day to find you."

Dick spoke with ardour and impetuosity. The deep feeling which he showed, and the mingled eagerness and delicacy which he exhibited, seemed not offensive to his companion. She looked up timidly.

"When to-morrow comes you will be thinking of something else — or perhaps away on those Alban mountains. You will forget all about me. What is the use of telling you? I ought to go now."

"I'll never forget!" burst forth Dick. "Never — never. Believe me. On my soul; and oh, Signorina, it is not much to ask!"

His ardour carried him away. In the broad street he actually made a gesture as though he would take her hand. The young girl drew back blushing deeply. She looked at him with a reproachful glance.

"You forget —"

Whereupon Dick interrupted her with innumerable apologies.

"You do not deserve forgiveness. But I will forgive you if you leave me now. Did I not tell you that I was in a hurry?"

"Will you not tell me where I can see you again?"

"I suppose I will be walking out about this time to-morrow."

"Oh, Signorina! and I will be at the gate."

"If you don't forget."

"Would you be angry if you saw me at the gate this evening?"

"Yes; for friends are going out with me. Addio, Signore."

The young girl departed leaving Dick rooted to the spot. After a while he went on to the Piazza del Popolo. A thousand feelings agitated him. Joy, triumph, perfect bliss, were mingled with countless tender recollections of the glance, the smile, the tone, and the blushes of Pepita. He walked on with new life.

After his meeting with Pepita, Dick found it extremely difficult to restrain his impatience until the following evening. He was at the gate long before the time, waiting with trembling eagerness.

It was nearly sundown before she came; but she did come at last. Dick watched her with strange emotions, murmuring to himself all those peculiar epithets which are commonly used by people in his situation. The young girl was unmistakably lovely, and her grace and beauty might have affected a sterner heart than Dick's.

"Now I wonder if she knows how perfectly and radiantly lovely she is," thought he, as she looked at him and smiled.

He joined her a little way from the gate.

"So you do not forget."

"*I forget!* Before I spoke to you I thought of you without ceasing, and now I can never forget you."

"Do your friends know where you are?" she asked timidly.

"Do you think I would tell them?"

"Are you going to stay long in Rome?"

"I will not go away for a long time."

"You are an American."

"Yes."

"America is very far away."

"But it is easy to get there."

"How long will you be in Rome?"

"I don't know. A very long time."

"Not in the summer?"

"Yes, in the summer."

"But the malaria. Are you not afraid of that? Will your friends stay?"

"I do not care whether my friends do or not."

"But you will be left alone."

"I suppose so."

"But what will you do for company? It will be very lonely."

"I will think of you all day, and at evening come to the gate."

"Oh, Signore! You jest now!"

"How can I jest with you?"

"You don't mean what you say."

"Pepita!"

Pepita blushed and looked embarrassed. Dick had called her by her Christian name; but she did not appear to resent it.

"You don't know who I am," she said at last. "Why do you pretend to be so friendly?"

"I know that you are Pepita, and I don't want to know anything more, except one thing, which I am afraid to ask."

Pepita quickened her pace.

"Do not walk so fast, Pepita," said Dick, beseechingly. "Let the walk be as long as you can."

"But if I walked so slowly you would never let me get home."

"I wish I could make the walk so slow that we could spend a lifetime on the road."

Pepita laughed. "That would be a long time."

It was getting late. The sun was half-way below the horizon. The sky was flaming with golden light, which glanced dreamily through the hazy atmosphere. Everything was toned down to soft beauty. Of course it was the season for lovers and lovers' vows. Pepita walked a little more slowly to oblige Dick. She uttered an occasional murmur at their slow progress, but still did not seem eager to quicken her pace. Every step was taken unwillingly by Dick, who wanted to prolong the happy time.

Pepita's voice was the sweetest in the world, and her soft Italian sounded more musically than that language had ever sounded before. She seemed happy, and by many little signs showed that her companion was not indifferent to her. At length Dick ventured to offer his arm. She rested her hand on it very gently, and Dick tremulously took it in his. The little hand fluttered for a few minutes, and then sank to rest.

The sun had now set. Evening in Italy is far different from what it is in northern latitudes. There it comes on gently and slowly, sometimes prolonging its presence for hours, and the light will be visible until very late. In Italy, however, it is short and abrupt. Almost as soon as the sun disappears the thick shadows come swiftly on and cover everything. It was so at this time. It seemed but a moment after sunset, and yet everything was growing indistinct. The clumps of trees grew black; the houses and walls of the city behind all faded into a mass of gloom. The stars shone faintly. There was no moon.

"I will be very late to-night," said Pepita, timidly.

"But are you much later than usual?"

"Oh, very much!"

"There is no danger, is there? But if there is you are safe. I can protect you. Can you trust me?"

"Yes," said Pepita, in a low voice.

It was too dark to see the swiftly-changing colour of Pepita's face as Dick murmured some words in her ear. But her hand trembled violently as Dick held it. She did not say a word in response. Dick stood still for a moment and begged her to answer him. She made an effort and whispered some indistinct syllables. Whereupon Dick called her by every endearing name that he could think of, and — Hasty footsteps! Exclamations! Shouts! They were surrounded! Twelve men or more — stout, strong fellows, magnified by the gloom. Pepita shrieked.

"Who are you?" cried Dick. "Away, or I'll shoot you all. I'm armed."

"Boh!" said one of the men, contemptuously.

"Off!" cried Dick, as the fellow drew near.

He put himself before Pepita to protect her, and thrust his right hand in the breast-pocket of his coat.

"Who is that with you?" said a voice.

At the sound of the voice Pepita uttered a cry. Darting from behind Dick she rushed up to him.

"It is Pepita Luigi!"

"Pepita! Sister! What do you mean by this?" said the man hoarsely. "Why are you so late? Who is this man?"

"An American gentleman who walked out as far as this to protect me," said Pepita, bursting into tears.

"An American gentleman!" said Luigi, with a bitter sneer. "He came to protect you, did he? Well, we will show him in a few minutes how grateful we are."

Dick stood with folded arms awaiting the result of all this.

"Luigi! dearest brother!" cried Pepita, with a shudder, "on my soul — in the name of the Holy Mother — he is an honourable American gentleman, and he came to protect me."

"Oh! we know, and we will reward him."

"Luigi! Luigi!" moaned Pepita, "if you hurt him I will die!"

"Ah! Has it come to that?" said Luigi, bitterly. "A half-hour's acquaintance, and you talk of dying. Here, Pepita; go home with Ricardo."

"I will not. I will not go a step unless you let him go. Promise me you will not hurt him."

"Pepita, go home!" cried her brother, sternly.

"I will not unless you promise."

"Foolish girl! Do you suppose we are going to break the laws and get into trouble? No, no. Come, go home with Ricardo. I'm going to the city."

Ricardo came forward, and Pepita allowed herself to be led away.

When she was out of sight and hearing Luigi approached Dick. Amid the gloom Dick did not see the wrath and hate that might have been on his face, but the tone of his voice was passionate and menacing. He prepared for the worst.

"That is my sister — wretch! what did you mean?"

"I swear —"

"Peace! We will give you cause to remember her."

Dick saw that words and excuses were useless. He thought his hour had come. He resolved to die game. He hadn't a pistol. His manoeuvre of putting his hand in his pocket was merely intended to deceive. The Italians thought that if he had one he would have done more than mention it. He would at least have shown it. He had stationed himself under a tree. The men were before him. Luigi rushed at him like a wild beast. Dick gave him a tremendous blow between his eyes that knocked him headlong.

"You can kill me," he shouted, "but you'll find it hard work!"

Up jumped Luigi, full of fury; half a dozen others rushed simultaneously at Dick. He struck out two vigorous blows, which crashed against the faces of two of them. The next moment he was on the ground. On the ground, but striking well-aimed blows and kicking vigorously. He kicked one fellow completely over. At last a tremendous blow descended on his head. He sank senseless.

When he revived it was intensely dark. He was covered with painful bruises. His head ached violently. He could see nothing. He arose and tried to walk, but soon fell exhausted. So he crawled closer to the trunk of the tree, and groaned there in his pain. At last he fell into a light sleep, that was much interrupted by his suffering.

He awoke at early twilight. He was stiff and sore, but very much refreshed. His head did not pain so excessively. He heard the trickling of water near, and saw a brook. There he went and washed himself. The water revived him greatly. Fortunately his clothes were only slightly torn. After washing the blood from his face, and buttoning his coat over his bloodstained shirt, and brushing the dirt from his clothes, he ventured to return to the city.

He crawled rather than walked, often stopping to rest, and once almost fainting from utter weakness. But at last he reached the city, and managed to find a wine-cart, the only vehicle that he could see, which took him to his lodgings. He reached his room before any of the others were up, and went to bed.

From *The Dodge Club; or Italy in 1859* (1860) by James de Mille 1836–1880. Born in St. John, N.B., he taught at Acadia and Dalhousie universities. In addition to *The Dodge Club*, he published four boys' books and (posthumously in 1888) a novel, *A Strange Manuscript.*

Sinai
by C.T. Currelly

In February of 1905 Frost and I took a group of the men and started out for what is called Mount Sinai. We soon came to the Wadi called Feran on most maps. I had met the Archbishop of Sinai in Cairo and he told me there was very little water at the great monastery, so I had visions of a dry area where even documents might be preserved if they were a foot or so under the surface. We had had altogether twenty-two days of rain, and though it was not heavy I felt it was quite enough to destroy parchment and paper. When we arrived at the Wadi Feran under Mount Serbal it turned out to be one of the most impressive places I have ever seen, and it would be natural enough to look upon it as the home of a god. The mountain is very high and everything seems to conspire to make it impressive. The wild, rocky scenery all around forms a vivid contrast to the exquisite beauty of the rich little oasis where a few acres of grain grew; there were also date palms and a few other trees. It is the only spot where the tribes of Sinai ever could gather, except along the coast. Coming out of the rock there is a stream about three inches in diameter which runs down the valley and provides water for irrigation. Further down the stream grows smaller and smaller and eventually disappears into the sandy ground, to come again to the surface some little distance away. It has a strange habit of changing its direction. By watching very carefully I became able to tell where it was likely to break out again.

The evening that I joined Petrie at the Valley of the Mines he said: "Well, I suppose you have already come to the conclusion that Moses never marched two million people through this country." My answer that there wouldn't have been a drink apiece for them was quite accurate. My mind goes back to a Sunday School picture showing a young girl in some vague Oriental drapery holding a pitcher on her shoulder and waiting for her turn to fill her pitcher. One so easily accepts such things without doing any mental arithmetic. With two million people the young lady would have had to wait sixteen years for her next pitcherful, if she were to get it from practically the only considerable source of water in the whole country.

At the Valley of the Mines we had discussed such questions a good deal. I was interested in the contrast between the attitude of Captain Weil, an outstanding reader of hieroglyphics and a French Jew, who pooh-poohed the whole story, and of Petrie, the trained archaeologist, who could not dismiss any serious ancient legend. Early stories can be altered according to the natural predilections of ancient tellers, but that this one could be completely rejected seemed to him out of the question. What puzzled him was the explanation of the enormous numbers in the Bible. All our talk led to nothing until Petrie began to play with the two census lists of the tribes that are given in Numbers: one when they entered Sinai and the other when they were leaving. The figures are strange for a census list. For instance, there seems no reason why there should be the definite relation that there is between the thousands and the hundreds. When Petrie returned to England he put this question to some of the best English scholars, and found that the word for thousand could also be used for tent, so the matter at once became clear. In other words, there were about six thousand men, and a general average to a tent, a perfectly possible number to live in Goshen, and to fight a successful battle with the local Sinai people, who could assemble at this spot only, because it is the only spot in the peninsula with enough water (except along the coast, where, by digging a few feet back from the edge of the Red Sea, there is plenty of brackish water. It will quench the thirst but is not pleasant to drink.).

I think the irregular movement of the stream that I noticed is the origin of the story of Moses smiting the rock (or ground) and bringing forth water. Moses had been in Sinai for a number of years and doubtless knew how this water acted, so it would be possible for him to strike the ground and a few minutes later for water to appear. Moses must have been one of the most remarkable men, and to keep his control over these twelve tribes must have been a difficult matter, so it is easy to understand his performing a bit of magic. The narrative says that he was not allowed to enter Canaan, because he took the glory to himself for producing the water, but this is a development of the story quite consistent with such an explanation.

After months spent among high rocks and dry, gravelly, sandy valleys, to enter the Wadi Feran gives one a feeling of awe. Deirel-Bahri, Delphi, the Grand Canyon and the Wadi Feran: of these, three were the homes of gods — one felt they had to be; certainly if the Grand Canyon had been in the old world it would have been the home of a god also. There were ruins of an enormous mud brick monastery which seems to have been destroyed by the early Mohammedan rush that came through, though the local Bedowi maintained that they were not conquered but became Mohammedans because the Prophet himself wrote them a letter. The fact that none of them could read (with the exception of the head chief, and I am not sure about him), didn't seem to worry them in the least, but if none of them could read in my time, their chances of being able to decipher the Prophet's letter were considerably less. There were some fair-sized walls remaining, and it must have been a big monastery in the days when so many men were going to the desert to become monks. I hunted around and found a good many coins of Constantine I, so it must have been fairly important in his period — say about 330 A.D.

I am convinced that at that time the place we were now in was considered the Mount of the Law: it was certainly the only place where the Hebrews could have been all together for Moses to have given them the Commandments. Near the monastery are numbers of little caves; in some places the side of the cliff was honeycombed with them. They looked much like empty tombs. This monastery had been under the Egyptian (Coptic) Church, but now the monks of the monastery of St. Catherine had got hold of a little property in the neighbourhood, had a monk living there, and were doubtless trying to establish their influence over the ancient site. The monks of St. Catherine are Greeks.

As we approached the valley in which the great monastery of St. Catherine is situated, we crossed a fairly high pass and a little snow fell. The excitement was tremendous. Men ran to me calling out, as the children of Israel did to Moses: "Master, what is it?" A very pious Ababdi, who was walking ahead of my camel, said with much indignation: "What is it? What is it? The Lord has sent us rice from heaven, that's what it is." None of these men had ever seen or heard of snow before. The men tried to catch it and taste it. I tried to explain what snow was, and said that in my country we had a foot or more of it covering the ground most of the winter, and that in the cold weather on the top of the rivers water turned so hard that a horse could go over it. Like many others who have tried to explain simple things to simple people, I made no impression, and when later the men returned to their homes I heard them describing to their relatives a miracle of rice coming down from heaven. That evening I got out my Bible and carefully read the two accounts of manna. Each characteristic fits the snow exactly except the last, and in this case the accounts differ, one stating that the waste was like wafers made with honey, and the other that it was like new oil. It was white; it fell in the night; it melted when the sun grew hot; it was like coriander seed. All these descriptions fit snow. Both accounts are accurate up to a point, but one version evidently came from someone with a sweet tooth and the other from one who liked rich foods.

As it would be impossible to keep on telling tales of snow from generation to generation without the question arising of what the children of Israel did with it, and what it tasted like, it seems to me inevitable that details should have been added, such as we have in the Biblical accounts. Any explanation that manna was something the Hebrews obtained from turfa bushes or from any other plant would make the Hebrews of the period a very stupid people. Manna fell from the skies: it is either an extraordinary miracle, or it is snow. As the Hebrews had the same food in Sinai as in the land of Goshen, plenty of meat and milk from their sheep and goats, there was no more reason for miraculous feeding in Sinai than there was before they entered it.

Presently we reached the monastery of St. Catherine, built by order of the Emperor Justinian, c. 550 A.D. It had been built without a gate, and everything had to be taken up over the wall in a basket with rope and pulley. The military engineer who laid it out had been wise, as it is impossible to keep such a guard on a gate that at some time or other it cannot be forced. A little time before we came, a hole had been cut through the wall and a doorway made, so that it was no longer necessary to go up over the wall. During the Mohammedan invasion, and in subsequent wars, this monastery was never once captured. Its proportions are grand and dignified. The huge blocks of granite of which it is built were quarried close by. As far as I can ascertain, Mt. St. Catherine, called on the map "Mt. Sinai," was not associated with the mount of Moses until after the Mohammedan conquest, when the great Coptic monastery of the Wadi Feran was seized. The monks of St. Catherine's monastery immediately made the claim that the mountain where St. Catherine's body had been found was the mountain of the Law. Some nonsense has been written about this being the only place where the Israelites could have been assembled, the writers not considering where they could have obtained water.

As far as I know, this Mount, which is most impressive, with the great monastery at its foot, was connected only with St. Catherine, whose body was miraculously deposited on top of it. Now, of course, everything connected with Moses has been moved to this monastery, and the Burnish Bush and the tree from which Aaron's rod was cut are still growing near the kitchen door. Petrie had the idea, which I think is right, that Aaron's rod and the pot of manna, which were placed in the Ark of the Covenant, were Hebrew units of measure and capacity, like our yardstick and quart pot. With most early peoples such units were invariably kept in the most sacred part of the temple and given some miraculous origin.

A short way up the mountain there is a peculiar stone with holes in it. I do not think any one of the holes would have held a gallon, but this is pointed out to the pilgrims as the rock struck by Moses from which the Hebrews got their water, and the story goes that it rolled along with the people as they marched, the different tribes getting their drink each from one of the holes. When one realizes that this story is accepted by many people, and has been for generations, one is amazed at human credulity; but that it is a very old story is clear from the fact that St. Paul seems to imply it.

The pride of the monastery of St. Catherine is its fine library, where one could sit in sixteenth-century chairs and turn over the leaves of ancient manuscripts. As far as I can remember, not more than ten books had been placed in the library since the Norman Conquest of England. The librarian was very proud of the beautiful manuscripts, some written entirely in gold, others beautifully illuminated. He told me he wanted me to know the true story of the famous *Codex Sinaiticus*.

Years ago, a monk had had a pan of charcoal in his room and had died in consequence. Hence it came to be believed that the wood in that region was poisonous, and no fire had been allowed in the monastery since that time except in the kitchen. But of course in this granite building the cold became intense in winter. The German-Russian scholar, Tischendorff, came to the library and was shown their books, and was particularly attracted by the famous codex, the value of which the monks thoroughly understood. He started to copy it, but complained that it was utterly impossible to work in such terrible cold, and begged them to allow him to take the codex to the Russian consul's house in Suez. He offered to pay the expenses of a monk to go with it, so that it could be said not to be out of their hands. After much deliberation, and rather timidly, they granted the request. The monk, therefore, went with Tischendorff to Suez, carrying the book. As soon as they were in the Russian consul's house the monk was told that he was now in Russian territory, and was kicked out. Tischendorff left at once for Russia and the book was gone. The monks set about entering a legal protest, but were told that they would never get the book back. The Russian Emperor was prepared to give them fifty thousand pounds, and to see that their superior was raised from a bishop to an archbishop. As they felt that this was the best they could hope for, they accepted the terms, but were very bitter at what they considered a robbery. I am inclined to think, from my knowledge of these monasteries, that the story so commonly told, that the monks were lighting the fire with this codex and that it was gradually being destroyed, is nonsense, as I would not like to try to light a fire with parchment; and I am prepared to believe that there is some truth in the librarian's story.

We started to dig the kitchen-midden at the monastery, but we soon stopped, for though the Archbishop was willing, the monks got thoroughly frightened. The little digging we did showed me that the midden contained nothing of any value, so I did not put up much resistance.

We continued our journey further east, beyond the region of maps, into country unknown to any of our Sinai camel-men. The first day's journey into the unknown, however, provided us with a guide whom we met trudging along one of the valleys. He told us that he knew where there were extraordinary things. When we camped the first night he told us that we were not quite half a day's journey from water. The next day Frost and I set out with the men and followed him to the spot, where his descriptions seemed to me to indicate the possibility of metalwork. I wasn't much surprised, though, when I found it was nothing more than a hole where a couple of blasts had been put in years before when the future President Hoover had been looking for copper. But within a few feet of this I saw what looked like signs of very ancient habitation, and we started to dig the ground over carefully. We found some beautiful flint drills that had been used in beadmaking, and a few partly made beads of carnelian. There was no sign of pottery or any household gear, and as there were no special stones for beadmaking nearby, and water was a long way off, it was difficult to understand why neolithic man should have stayed there for what was evidently a considerable time. We finished the digging in one day, and towards evening started home. It was a roundabout way of a few miles, and when we got home I started to wrap the delicate flints and to make what notes I could.

In the midst of this job Yusef came in to tell me that Ali wasn't in. I said: "Surely that's all right, Yusef, he's a desert man, he can't have gone far." With this he went away. When it was dark, he came in again, and I said: "Really, Yusef, what's the matter? Ali can't have wandered any distance away." "Oh," he said, "he didn't come back with us." I said: "What in the world do you mean?" He replied: "Soon after we started on the way home, Ali said he wouldn't walk all the way home as we came, as he could go straight over the hills to the camp, so he stepped behind a rock till you had gone on, and then started to go straight across."

This was serious, because I felt that there were ten chances to one that he would be lost, and being lost meant death, which meant the end of everything for us, as the men would refuse to go on. I tried to follow Moses' plan of showing where the camp was with a "pillar of fire" on the highest point, but though we gathered a lot of dead bushes and made a fire, the wind was strong and blew the fire down at right angles, and I knew it wouldn't be seen at any distance away. It was now dark, and I told the men to get their suppers and go to sleep. They had declared a fast, which I discouraged as much as I could, by telling them that we would need every bit of strength in the morning for a hunt. As I knew I could do nothing more then, I went to sleep, having seen the men in their blankets; but as soon as I was asleep, the Ababdis got up and started a search. When I woke up they were coming back, and one more man was lost. There was only one water-hole some distance away, with nothing to mark the spot, and though I had a vague hope of tracking the first man who was lost, of the second I had no hope whatever.

At daybreak I started what was the most difficult tracking I have ever done, as the only clue was an occasional overturned stone that showed a different colour on the under surface. Later in the afternoon I had made less than half a mile of progress, when a shot was heard coming along one of the valleys. Our man going for water had found both our lost men, sitting by the only water-hole within miles. Being desert men, the moment they were lost they knew that it meant death. They said a great fear came upon them, and they pushed straight ahead, and Allah led them to the water. The two men were lost miles apart, not only in country with which they were unfamiliar, but in geological conditions quite unknown to them, and the water-holes were always in some obscure spot in a valley, usually against the edge of a cliff, and with nothing whatever to mark them. Yet in the pitch dark these men went straight to water. A somewhat similar thing happened to Lepsius when he and his man were lost in the desert across the Red Sea, but his man went to water only after he was insane. I discussed the matter with the men, but could find no explanation.

As there seemed nothing from an archaeological standpoint in the region, we started for Tor. The men began to play out badly, and more than the usual number had to be put up on the camels. This started a series of rows with the camel-men, who claimed that their camels couldn't carry the extra load. This was untrue, because our supplies were getting lighter every day. One night a Bedowi stole a whole skin of dates, a serious loss for us. When we discovered the loss, I told Yusef, and quietly each Bedowi was isolated from his camel while his saddlebags were examined. The thief was soon found, and charged with the theft, which he denied in the name of God and Mohammed and everyone else he could think of, but his camel bags were opened, and, as happened to Benjamin, the dates were found.

As things were getting troublesome, I felt I had to be dramatic, so I told my men to give him enough food and water to take him home, and ordered him to leave us at once, under threats of dire punishment. I paid him for what he had done. Next morning he left for home, and I heard afterward that he got home all right, but his camel died the day after his arrival. This was clearly a piece of magic on my part, designed not to take his life but to cause him great loss.

The last few days before we reached Tor things got very bad. One of the Bedowi swung a gun on one of my men, but the quickness of the Ababdis is extraordinary; the gun was out of his hand before he knew what had happened. It proved to be a long matchlock, with a broken lock, and was dangerous only as a club. The poor chap had been carrying it for months. It was half as heavy again as the modern service rifle, useless, of crushing weight, and yet in his temper he had whisked it off his back, where it hung by a strap, and was getting it to his shoulder when it was seized.

I wasn't afraid of the guns, because it took too long to do anything with them, but a sword or dagger can be drawn much more quickly. But I felt it was time to think up some punishment, if it were only to relieve my own feelings. When we arrived at Tor I got money and supplies from the French engineers, and carefully calculating what I owed the Bedowi I divided it into sovereigns and silver, called them together, handed the whole amount of it to one of them, and said: "Now that is what I owe all of you, go!" This was in the morning. We had to wait a couple of days for a boat to Suez. Next day the Bedowi came to me with great lamentations. They said they had been very wicked, but would I not forgive them? The fellow to whom the money had been given had been forced to sit in a circle with the other camel-men; they were afraid even to let him close his hand, afraid to take their eyes off the money, afraid to go away to get food or anything else. None of them could count, so they were unable to divide the money, and all day and all night they sat in the circle watching the gold and silver. If I had whipped them all black and blue I couldn't have subdued them more effectively.

From Tor we went to Suez and then up to Pithom, in the land of Goshen, that the Hebrews had built for Rameses II as a store place and base for his Syrian campaign. It was from this neighbourhood that the Hebrews set out for the Promised Land. We wished to see if it were possible to do anything with what remained of this city of Pithom. Naville had worked there and had published a report showing the great store chambers and a few other walls. Naville was one of the best hieroglyph scholars of his day, but there were few good linguists of that time who had any mechanical knowledge, with the exception of Sir William Ridgeway. I was eager to go because of the Biblical associations. As I had Naville's plans, I was able to see the form of these so-called store chambers. A couple of pits were sunk to the original ground level and the plans showed that the walls were of late Roman period. The large mass of thick walls in the middle of the place was no doubt the central castle-like structure, where the more destructible materials were probably stored, the fodder and such being placed anywhere in the town, which was itself also protected by a thick wall. This outer wall had been cut down to the level of the surrounding country by the fierce blowing sand — the fiercest, I think, I have ever seen. In connection with the destruction of the upper part of the castle-like structure it has often been stated that whereas the bottom bricks were made with straw, the upper ones were not. This is merely amusing, as only the lower parts of the wall were left anyway — in any case the Biblical narrative says that the Hebrews gathered their own straw. I broke up half a dozen bricks, and found every one full of holes where the straw had been, but the moisture from occasional rains had caused the straw to decay. The statement, made by a prominent engineer who visited Naville's excavations, has been taken more seriously than it deserves.

There was a railway some miles away, and a little desert station, from which it was possible to send letters. One day I had sent a man to see if there was any mail for us. When he came back at night I heard a great commotion. One man of the group, an Egyptian, could read, and the Ababdis, with some Egyptians in the rear, came rushing over to me in a state of great excitement, all talking at once; the one sentence that was repeated again and again was: "Ali has been struck!" As soon as I could quiet them, I said: "Yusef, you tell me what the trouble is." Yusef said that when his brother had taken Porch and his Italian servant to the Nile, they asked him to remain with them, as Porch was hunting palaeolithic flints. Something happened, and the Italian servant had slapped Ali's face. I said: "But what's the difference? I have been slapped plenty of times." They explained that their tribal law on this matter was very severe. Anyone who struck one of their tribe had to be killed to wipe out the disgrace to the tribe, and if any tribesman had it in his power to kill the offender and did not do so, he lost his tribesmanship, and became an outcast. Now the question was, what was I going to do about it? I had got them into the trouble. I sent a letter to the station-master with a telegram to be sent off to Porch, telling him that the Italian must be shipped out of the country at once. As these men, who had become real friends of mine, would have stood by me in any pinch of safety or honour, they naturally expected me to do the same.

This incident set me thinking about the flight of Moses from the court of the Egyptian governor into Sinai. I had puzzled for years about this story and could make nothing of it. In the light of what had just occurred, it seemed clear. Here is a young man brought up at the court of Pharaoh, whose daughter, Moses' patron, was no doubt married to the governor guarding the eastern borders near Goshen. He wanders out among his own people, who are building the huge storehouses for Pharaoh's base, and sees an Egyptian, probably an overseer, strike one of his own tribe. Though Moses was a young blood of the Egyptian court and knew the Egyptian law, he killed the Egyptian and buried him in the sand. When he found that the Hebrew, in spite of his warning, had talked, he had to flee the country and make his escape into Sinai. St. Paul's allusion had also puzzled me when he said that Moses had preferred to throw in his lot with his own people rather than have the wealth of the Egyptians. The desert law would have made Moses lose his tribesmanship and become an outcast from his own people unless he had avenged the insult. As all Egyptian gentlemen carried a stone-headed mace, it would have been easy enough for Moses to kill the Egyptian — the poor fellow probably bowed his head and submitted his fate to the favourite of Pharaoh's daughter. Much nonsense has been written about the impossibility of this story of Moses, on the assumption that Pharaoh's daughter must have been living with the Pharaoh, hundreds of miles away. None of the writers seems to have realized that a girl often leaves home when she marries.

We had incessant sand storms that blew the tents down and filled the food with sand. About three times a week we could see a pea-soup-coloured cloud coming toward us, and would make for whatever shelter we could and try to endure it. It was difficult to eat, and I became weak from malnutrition. As we were encamped on the Sweet Water Canal, which runs from the Nile into the gulf of Suez, a few stragglers were occasionally met with. One day a magician arrived with an old book of magic, and tried to sell copies of formulas that looked as though noughts and crosses had been played all over the page. For a sum he would copy one out and sell it, and like the old patent medicine man's preparation, it would cure "whatever ailed yuh." These scoundrels prey on the Egyptians continually, and there is no getting back at them. You buy a charm, and the magician disappears. If he comes round again and you complain, he says: "How did you wear it?" Of course you wore it the wrong side up or down, or in or out, so if the charm didn't work it was your fault. The people are much afraid of them. When he tried to sell charms to my men I ordered him off, telling him that if he didn't go at once I would whip him. The magician, who had been feared for so many years, couldn't grasp this, and looked at my men as though he must have misunderstood me. The answer was: "He will, you know." As soon as he was a little distance away I received a scream of abuse that reached heights almost of grandeur in its inventiveness.

One day a few Bedowi turned up and asked an Egyptian if two men in the distance were Ababdi. The Egyptian swore he had never heard of any such people, but one of the Bedowi, pointing to three of the men, called one of them by name. I appeared on the scene and ordered the Bedowi away with threats, but the Ababdi who had been recognized felt that he had better leave.

Petrie was kind enough to pay me a visit, but it seemed as if we weren't getting anywhere, and moreover Sir Gaston Maspero had wanted him to get me to go back to Sinai and remove the inscriptions from over the mines at the Wadi Magareh. We took a few of the men down to Suez and arranged to have a sailing boat take a quantity of timber down to make scaffolds that could later be used for packing. We arranged passage to Tor. When we came to go on the boat, as I thought in plenty of time, I found that we were supposed to go to some fumigating, quarantine type of place, although we had just come out of the desert. The officials, anxious to show off, were very firm and drew a line of Egyptian soldiers across the gangway. Frost and I went up quietly and told the men to keep straight behind us. We grabbed two of their rifles and pushed them aside and burst through. A very official person then demanded our names and ages, and everything else he could think of. After Frost and I were disposed of, it was the turn of Yusef. "How old?" "I don't know; God knows." The official looked to me, so I gave a guess at Yusef's age. When Ali came through next, I added ten years to my former guess, and so with the rest. Soon the official said: "Are you all brothers?" I answered: "No, it's the tribe." A comparative youth came through when the age had reached 104, whereupon the official looked at me very seriously, and then it dawned on him what I was doing.

At Suez we got long chisels and obtained the lumber, ropes and other equipment. A sailing boat was engaged to drop them off as near the Valley of the Mines as possible. Most of the men were to come by sail boat, but we took four with us to Tor. When we arrived at Tor we found that the pilgrims had begun to come up from Mecca. Here was a wonderful hospital under an international board. The famous Doctor Ruffer was in charge with a few other doctors appointed by the boards, one a most charming Russian, who didn't know any medicine and made no pretence of doing anything. Ruffer had a comfortable little home, which his wife managed expertly, and placed at our disposal a convenient Indian tent. Barbed wire enclosures kept each shipload of passengers well apart from the next. The Ruffers welcomed us most kindly, but that afternoon Frost was thrown from his mount, and, when the excitement was over, I nearly collapsed. Ruffer examined me and found me in a very low state with malnutrition and refused to allow me to go on for a week.

My rest gave me an excellent chance to see the pilgrims. About forty-five thousand had gone to Mecca, and of these about fifteen thousand were already dead. It was very hot, running around 120 in the shade, and dysentery was the main cause, though a number were suffering from shot wounds. Every year an elaborate carpet is made in Egypt and sent to hang on the Sacred Stone of Mecca for a year, and then brought back. A contingent of soldiers guards it. As the pilgrims made their way from the sea, it became a favourite sport of the local Bedowi to lie on the cliffs and take pot shots at them plodding through the valleys. One day at a turn in the valley, the soldiers came on an encampment of Bedowi, and, furious for vengeance, they let blaze into the women and children. Now of course there was no longer any question of trying to stampede the pilgrims with the hope of picking up whatever the killed or wounded had on them, but a real blood feud. On the return journey things had been just as bad, and with the heat even small wounds became serious. At the hospital the dead were piled up like cordwood, and one day nearly every patient died in spite of all the doctors could do. The staff detailed for the purpose could not bury them fast enough. The diggers were working to the limit of their strength, but the death rate continued to rise with the temperature.

From *I Brought the Ages Home* (1956) by Charles Trick Currelly, 1876-1957. Born in Exeter, Ontario, Currelly went with the archaeologist Flinders Petrie to Egypt in 1901. In 1912 he became the first director of the Royal Ontario Museum, founded that year on his initiative.

LONDON
by Stephen Leacock

Before setting down my impressions of the great English metropolis — a phrase which I have thought out as a designation for London — I think it proper to offer an initial apology. I find that I receive impressions with great difficulty and have nothing of that easy facility in picking them up which is shown by British writers on America. I remember Hugh Walpole telling me that he could hardly walk down Broadway without getting at least three dollars' worth and on Fifth Avenue five dollars' worth; and I recollect that St. John Ervine came up to my house in Montreal, drank a cup of tea, borrowed some tobacco, and got away with sixty dollars' worth of impressions of Canadian life and character.

For this kind of thing I have only a despairing admiration. I can get an impression if I am given time and can think about it beforehand. But it requires thought. The fact was all the more distressing to me in as much as one of the leading editors of America had made me a proposal, as honourable to him as it was lucrative to me, that immediately on my arrival in London — or just before it — I should send him a thousand words on the genius of the English, and five hundred words on the spirit of London, and two hundred words of personal chat with Lord Northcliffe. This contract I was unable to fulfil except the personal chat with Lord Northcliffe, which proved an easy matter as he happened to be away in Australia.

But I have since pieced together my impressions as conscientiously as I could and I present them here. If they seem to be a little bit modelled on British impressions of America I admit at once that the influence is there. We writers all act and react on one another; and when I see a good thing in another man's book I react on it at once.

London, the name of which is already known to millions of readers of this book, is beautifully situated on the river Thames, which here sweeps in a wide curve with much the same breadth and majesty as the St. Jo River at South Bend, Indiana. London, like South Bend itself, is a city of clean streets and admirable sidewalks, and has an excellent water supply. One is at once struck by the number of excellent and well appointed motor cars that one sees on every hand, the neatness of the shops and the cleanliness and cheerfulness of the faces of the people. In short, as an English visitor said of Peterborough, Ontario, there is a distinct note of optimism in the air. I forget who it was who said this, but at any rate I have been in Peterborough myself and I have seen it.

Contrary to my expectations and contrary to all our transatlantic precedents, I was *not* met at the depot by one of the leading citizens, himself a member of the Municipal Council, driving his own motor car. He did *not* tuck a fur rug about my knees, present me with a really excellent cigar and proceed to drive me about the town so as to show me the leading points of interest, the municipal reservoir, the gas works and the municipal abattoir. In fact he was not there. But I attribute his absence not to any lack of hospitality but merely to a certain reserve in the English character. They are as yet unused to the arrival of lecturers. When they get to be more accustomed to their coming, they will learn to take them straight to the municipal abattoir just as we do.

For lack of better guidance, therefore, I had to form my impressions of London by myself. In the mere physical sense there is much to attract the eye. The city is able to boast of many handsome public buildings and offices which compare favourably with anything on the other side of the Atlantic. On the bank of the Thames itself rises the power house of the Westminster Electric Supply Corporation, a handsome modern edifice in the later Japanese style. Close by are the commodious premises of the Imperial Tobacco Company, while at no great distance the Chelsea Gas Works add a striking feature of rotundity. Passing northward, one observes Westminster Bridge, notable as a principal station of the underground railway. This station and the one next above it, the Charing Cross one, are connected by a wide thoroughfare called Whitehall. One of the best American drug stores is here situated. The upper end of Whitehall opens into the majestic and spacious Trafalgar Square. Here are grouped in imposing proximity the offices of the Canadian Pacific and other railways, the International Sleeping Car Company, the Montreal *Star*, and the Anglo-Dutch Bank. Two of the best American barber shops are conveniently grouped near the Square, while the existence of a tall stone monument in the middle of the Square itself enables the American visitor to find them without difficulty. Passing eastward towards the heart of the city, one notes on the left hand the imposing pile of St. Paul's, an enormous church with a round dome on the top, suggesting strongly the First Church of Christ (Scientist) on Euclid Avenue, Cleveland. But the English churches not being labelled, the visitor is often at a loss to distinguish them.

A little further on one finds oneself in the heart of financial London. Here all the great financial institutions of America — the First National Bank of Milwaukee, the Planters National Bank of St. Louis, the Montana Farmers Trust Co., and many others — have either their offices or their agents. The Bank of England — which acts as the London agent of the Montana Farmers Trust Company — and the London County Bank, which represents the People's Deposit Co., of Yonkers, N.Y., are said to be in the neighbourhood.

This particular part of London is connected with the existence of that strange and mysterious thing called "the City." I am still unable to decide whether the City is a person, or a place, or a thing. But as a form of being I give it credit for being the most emotional, the most volatile, the most peculiar creature in the world. You read in the morning paper that the City is "deeply depressed." At noon it is reported that the City is "buoyant" and by four o'clock the City is "wildly excited."

I have tried in vain to find the causes of these peculiar changes of feeling. The ostensible reasons, as given in the newspaper, are so trivial as to be hardly worthy of belief. For example, here is the kind of news that comes out from the City. "The news that a *modus vivendi* has been signed between the Sultan of Kowfat and the Shriek-ul-Islam has caused a sudden buoyancy in the City. Steel rails which had been depressed all morning reacted immediately while American mules rose up sharply to par." . . . "Monsieur Poincaré, speaking at Bordeaux, said that henceforth France must seek to retain by all possible means the ping-pong championship of the world: values in the City collapsed at once." . . . "Despatches from Bombay say that the Shah of Persia yesterday handed a golden slipper to the Grand Vizier Feebli Pasha as a sign that he might go and chase himself; the news was at once followed by a drop in oil, and a rapid attempt to liquidate everything that is fluid. . . ."

But these mysteries of the City I do not pretend to explain. I have passed through the place dozens of times and never noticed anything particular in the way of depression or buoyancy, or falling oil, or rising rails. But no doubt it is there.

A little beyond the City and further down the river the visitor finds this district of London terminating in the gloomy and forbidding Tower, the principal penitentiary of the city. Here Queen Victoria was imprisoned for many years.

Excellent gasoline can be had at the American Garage immediately north of the Tower, where motor repairs of all kinds are also carried on.

These, however, are but the superficial pictures of London, gathered by the eye of the tourist. A far deeper meaning is found in the examination of the great historic monuments of the city. The principal ones of these are the Tower of London (just mentioned), the British Museum and Westminster Abbey. No visitor to London should fail to see these. Indeed he ought to feel that his visit to England is wasted unless he has seen them. I speak strongly on the point because I feel strongly on it. To my mind there is something about the grim fascination of the historic Tower, the cloistered quiet of the Museum and the majesty of the ancient Abbey, which will make it the regret of my life that I didn't see any one of the three. I fully meant to: but I failed: and I can only hope that the circumstances of my failure may be helpful to other visitors.

The Tower of London I most certainly intended to inspect. Each day, after the fashion of every tourist, I wrote for myself a little list of things to do and I always put the Tower of London on it. No doubt the reader knows the kind of little list I mean. It runs:

1   Go to bank
2   Buy a shirt
3   National Picture Gallery

4   Razor blades

5   Tower of London

6   Soap

This itinerary, I regret to say, was never carried out in full. I was able at times both to go to the bank and buy a shirt in a single morning: at other times I was able to buy razor blades and almost to find the National Picture Gallery. Meantime I was urged on all sides by my London acquaintances not to fail to see the Tower. "There's a grim fascination about the place," they said; "you mustn't miss it." I am quite certain that in due course of time I should have made my way to the Tower but for the fact that I made a fatal discovery. I found out that the London people who urged me to go and see the Tower had never seen it themselves. It appears they never go near it. One night at a dinner a man next to me said, "Have you seen the Tower? You really ought to. There's a grim fascination about it." I looked him in the face. "Have you seen it yourself?" I asked. "Oh, yes," he answered. "I've seen it." "When?" I asked. The man hesitated. "When I was just a boy," he said, "my father took me there." "How long ago is that?" I inquired. "About forty years ago," he answered. "I always mean to go again but I don't somehow seem to get the time."

After this I got to understand that when a Londoner says, "Have you seen the Tower of London?" the answer is "No, and neither have you."

Take the parallel case of the British Museum. Here is a place that is a veritable treasure house. A repository of some of the most priceless historical relics to be found upon the earth. It contains, for instance, the famous Papyrus Manuscript of Thotmes II of the first Egyptian dynasty — a thing known to scholars all over the world as the oldest extant specimen of what can be called writing; indeed one can here see the actual evolution (I am quoting from a work of reference, or at least from my recollection of it) from the ideographic cuneiform of the phonetic syllabic script. Every time I have read about that manuscript and have happened to be in Orillia (Ontario) or Schenectady (N.Y.) or any such place, I have felt that I would be willing to take a whole trip to England to have five minutes at the British Museum, just five, to look at that papyrus. Yet as soon as I got to London this changed. The railway stations of London have been so arranged that to get to any train for the north or west, the traveller must pass the British Museum. The first time I went by it in a taxi, I felt quite a thrill. "Inside those walls," I thought to myself, "is the manuscript of Thotmes II." The next time I actually stopped the taxi. "Is that the British Museum?" I asked the driver. "I think it is something of the sort, sir," he said. I hesitated. "Drive me," I said, "to where I can buy safety razor blades."

After that I was able to drive past the Museum with the quiet assurance of a Londoner, and to take part in dinner table discussions as to whether the British Museum or the Louvre contains the greater treasures. It is quite easy any way. All you have to do is to remember that the Winged Victory of Samothrace is in the Louvre and the papyrus of Thotmes II (or some such document) is in the Museum.

The Abbey, I admit, is indeed majestic. I did not intend to miss going into it. But I felt, as so many tourists have, that I wanted to enter it in the proper frame of mind. I never got into the frame of mind; at least not when near the Abbey itself. I have been in exactly that frame of mind when on State Street, Chicago, or on King Street, Toronto, or anywhere three thousand miles away from the Abbey. But by bad luck I never struck both the frame of mind and the Abbey at the same time.

But the Londoners, after all, in not seeing their own wonders, are only like the rest of the world. The people who live in Buffalo never go to see Niagara Falls; people in Cleveland don't know which is Mr. Rockefeller's house, and people live and even die in New York without going up to the top of the Woolworth Building. And anyway the past is remote and the present is near. I know a cab driver in the city of Quebec whose business in life it is to drive people up to see the Plains of Abraham, but unless they bother him to do it, he doesn't even show them the spot where Wolfe fell: what he does point out with real zest is the place where the Mayor and the City Council sat on the wooden platform that they put up for the municipal celebration last summer.

No description of London would be complete without a reference, however brief, to the singular salubrity and charm of the London climate. This is seen at its best during the autumn and winter months. The climate of London and indeed of England generally is due to the influence of the Gulf Stream. The way it works is thus: the Gulf Stream, as it nears the shores of the British Isles and feels the propinquity of Ireland, rises into the air, turns into soup, and comes down on London. At times the soup is thin and is in fact little more than a mist; at other times it has the consistency of a thick Potage St. Germain. London people are a little sensitive on the point and flatter their atmosphere by calling it a fog; but it is not; it is soup. The notion that no sunlight ever gets through and that in the London winter people never see the sun is of course a ridiculous error, circulated no doubt by the jealousy of foreign nations. I have myself seen the sun plainly visible in London, without the aid of glasses, on a November day in broad daylight; and again one night about four o'clock in the afternoon I saw the sun distinctly appear through the clouds. The whole subject of daylight in the London winter is, however, one which belongs rather to the technique of astronomy than to a book of description. In practice daylight is but little used. Electric lights are burned all the time in all houses, buildings, railway stations and clubs. This practice which is now universally observed is called Daylight Saving.

But the distinction between day and night during the London winter is still quite obvious to any one of an observant mind. It is indicated by various signs such as the striking of clocks, the tolling of bells, the closing of saloons, and the raising of taxi rates. It is much less easy to distinguish the technical approach of night in the other cities of England that lie outside the confines, physical and intellectual, of London and live in a continuous gloom. In such places as the great manufacturing cities, Buggingham-under-Smoke, or Gloomsbury-on-Ooze, night may be said to be perpetual.

I had written the whole of the above chapter and looked on it as finished when I realized that I had made a terrible omission. I neglected to say anything about the Mind of London. This is a thing that is always put into any book of discovery and observation and I can only apologize for not having discussed it sooner. I am quite familiar with other people's chapters on "The Mind of America," and "The Chinese Mind," and so forth. Indeed, so far as I know it has turned out that almost everybody all over the world has a mind. Nobody nowadays travels, even in Central America or Tibet, without bringing back a chapter on "The Mind of Costa Rica," or on the

"Psychology of the Mongolian." Even the gentler peoples such as the Burmese, the Siamese, the Hawaiians, and the Russians, though they have no minds, are written up as souls.

It is quite obvious then that there is such a thing as the mind of London: and it is all the more culpable in me to have neglected it in as much as my editorial friend in New York had expressly mentioned it to me before I sailed. "What," said he, leaning far over his desk after his massive fashion and reaching out into the air, "what is in the *minds* of these people? Are they," he added, half to himself, though I heard him, "are they thinking? And, if they think, *what* do they think?"

I did therefore, during my stay in London make an accurate study of the things that London seemed to be thinking about. As a comparative basis for this study I brought with me a carefully selected list of the things that New York was thinking about at the moment. These I selected from the current newspapers in the proportions to the amount of space allotted to each topic and the size of the heading that announced it. Having thus a working idea of what I may call the mind of New York, I was able to collect and set beside it a list of similar topics, taken from the London Press to represent the mind of London. The two placed side by side make an interesting piece of psychological analysis. They read as follows:

THE MIND OF NEW YORK
What is it thinking?

1 Do chorus girls make good wives?
2 Is red hair a sign of temperament?
3 Can a woman be in love with two men?
4 Is fat a sign of genius?

THE MIND OF LONDON
What is it thinking?

1 Do chorus girls marry well?
2 What is red hair a sign of?
3 Can a man be in love with two women?
4 Is genius a sign of fat?

Looking over these lists, I think it is better to present them without comment; I feel sure that somewhere or other in them one should detect the heart throbs, the pulsations of two great peoples. But I don't get it. In fact the two lists look to me terribly like "the mind of Costa Rica."

The same editor also advised me to mingle, at his expense, in the brilliant intellectual life of England. "There," he said, "is a coterie of men, probably the most brilliant group east of the Mississippi." (I think he said the Mississippi.) "You will find them," he said to me, "brilliant, witty, filled with repartee." He suggested that I should send him back, as far as words could express it, some of this brilliance. I was very glad to be able to do this, although I fear that the results were not at all what he had anticipated. Still, I held conversations with these people and I gave him, in all truthfulness the result. Sir James Barrie said, "This is really very exceptional weather for this time of year." Cyril Maude said, "And so a Martini cocktail is merely gin and vermouth." Ian Hay said, "You'll find the underground ever so handy once you understand it."

I have a lot more of these repartees that I could insert here if it was necessary. But somehow I feel that it is not.

From *My Discovery of England* (1922) by Stephen Leacock, 1869–1944. Born in England, he grew up in Ontario from age six to become a professor of economics and political science at McGill University, but won lasting fame with his unflagging output of funny books. He had visited London in 1907 and 1921 when he wrote this sketch.

PARIS
by Morley Callaghan

The Quarter was like a small town. It had little points of protocol, little indignities not to be suffered. There was a general
awareness of what was going on in everyone else's life, a routine to
be followed if the café was to be the centre of your social life. For
the Joyces or Gertrude Stein, the café was not the place where one
entertained one's friends, or the place where wives showed up to meet
their husbands. Nor did the Fitzgeralds, as we were to discover, belong
to the Left Bank café set. But for us, not having the family respon-
sibilities of the Hemingways and the Fitzgeralds, the late hours at
the café were a happy time — unless a neighbourhood indignity was
being endured by a friend.

We had a friend, a middle-aged man named Edward Titus, who
was the husband of Helena Rubenstein, the rich beautician. He lived
by himself in a comfortable apartment just around the corner at 4
rue Delambre. He was a famous book collector and the publisher
of the Black Maniken Press. An agreeable quiet man, with graying
hair combed straight back, he had grown tired of the opulent display,
the chauffeurs, and all the business detail that took up his time in
the great cosmetic firm of Helena Rubenstein. He had chucked it
all. He was living his own life. When the editor of the magazine *This
Quarter* had died, Titus, not wanting the magazine to die too, had
taken it over.

At nine thirty in the evening, Loretto and I would come along the
boulevard to the Sélect. Within half an hour Titus would join us.
Sometimes Helena Rubenstein would come over to the Quarter from
the Right Bank. She came to the parties with a tall dark opera singer
named d'Alvarez, who wore evening dresses showing a broad and

fascinating expanse of bare back. Sometimes Madame Rubenstein would come to the café with Titus, and he would have her sit with us. In those days she was a very busy woman, growing stout, but still dark, handsome and full of energy. Too much energy, I suppose, for sometimes she gave the impression of wanting to take a little nap. When she was with us there was always an amusing interplay about paying for the saucers. Titus was an old resident of the Quarter; no one treated him as a visiting businessman who was expected to pay the shot, and he seemed to know that if he ever gave in and picked up the tab just because he was rich, he would lose all caste with the people whose respect he wanted. Quite properly he paid for his own saucers as I for mine.

At the end of an evening Helena Rubenstein would watch, aloof and impatient, while the waiter busily counted up our separate piles of saucers. "Pay for them, Edward," she would say imperiously. Did she ever understand his reluctance? I wonder. Maybe she didn't care. As a grand dame, a figure of opulence, she could hardly sit there listening to the public bookkeeping. One way or another, only a couple of dollars was involved. Whenever she intervened, Titus understood that protocol was being broken; he was being made to look like an alien in the Quarter, and he didn't like it.

Though he was established in the neighbourhood, and published in his own right, Titus did not know Joyce, Pound, Wyndham Lewis, Hemingway, Fitzgerald or McAlmon. It was hard to explain why he didn't know any of these people. I used to wonder if there was a lot of anti-Semitism in the Quarter.

McAlmon, having returned to Paris, had quickly looked us up. I liked McAlmon. No matter what they say about him, his judgment of other writers was respected by some of the best people on earth. His destructive malice didn't bother me at all. If a man of talent was in any kind of trouble, McAlmon would help him if he could.

When he met my wife, he showed he was pleased with her; then he had to jab his little needle into me, or her, and sow the seeds of discord. "You had me fooled," he said to her some hours after meeting us. "I thought you were Spanish. You're Irish." And then he added with a touch of weary disdain, "You ought to be always dressed well, be seen in *Vogue* and *Harper's Bazaar*. It's too bad. Morley won't bother. You might as well know it now." When he saw we were laughing at him, he didn't mind; he laughed too.

I had asked Titus if he would like to meet McAlmon. Indeed he would, he said. That night McAlmon came to the Sélect.

Alone with me, or even when my wife was along, McAlmon never behaved badly, or got outrageously drunk. Maybe he felt ill at ease with Titus, or wasn't sure how he felt about him, therefore he had to drink a lot very quickly. I had asked if he had heard whether Fitzgerald was in Paris. It set him off. He told of a meeting with the Fitzgeralds when Zelda had cast a lustful eye at him. Titus, who had said little, and no wonder, pricked up his ears. I laughed cynically and shook my head at Titus. When Bob McAlmon had had a drink or two he seemed to believe every good-looking citizen, man or woman, postman or countess, wanted to make a pass at him.

Along the street came those two willowy graceful young men from Montreal whom McAlmon called affectionately "the clever little devils." Sauntering into the café with their bland and distinguished air, they saw us and bowed. My lighthearted wave of the hand piqued McAlmon. "Oh, you don't understand those two at all," he jeered. But I did understand that the two boys shared his snickering wit. Friends of his they might be, but it didn't stop them from laughing at him. Just before his return, his Contact Press had printed one of his own poems. One boy would look at the other solemnly, quote a line from the poem, "Is this the Aztec heart that writhes upon the temple floor," then they would both kill themselves laughing.

His view of the boys amused me and I said so. We kept jibing and jeering at each other, offering contrasting views of the boys. Titus, brightening and becoming an alert editor, suggested we should both write stories; he would publish two stories side by side in the next issue of *This Quarter*. Immediately I agreed to do it. So did McAlmon.

By the way, I did write the story, "Now That April's Here," and Titus did publish it. Ezra Pound wrote me a letter from Rapallo expressing his admiration of the story and suggesting that I go to Washington and write about the politicians in the same manner.

By now McAlmon, exhilarated by our debate, and getting tight, had become truly expansive. He ordered another champagne cocktail and a Welsh rarebit. When the waiter brought the rarebit McAlmon tasted it, and dropped his fork. "Tell Madame Sélect," he said in a disgusted tone, "that this rarebit did not come from the kitchen. It came from the toilet." The waiter hurried to Madame Sélect.

She was a plump, dark, determined-looking woman with a round high-coloured face, who watched over the cash register and the waiters. Indeed she was the café boss. Approaching our table, quivering with rage, she told McAlmon she, herself, had made the rarebit. In that case, said McAlmon, waving his hand disdainfully, she ought to know where it came from. Aghast, she snatched the plate off the table and fled to the kitchen. In a little while she came out and stood back from the terrace at the door, watching us balefully, muttering, throwing glances of hatred at McAlmon, who had kept on laughing.

McAlmon's real target, and I couldn't put it past him if he was in one of his contemptuous moods, may have been Titus. Half drunk as he was, did he feel compelled to show some disrespect to this other publisher whose aims were so different from his own? In the meantime I had turned to watch a group of young homosexuals two tables away. The expression on my face must have irritated McAlmon. Maybe I did look too concerned. Four of the young homosexuals were commiserating with a sad-looking young fellow of twenty-five, whose story we knew. His wife, now on her way from the States to join him, did not know that in the months he had been without her, he had been corrupted by these boys. Now he had no desire to see her. McAlmon evidently resenting my expression of concern or pity, wanted to offend me. Knowing I had kept all my good feeling for Hemingway, he struck very deftly at him. In *The Sun Also Rises*, why had Hemingway treated these homosexuals in such a vulgar orthodox manner? he asked. The answer was simple: he had been catering to all the virile men of the Middle West. All he had been really doing was strutting and flexing his own big powerful muscles, asserting his own virility — something, said McAlmon, looking down his nose, that was open to question. "So, Morley old boy, don't you start turning up your nose at homosexuals," he said, "or I'll suspect you too."

"It's the one boy there, Bob. I feel sorry for him."

"You're ridiculous," he said, and he began a funny, mocking, eloquent, but often loud defense of homosexuals. As Titus showed his embarrassment, McAlmon went on talking grandly about Plato and Michelangelo. Our objections only aroused his chuckling disdain. He was happily drunk. Suddenly he cried exuberantly, "I'm bisexual myself, like Michelangelo, and I don't give a damn who knows it." He hurled his glass out to the sidewalk where it splintered in front of an elderly man who stopped, rattled, waving his hand as if he were calling the police.

Madame Sélect, who had been standing at her post, watching and scowling at McAlmon and brooding over the insult to her rarebit, now came rushing over to the table. McAlmon would pay for the glass, she cried. Not only would he pay, she added grimly, he would leave the café at once. With a patient, tolerant smile, McAlmon rose, tried to bow, then had to sit down quickly — he couldn't move. While he sat there staring earnestly at the table top, his face chalk white, I went for a taxi. When I returned, Titus told me Madame Sélect had said my friend was not welcome at her café any more.

Glancing at Madame Sélect, who waited, her arms folded, grim, solid and unyielding, Titus urged me to hurry and get McAlmon into a taxi. I did. But again for Titus, the protocol was broken; being treated as a businessman, he was left paying for McAlmon's drinks, the Welsh rarebit, the broken glass, and our drinks too. Though McAlmon, in the taxi, was in a stupor, as I looked at him I wondered if he hadn't actually wanted this to happen.

Now a matter of the greatest dignity began to concern our little neighbourhood. Next night at nine thirty when Loretto and I came along the boulevard, Titus, in his chair at the Sélect, stood up and beckoned. We bowed apologetically. We went to a new little café between the Rotonde and the Sélect. Each night we followed this procedure. From his chair at the Sélect, Titus could see us sitting at the new place. We hated this little café. No one we knew sat there. Sometimes one of our friends, feeling sympathy for the grandeur of our position — the support of a drunken friend — would come and sit with us.

Each night Titus watched us with a lonely and disgusted expression on his face. Sometimes we saw him arguing with Madame Sélect. They would both grow vehement. One night, after they had had one of these cold grim arguments, we saw Madame Sélect and her head-waiter come out to the sidewalk, look along to the café where we sat, and contemplate us in silence.

It went on like this all week. On Saturday night as we were passing the Sélect at nine thirty, Titus came hurrying from his place on the terrace. "Madame Sélect would like a word with you," he said coaxingly and he beckoned to her.

We waited, aloof, dignified, beyond reproach as she came toward us, all grace, smiles and kindly benevolence. Would we sit down and have a drink on her? she asked. Would we invite our friend McAlmon to come and have a drink on her? There was much handshaking all around and so we sat down at the Sélect again, confident that a great victory for something or other had been won.

On the boulevard one night at the *aperitif* hour we encountered McAlmon. "What are you doing tonight?" he asked.

"Nothing, as usual."

"I'm having dinner with Jimmy Joyce and his wife at the Trianon. Why don't you join us?"

Jimmy Joyce! "No," I said quickly. "I understand he hates being with strangers and won't talk about anybody's work."

"Who told you all this?"

"Hemingway."

"Oh, nuts," he said, curling his lip. "Don't you want to see Jimmy? You'll like him. You'll like Nora, too."

"Well, of course we want to meet Joyce."

"See you in about an hour and a half at the Trianon," and he went on his way.

He had made it sound as if anyone could drop in on the Joyces at any time. Jimmy, he had called him. Yet Sylvia Beach kept on throwing up her protective screen as dozens of English and American scholars tried to get close to the Irish master. What kind of magic touch did McAlmon have? Was it possible that Joyce had the same sneaking respect for McAlmon that I had myself and liked drinking with him? We'd soon see. At twilight we approached the Trianon just as casually as we might approach a bus stop.

It was a restaurant near the Gare Montparnasse, where the food was notably good. Just to the right as you go in we saw McAlmon sitting with the Joyces. The Irishman's picture was as familiar to us as any movie star's. He was a small-boned, dark Irishman with fine features. He had thick glasses and was wearing a neat dark suit. His courtly manner made it easy for us to sit down, and his wife, large bosomed with a good-natured face, offered us a massive motherly ease. They were both so unpretentious it became impossible for me to resort to Homeric formalities. I couldn't even say, "Sir, you are the greatest writer of our time," for Joyce immediately became too chatty, too full of little bits of conversation, altogether unlike the impression we had been given of him. His voice was soft and pleasant. His humour, to my surprise, depended on puns. Even in the little snips of conversation, he played with words lightly. However, none of his jokes made his wife laugh out loud, and I was reminded of McAlmon's story that she had once asked the author of the comic masterpiece *Ulysses*, "Jimmy, have we a book of Irish humour in the house?"

No matter what was being said, I remained aware of the deep-bosomed Nora Joyce. The food on the table, the white tablecloths, our own voices, everything in the restaurant seemed to tell me Joyce had got all the stuff of Molly Bloom's great and beautiful soliloquy at the close of *Ulysses* from this woman sitting across from me; all her secret, dark night thoughts and yearning. Becoming a little shy, I could hardly look at her. But the quiet handsome motherly woman's manner soon drove all this nonsense out of my head. She was as neighbourly and sympathetic as Joyce himself. They both gossiped with a pleasant ease.

The sound of Joyce's voice suddenly touched a memory of home which moved me. My father, as I have said, didn't read modern prose, just poetry. Fond of music as he was, he wouldn't listen to jazz. He wouldn't read Anderson. I had assumed he would have no interest in experimental prose. When that copy of *This Quarter* carrying my first story, along with the work of Joyce, Pound, Stein, Hemingway and others, had come to our house, my father sat one night at the end of the kitchen table reading it. Soon he began to chuckle to himself. The assured little smirk on his face irritated me. Passing behind his shoulder, I glanced down at the page to see what he was reading. "Work In Progress," by James Joyce, which was a section from *Finnegans Wake*. Imagining he was getting ready to make some sarcastic and belittling remark, I said grimly, "All right. What's so funny?"

But he looked up mildly; he had untroubled blue eyes; and he said with genuine pleasure, "I think I understand this. Read it like Irish brogue. . . . Shem is short for Shemus just as Jem is joky for Jacob.

A few toughnecks are gettable. . . . It's like listening to someone talking in a broad Irish brogue, isn't it, Son?" "Yeah," I said. But I felt apologetic.

And now, after listening to Joyce in our general gossiping, I blurted out that my father had said the new Joyce work should be read aloud in an Irish brogue. Whether it was Joyce or McAlmon who cut in quickly, agreeing, I forget. It came out that Joyce had made some phonograph records of the work; in the way he used his voice it had been his intention to make you feel you were listening to the brogue; much of the music and meaning was in the sound of the brogue. So my father had helped me; I wanted to go on: had Joyce read those proofs of *A Farewell to Arms* which I knew Hemingway had taken to him? Why not ask him? But there had been that warning from Hemingway, "He doesn't like to talk about the work of other writers." I felt handcuffed, exasperated, and therefore was silent. So Joyce had to make most of the conversation. Were we going to London? Sooner or later? He wrote down the name of an inexpensive hotel near the Euston Station.

McAlmon, who had been drinking a lot as usual, suddenly got up, excused himself and went toward the washroom. And then, almost as soon as McAlmon's back was turned, Joyce, leaning across the table, asked quietly, "What do you think of McAlmon's work?"

Surprised, I couldn't answer for a moment. Joyce? Someone else's work? Finally I said that McAlmon simply wouldn't take time with his work; he had hypnotized himself into believing the main thing was to get down the record.

"He has a talent," Joyce said. "A real talent; but it is a disorganized talent." And as he whispered quickly about this disorganized talent, trying to get it all in before McAlmon could return, I wanted to laugh. How had the story got around that the man wouldn't talk about another writer? Then Joyce suddenly paused, his eyes shifting away. McAlmon was on his way back from the washroom and like a conspirator Joyce quickly changed the subject.

As McAlmon came sauntering over to us with his superior air, I noticed a change in his appearance. He looked as if he had just washed his face and combed his hair. From past experience I knew what it meant. When with people he respected he would not let himself get incoherently drunk; he would go to the washroom; there he would put his finger down his throat, vomit, then wash his face, comb his hair and return sober as an undertaker.

It was now about ten o'clock. Turning to his wife, Joyce used the words I remember so well. "Have we still got that bottle of whiskey in the house, Nora?"

"Yes, we have," she said.

"Perhaps Mr. and Mrs. Callaghan would like to drink it with us."

Would we? My wife said we would indeed and I hid my excitement and elation. An evening at home with the Joyces, and Joyce willing to talk and gossip about other writers while we killed a bottle! Stories about Yeats, opinions about Proust! What would he say about Lawrence? Of Hemingway? Did he know Fitzgerald's work? It all danced wildly in my head as we left the restaurant.

Looking for a taxi, McAlmon had gone ahead with Mrs. Joyce and Loretto. Joyce and I were trailing them. The street was not lighted very brightly. Carried away by the excitement I felt at having him walking beside me, I began to talk rapidly. Not a word came from him. I thought he was absorbed in what I was saying. Then far back of me I heard the anxious pounding of his cane on the cobblestones and turned. In the shadows he was groping his way toward me. I had forgotten he could hardly see. The headlights of an approaching taxi picked him up, and in the glaring light he waved his stick wildly. Conscience-stricken, I wanted to cry out. Rushing back, I grabbed him by the arm as the taxi swerved around us. I stammered out an apology. He made some pun on one of the words I used. I don't remember the pun, but since I was trembling the poor quick pun seemed to make the situation Joycean and ridiculous.

The Joyces lived in a solid apartment house, and in the entrance hall Mrs. Joyce explained we would have to use the lift in shifts; it was not supposed to carry more than two people at one time. For the first ascension my wife and Mrs. Joyce got into the lift. When it returned, McAlmon offered to wait while Joyce and I ascended. No, said Joyce, the three of us would get in. The lift rose so slowly I held my breath. No one spoke. Out of the long silence, with the three of us jammed together, came a little snicker from Joyce. "Think what a loss to English literature if the lift falls and the three of us are killed," he said dryly.

The Joyce apartment, at least the living room in which we sat, upset me. Nothing looked right. In the whole world there wasn't a more original writer than Joyce, the exotic in the English language. In the work he had on hand he was exploring the language of the dream world. In this room where he led his daily life I must have expected to see some of the marks of his wild imagination. Yet the place was conservatively respectable. I was too young to have discovered then that men with the most daringly original minds are rarely eccentric in their clothes and their living quarters. This room was all in a conventional middle-class pattern with, if I remember, a brown-patterned wallpaper, a mantel, and a painting of Joyce's father hanging over the fireplace. Mrs. Joyce had promptly brought out the bottle of Scotch. As we began to drink, we joked and laughed and Joyce got talking about the movies. A number of times a week he went to the movies. Movies interested him. As he talked, I seemed to see him in a darkened theatre, the great prose master absorbed in camera technique, so like the dream technique, one picture then another flashing in the mind. Did it all add to his knowledge of the logic of the dream world?

As the conversation began to trail off, I got ready. At the right moment I would plunge in and question him about his contemporaries. But damn it all, I was too slow. Something said about the movies had reminded McAlmon of his grandmother. In a warm, genial, expansive mood, and as much at home with the Joyces as he was with us, he talked about his dear old grandmother, with a happy nostalgic smile. The rich pleasure he got out of his boyhood recollections was so pure that neither the Joyces nor my wife nor I could bear to interrupt. At least not at first. But he kept it up. For half an hour he went on and on. Under my breath I cursed him again and again. Instead of listening to Joyce, I was listening to McAlmon chuckling away about his grandmother. Quivering with impatience I looked at Joyce, who had an amused little smile. No one could interrupt McAlmon. Mrs. Joyce seemed to have an extraordinary capacity for sitting motionless and looking interested. The day would come, I thought bitterly, when I would be able to tell my children I had sat one night with Joyce listening to McAlmon talking about his grandmother.

But when McAlmon paused to take another drink, Joyce caught

him off balance. "Do you think Mr. and Mrs. Callaghan would like to hear the record?" he asked his wife.

"What record?" asked McAlmon, blinking suspiciously, and for a moment I, too, thought Joyce had been referring to him. Now Mrs. Joyce was regarding my wife and me very gravely. "Yes," she said. "I think it might interest them."

"What record?" McAlmon repeated uneasily.

Mrs. Joyce rose, got a record out of a cabinet and put it on the machine. After a moment my wife and I looked at each other in astonishment. Aimee Semple McPherson was preaching a sermon! At that time everyone in Europe and America had heard of Mrs. McPherson, the attractive, seductive blond evangelist from California. But why should Joyce be interested in the woman evangelist? and us? and McAlmon? Cut off, and therefore crestfallen, he, too, waited, mystified. Joyce had nodded to me, inviting my scholarly attention. And Mrs. Joyce, having sat down, was watching my wife with a kind of saintly concern.

The evangelist had an extraordinary voice, warm, low, throaty and imploring. But what was she asking for? As we listened, my wife and I exchanging glances, we became aware that the Joyces were watching us intently, while Mrs. McPherson's voice rose and fell. The voice, in a tone of ecstatic abandonment, took on an ancient familiar rhythm. It became like a woman's urgent love moan as she begged, "Come, come on to me. Come, come on to me. And I will give you rest . . . and I will give you rest . . . Come, come . . ." My wife, her eyebrows raised, caught my glance, then we averted our eyes, as if afraid the Joyces would know what we were thinking. But Joyce, who had been watching us so attentively, had caught our glance. It was enough. He brightened and chuckled. Then Mrs. Joyce, who had also kept her eyes on us, burst out laughing herself. Nothing had to be explained. Grinning mischievously, in enormous satisfaction with his small success, Joyce poured us another drink.

Before we could comment his daughter, a pretty, dark young woman, came in. And a few minutes later, his son too joined us. It was time for us to leave.

When we had taken Robert McAlmon, publisher of the city of Paris, home, we wandered over to the Coupole. That night we shared an extraordinary elation at being in Paris. We didn't want to go back to the apartment. In the Coupole bar we met some friends. One of them asked Loretto if she could do the Charleston. There in the bar she gave a fine solo performance. A young, fair man, a Servian count, who had been sitting at the bar holding a single long-stemmed red rose in his hand, had been watching her appreciatively. But one of our friends told him the dancing girl was my wife. With a shy, yet gallant bow to me from a distance, he asked if he had permission to give Loretto the rose. It was a good night.

From *That Summer in Paris* (1963) by Morley Callaghan, born 1903 in Toronto. Contemporary with Ernest Hemingway on the Toronto *Star*, he followed his friend to Paris in 1929, returning the same year to Toronto, where he has been writing novels ever since.

PARIS
by John Glassco

'TODAY we're meeting the white hope of North American literature,' said Bob next morning. 'His name is Callaghan, and he's just come to town with a pisspot full of money from a book called *Stranger Interlude*. Have you read it?'

'No,' said Graeme. 'But I know his stories in the *New Yorker*. Very fine and sophisticated. Just like Hemingway's, only plaintive and more moral.'

'Well, Fitzgerald says he's good, so he's probably lousy. Anyway he has a lot of dough, so we might get a dinner out of him. He's Canadian too. What do you think he's like?'

'Well,' said Graeme, 'I see him as tall, thin, blond, cynical, in a pin-striped suit. It's the way he writes anyway.'

'Rats,' said Bob, 'that doesn't scare me. I know these sophisticated *New Yorker* types. They're just a bunch of *arrivistes*.'

However, he shaved carefully, running the razor up to his eyes, shined his shoes with his socks, and put on a new polka-dot bow tie before going to meet Callaghan at the hotel-room he was still keeping on the rue de Vaugirard.

'Join us in the Coupole Bar around four,' he said. 'I'll have him softened up by then. *Sophisticated*, what the hell! I've handled John Barrymore in my day. But look, for God's sake, both of you get your hair cut.'

Graeme and I went to a barber shop and then idled around the quarter until four o'clock. We looked into the Coupole, the Dôme, the Sélect, and the Rotonde without seeing Bob; by five o'clock we had also done the Dingo, the College Inn, and the Falstaff, still without success. Coming from the Falstaff we saw Bob sitting with a couple at the little *tabac* on the corner. He hailed us and we sat down.

Morley Callaghan was short, dark, and roly-poly, and wore a striped shirt without a collar; with his moon face and little moustache he looked very like Hemingway; he had even the same shrewd little politician's eyes, the same lopsided grin and ingratiating voice. His wife was also short and thickset, and wore a coral dress and a string of beads. Both of them were so friendly and unpretentious that I liked them at once. It was like meeting people from a small town. We apologized for not finding them sooner, saying we had looked in the Coupole.

'I didn't like that Coupole, it's too much of a clip-joint,' said Callaghan. 'The drinks here are just as good, and a lot cheaper. Eh, Loretto?'

'Yes, about fifteen per cent less, Morley. And you have just the same view here. My, this is a lovely city, but the French are right after you for all they can get. You find that, Mr. Taylor?'

'Yes,' said Graeme. 'You get used to it.'

'Like hell we will,' said Morley. 'Right now we're looking for an apartment. The hotel we're at charges like the dickens.' Suddenly changing the subject, he asked, 'Say, how do you get to meet James Joyce? McAlmon, you know him, I'm told.'

'You're damn right I do,' said Bob. 'But what do you want to do in Paris, go around like a literary rubberneck meeting great men? I'm a great man too, for God's sake. And here I am. Ask me your questions. I'll even give you my autograph.'

'You're a good writer,' said Morley, all his strength of character appearing, 'but you're not Joyce — not yet. What the hell,' he went on, 'this guy Joyce is great. *Ulysses* is the greatest novel of the century. I wouldn't compare myself to him. Why should you?'

'Oh,' said Bob, 'now you're getting modest. Well, you can't fool me. You think you're one hell of a writer, why don't you admit it? Why do you give me all this crap about Joyce? You're more important to yourself. If you think so much of Joyce, why don't you write like him instead of your constipated idol Hemingway? Lean, crisp, constipated, dead-pan prose. The fake naive.'

'Now, McAlmon, let's go into this properly. First thing, I don't write like Joyce for the simple reason that I can't, it's not my line. But I can admire him, can't I?'

'No, you can't. You can't admire Joyce and write like Hemingway. If you do, you're a whore.'

Morley reddened. 'You're a funny guy. I don't know if you're talking seriously, but let me tell you I write as well as I can, and though you may not like my stuff —'

'I've never read your stuff. I don't read the *New Yorker*.'

'Well then what in heck are you talking about? Perhaps you haven't read Joyce either.'

'Right! I haven't read Joyce or Hemingway. I don't have to, I *know* them — and I know you too, Morley, and I like you. Especially when you get mad. I know you're a good writer. The test of a good writer is when he gets mad.'

'Are you boys all through arguing?' said Loretto. 'Shall we all go and have supper somewhere?'

'Sure, but none of these clip-joints. McAlmon, where's a good cheap restaurant? Fitzgerald told me you know Paris inside out.'

'My generation doesn't eat supper,' said Bob. 'I'm having another drink. Waiter, five whiskies and water!'

The conversation continued in the same way. Bob was unreasonable and outrageously rude; Morley remained patient and serious. At last things became boring and I let my attention wander.

A little old man in rags came by, holding up a sheaf of pink papers. '*Guide des poules de Paris!*' he cried in a shrill quavering voice. 'All the girls in Paris, only ten francs! The names, the addresses!' He broke into a tittering sing-song, smacking his lips. '*Ah, les jolies pou-poules, fi-filles de joie de Paris! Achetez, achetez le guide rose! Toutes les jolies petites pou-poules de Paris! Dix francs, dix francs!*'

Two Americans sitting nearby began to laugh. The little man pounced on them, fluttering his pink sheets.

'All the girls in Paris for only ten francs,' one of them said. 'It's a bargain.' He held out a blue ten-franc bill, the little man seized it, peeled off one of the pink sheets and ran away. The two men bent over the *guide rose* for several minutes. 'Say, this is the real thing.

Listen: "Pierrette gives aesthetic massage." "Chez Suzy, everything a man wants." "Visit Mademoiselle Floggi, in her Negro hut: specialities —"'

'Boy, where do these girls hang out?'

'Here are all the phone numbers —'

'Man, these are just numbers — they don't give the exchange . . .'

They both studied the sheet carefully, then one of them pointed to the foot of it in disgust. 'No wonder there's no exchange! Look, this goddamn thing was printed in 1910.'

'Well for Christ's sake. The little bastard!'

Loretto Callaghan was shaking her head at me. 'Now isn't that just like the French,' she said. 'Always cheating!'

'Well, there goes your sophisticated *New Yorker* type,' said Bob when Morley and Loretto had left in search of a cheap restaurant.

'They're both very nice,' said Graeme. 'He's got brains and determination and a devoted wife. He'll go far.'

'Rats, he's just a dumb cluck, an urban hick, a sentimental Catholic. All he's got is a little-boy quality.'

'I'll bet he works like a dog,' I said. 'I wish I could.'

'Don't you ever work like he does, kid! Hard work never got anyone anywhere. A real writer just keeps on putting the words down! He gets the emotion *straight*, the scene, the quality of life — the way I do. Nuts to all that literary business.'

I thought of the inchoate maunderings of *The Politics of Existence* and said nothing. I was thinking that if Bob would only condescend to work, his books would be very fine. I see now, of course, that if he had done so they would be still worse than they were.

'All this literary talk is boring,' said Graeme. 'It's almost as bad as the chatter of poets — they're all so earnest, smelling trends, clawing or kissing each other —'

'Keep your skirts clean,' said Bob. 'That's all a writer has to do. — Hello, Caridad, sit down and have a drink.'

'Yes, I will. Graeme, my dear pussycat, you look very serious. You all do! You must stop it at once. And you must all come to a nice party with me — a real party of poets and painters and writers.'

'Not me,' said Bob. 'I know those lousy parties.'

'Oh, but this is a very distinguished party — and very, very wealthy.

Our hostess will be the great American lady-writer, Miss Gertrude Stein.'

'That old ham! You three go there and lap up the literary vomit. Not me.'

'Let us have dinner first anyway,' said Caridad. 'You will have to pay for mine because I haven't any money. But please, Bob, let us not have one of those awful ducks at the Coupole. We'll go to a nice cheap place like Salto's where I can eat a lot of spaghetti.'

We went around the corner to Salto's, just above the Falstaff, famous for the size of its portions and its coarse red wine. Here the food was good; there was always a *minestrone* that was a meal in itself and a wonderful *gateau maison* made of some kind of yellow cake filled with raisins and drenched with marsala. Caridad ate her way through a plate of anchovies, a bowl of *minestrone*, a mound of spaghetti, an *osso buco*, and the *gateau*, chattering all the time; Bob toyed with a veal cutlet; Graeme and I had a fine spicy rabbit stew made with green peppers, celery and lima beans. We went to the Dôme for coffee.

'Now,' said Caridad, pouring a ten-cent rum into her coffee, 'we shall go soon to Miss Gertrude Stein's and absorb an international culture. Her parties are very well behaved and there are always plenty of rich men — which I find very agreeable. A girl must live. Bob, you must show yourself there — you, celebrated man of letters, publisher, man of the world. It will also make my own entrance so much more impressive — with three cavaliers. Come, it is only a few streets away —'

'Rats, I know the place. I've been to her parties. Never again. Gertrude paid me to publish her lousy five-pound book and we've never been the same since. She thinks I held back some of the proceeds. No, you three run along.'

Although neither Graeme nor I cared for Gertrude Stein's work, we really wanted to see the great woman. I was thinking too of how I could write my father about meeting her, and that (once he had checked her credentials with the English Department at McGill) he might just raise my allowance. The business of living on fifty dollars a month was becoming almost impossible: we were always short of money, we were never able to eat or drink enough, and while Bob was often generous it was apparent his own resources were running low and he would soon have to make another requisition on his father-in-law. As foreigners we could take no regular work, and while Graeme's skill with the poker dice seldom failed, it often took him over an hour to win 100 francs and obliged him to endure as well the conversation of the dreariest types of American barfly; the worst of it was that he had to spend almost a quarter of his winnings drinking with them during his operations.

Accordingly we set off with Caridad down the boulevard Raspail in the plum-blue light of the June evening, arrived at the rue de Fleurus, and were greeted at the door by a deciduous female who seemed startled by the sight of Caridad.

'Miss Toklas!' Caridad cried affectionately. 'It is so long since we have not met. I am Caridad de Plumas, you will remember, and these are my two young Canadian squires to whom I wish to give the privilege of meeting you and your famous friend. We were coming with Mr. Robert McAlmon, he is unavoidably detained.'

As she delivered this speech she floated irresistibly forward, Miss Toklas retreated, and we found ourselves in a big room already filled with soberly dressed and soft-spoken people.

The atmosphere was almost ecclesiastical and I was glad to be wearing my best dark suit, which I had put on to meet Morley Callaghan. I had begun to suspect that Caridad had not been invited to the party and all of us were in fact crashing the gate. But Caridad, whether invited or not, was in a few minutes a shining centre of the party: her charm coruscated, her big teeth flashed, her dyed hair caught the subdued light. She paid no further attention to Graeme or myself, and I understood that she was as usual looking for rich men.

The room was large and sombrely furnished, but the walls held, crushed together, a magnificent collection of paintings — Braques, Matisses, Picassos, and Picabias. I only recovered from their cumulative effect to fall under that of their owner, who was presiding like a Buddha at the far end of the room.

Gertrude Stein projected a remarkable power, possibly due to the atmosphere of adulation that surrounded her. A rhomboidal woman dressed in a floor-length gown apparently made of some kind of burlap, she gave the impression of absolute irrefragability; her ankles, almost concealed by the hieratic folds of her dress, were like the pillars of a temple: it was impossible to conceive of her lying down. Her fine close-cropped head was in the style of the late Roman Empire, but unfortunately it merged into broad peasant shoulders without the aesthetic assistance of a neck; her eyes were large and much too piercing. I had a peculiar sense of mingled attraction and repulsion towards her. She awakened in me a feeling of instinctive hostility coupled with a grudging veneration, as if she were a pagan idol in whom I was unable to believe.

Her eyes took me in, dismissed me as someone she did not know, and returned to her own little circle. With a feeling of discomfort I decided to find Graeme and disappear: this party, I knew, was not for me. But just then Narwhal came up and began talking so amusingly that I could not drag myself away.

'I have been reading the works of Jane Austen for the first time,' he said in his quiet nasal voice, 'and I'm looking for someone to share my enthusiasm. Now these are very good novels in my opinion. You wouldn't believe it but here — among all these writers, people who are presumably literary artists — I can't find anyone who has read her book with any real attention. In fact most of them don't seem to like her work at all. But I find this dislike is founded on a false impression that she was a respectable woman.'

'Jane Austen?'

'I don't mean to say she was loose in her behaviour, or not a veuhjin. I'm sure she was veuhjin. I mean she was aristocratic, not bourgeoise, she was no creep, she didn't really give a darn about all those conventions of chastity and decorum.'

'Well, her heroines did.'

'Oh sure, they *seem* to, they've got to, or else there'd be no story. But Austen didn't herself. Who is the heroine, the Urheroine of *Sense and Sensibility*? It's Marianne, not Elinor. Of *Pride and Prejudice*? It's the girl that runs off with the military man. What's wrong with *Emma*? Emma.'

'You mean Willoughby and Wickham are her real heroes?'

'No, they're just stooges, see? But they represent the dark life-principle of action and virility that Austen really admired, like Marianne and Lydia stand for the life force of female letting-go. And when Ann Elliott falls for Captain Wentworth — you'll notice he's the third W of the lot — it's the same thing, only this time he's tanned.

It's a new conception of Austen's talent which I formed yesterday, and which was suggested to me by the fact that Prince Lucifer is the real hero of *Paradise Lost*, as all the savants declare.'

This idea of Jane Austen as a kind of early D.H. Lawrence was new. Never had the value of her books been so confirmed as by the extraordinary interpretation of them: it was a real tribute.

'Do you happen to know if there were any portraits of Austen made?' he asked.

'A water colour by a cousin, I think.'

'Good! I guess it's lousy then,' he said with satisfaction. 'Because I've been thinking of doing an imaginary portrait of her too. I see her in a wood, in a long white dress. She's looking at a mushroom. But all around her are these thick young trees growing straight up — some are black with little white collars and stand for ministers of the church and some are blue and stand for officers in the Royal English Navy. I'm also thinking of putting some miniature people, kind of elves dressed like witches and so forth, in the background — but I'm not sure.'

'It sounds good.'

'The focus of the whole thing will be the mushroom,' he said. 'It represents the almost overnight flowering of her genius — also its circumscribed quality, its suggestion of being both sheltered *and* a shelter — see? — and its economy of structure.'

'An edible mushroom?'

'You've got it. That will be the whole mystery of the portrait. The viewer won't know and she won't know either. We will all partake of Jane Austen's doubt, faced with the appalling mystery of sex.'

We must have been talking with an animation unusual for one of Gertrude Stein's parties, for several of the guests had already gathered around us.

'You are talking of Jane Austen and sex, gentlemen?' said a tweedy Englishman with a long ginger moustache. 'The subjects are mutually exclusive. That dried-up lady snob lived behind lace curtains all her life. She's of no more importance than a chromo. Isn't that so, Gertrude?'

I was suddenly aware that our hostess had advanced and was looking at me with her piercing eyes.

'Do I know you?' she said. 'No. I suppose you are just one of those silly young men who admire Jane Austen.'

Narwhal had quietly disappeared and I was faced by Miss Stein, the tweedy man and Miss Toklas. Already uncomfortable at being an uninvited guest, I found the calculated insolence of her tone intolerable and lost my temper.

'Yes, I am,' I said. 'And I suppose you are just one of those silly old women who don't.'

The fat Buddha-like face did not move. Miss Stein merely turned, like a gun revolving on its turret, and moved imperturbably away.

The tweedy man did not follow her. Leaning towards me, his moustache bristling, he said quietly. 'If you don't leave here this moment, I will take great pleasure in throwing you out, bodily.'

'If you really want,' I said, 'I'll wait outside in the street for three minutes, when I'll be glad to pull your nose.'

I then made my exit, and after standing for exactly three minutes on the sidewalk (by which time I was delighted to find he did not appear), I took my way back to the Dôme. Graeme joined me there fifteen minutes later.

'That's the last party we go to without being invited,' he said.

From *Memoirs of Montparnasse* (1970) by John Glassco, 1909-1979. Born in Montreal, he went to Paris in 1928, returning after three years to a lengthy battle with tuberculosis. His unique career as poet, pornographer and man of letters was conducted largely from Foster, Quebec, where he was at various times postman, mayor and fancier of harness horses.

NEW YORK, NEW YORK
by Hugh MacLennan

T he first time I understood that New York taxi-drivers are a
unique tribe within the human family was in 1929 on the occasion of my first visit there. I was with my father, who hated New York
and never missed an opportunity of saying so, who dreaded New York
not for its own sake but for all of our sakes, because New York by
its very colossality seemed a constant temptation inviting Providence
to get to work on it. On the way to Penn Station, my father grum-
bling with some justification about the way the traffic was not being
handled — they used cops then instead of lights and prohibition had
softened the cops up — the driver stopped his car and turned around.

"Listen mister, you wanna know what is the trouble with New York?
It is very simple. New York is the trouble with New York."

At the time this struck me as a courteous way of suggesting that
what was the trouble with my father was my father, but I don't really
think this is what the man meant. He simply meant that New York
is New York, and as such that it is so transcendent, so irrefragably
self-confident, that for most of us it has an unrivalled capacity among
cities for arousing extreme sensations of love, hate, admiration and
nausea. I don't know what your experience has been with this city,
but mine is nearly always the same. I arrive full of excited anticipa-
tion; I depart frustrated and with my pockets empty. I can't imagine
a world without New York; I find it increasingly difficult to imagine
the world surviving indefinitely with New York a part of it. New York,
for years, has been my Great White Whale. Year after year between
my first visit and 1952 I kept going down to New York and once I
lived there for eight consecutive months, during which it seemed
entirely different from the city I knew when I visited it. Then for

five years I stayed secure in Montreal and left the Whale to itself and the rest of humanity.

But a time came — it always does — when I had to return to New York, and on this occasion it was because I had finished a novel on which I had been working for five years. I was tired and with reason. During the previous five months I had been working night and day in the most intense creative drive I had ever known. So I slept for a week, then bought a ticket for the Great White Whale because it seemed essential that I consult my agent. "With this little book," whispered a little thought in the back of my little mind, "I will stick my little bodkin into the Whale. This little book will make the Whale admit that I exist."

So I slept soundly on the train, and with the usual feeling of expectant excitement I stepped out of Grand Central into a cab driven by Joe Przwyk, to whom I carelessly mentioned that I had not been in New York for five years.

"Where you bin?" said Przwyk. "In jail?"

There it was again: that cheerful, humiliating, friendly assumption that if you are absent from New York you are not alive, and that only the most ignominious failure or the direst calamity can keep you away until, after having been preserved on ice, you return. No wonder Moby Dick heaped Ahab; no wonder the Whale was his wall. Ahab was a whaler by trade; I am a writer by trade, and New York, among other things, happens to be the centre of the book market.

Przwyk drove with a competent insouciance delightful after the paranoic behaviour of Montreal taxi-drivers, and the familiar kaleidoscope unreeled, historical climacterics of a quarter century flashing past as he drove from Grand Central to my hotel. There was the corner on which I had stood, that November night in 1932, when Franklin Roosevelt was elected president and the New York crowd, anticipating 3.2 beer and everything else that happened during Roosevelt's régime, sang *Happy Days Are Here Again*. There was the barbershop where I read about Dollfuss' bombardment of the Viennese workers in 1934. Coming out of that theatre I had seen displayed in banner headlines the news that Adolf Hitler had become the master of Germany. In this block my shoes were shined while I looked at a *Daily News* photo of Hitler doing a jig in the Forest of Compiègne. New York had certainly appreciated the news value of the war, but it was from another member of its taxi-driving tribe that I learned what I believe was its real attitude towards that half-forgotten conflict.

"This town," the man said, "is pretty big for the war."

The news in New York on this particular occasion was widely analysed elsewhere on the continent and will be analysed in special circles long after New York has forgotten it. In Brooklyn, which might be described as the belly of the Great White Whale, a prominent school authority had just committed suicide; a famous judge had just been accused of calling the Superintendent of Schools a bastard; a grand jury had announced that the schools were rife with "hoodlums, rapists, thieves, extortionists, arsonists and the vandals"; the mayor had ordered policemen into some of these schools to protect the teachers against their pupils.

"Naw," said Przwyk, "that stuff has always been here. I could tell you a story."

He deposited me in front of the hotel where, in the spring of 1933, I had lived on credit for eight days while the nation's banks were closed. The hinterland had trembled, several Wall Street bankers had contemplated a choice between suicide and the penitentiary, but the Great White Whale had basked blissfully indifferent and carried on as usual while the world panicked. The most disreputable strangers were given almost unlimited credit in the hotels. New York, after all, had to continue being New York just as it now had to continue being New York in spite of the blackboard jungle.

"Yeah," said Dominick Tintoretto as he drove me that night to a remembered jazz-spot in the Village, "definitely and strictly it is a very wonnerful thing people like you coming from all over here. You see how things is done here, you go home and you make your improvements. It is all very wonnerful. Seeing how things is done here, you *gotta* make improvements or how can you odderwise live? Up in Mo-ree-al how are things?"

I asked him how he knew I was from Montreal, since I had not told him.

"You talk like an English fella," said Tintoretto, "only you don't talk like an English fella, so I figure it is from Mo-ree-al that you come."

I asked how he knew how an English fella talked.

"I bin all over, First World War Wincheser, Durby, Oggsferd, Wales. I guess England's okay if you like the Village. The Mayor is gonna do something about the Village. Now take the Mayor."

He arrived at my destination before he had time to take the Mayor, and I entered the familiar place to find it with a new decor, a quadrupled cover charge, but the same sprightly, spring-fresh jazz played by young negroes who looked just like the ones I had first heard a quarter century ago before they became middle-aged and famous and much duller than they had been when they played here. Next to me was a couple holding hands sitting opposite another couple doing the same, and they all seemed so intimate I thought they were old friends until the second couple departed for the bar and I overheard that the first couple had met them only half an hour before. The girl, speaking a beautiful English in a Dutch accent, was explaining something to her inarticulate American escort.

"But New York is the *only* place where people don't have to live with *each other*. They only have to live with *themselves*."

Her escort, who admitted that his home town was Washington Courthouse, Ohio, opined that New York had everything, and the Dutch girl said she wasn't sure about that, but she was certainly sure — a glance from lowered lids into the eyes of the Washington Courthouse man — that New York was a place where the most delicious things could happen to a girl night after night.

"You know what's the trouble with Arnold Toynbee?" said Isadore Goldberg three hours later as he drove me back to my hotel.

I have been driven through New York by a student of Immanuel Kant, by several Marxian scholars, by one anthropologist, by a variety of ex-pugs and bootleggers, but now, in Goldberg, I had discovered someone who outmoded the lot of them.

"What's history," said Goldberg, "but psychology, and what's psychology but the ree-searches of Sigmund Freud? Toynbee writes history like Freud was not in it. That's what's the trouble with Toynbee."

New York, which is everything, is also the Metropolitan Museum, and I spent four hours there on my second day, my chief purpose being to revisit the Rembrandts and the Grecos. They were there, they were cleaned and they were wonderful, but once again I found that the White Whale had continued its habit of surpassing and out-moding even itself. I left the Museum overwhelmed, not by Rembrandt and Greco, but by the colossal, nude, bronze statue of the Emperor Trebonianus Gallus, who was the greatest man in the world between 251 A.D. and 253 A.D., when he was murdered by his own soldiers. Black, terrible, huge and naked — the nakedest statue I ever saw — this awful apparition dominates the atrium of the Metropolitan, his face and horrible labourer's body telling more about the decline and fall of the Roman Empire than Gibbon and Toynbee put together. Was it always there in the Metropolitan and I had not seen it? But New York had incorporated Gallus now, and Goldberg, who as a Freudian understands that history is a prolonged process of gods eating gods, religions eating religions, civilizations eating civilizations, might possibly agree with my terrified apprehension that the Great Whale has now swallowed the Roman Empire along with the British.

The Whale, I discovered a few hours later, had swallowed and incorporated another big fish: Franklin Roosevelt, together with his whole family which has survived him and still lives, I understand, interesting and exciting lives of their own, had been legendized into a show off Broadway with Ralph Bellamy in the lead. Mr. Bellamy had never seemed to me to resemble Franklin Roosevelt in any way whatever, but there he was, and I had the odd sensation that so far as the Whale was concerned, the Thirty-first President had never been quite real until he was dead enough to be converted into The Roosevelt Story. The Whale was browsing as usual on a large variety of sexual shows (when will it outmode sex?) and also on the dramatized versions of two novels which seemed to me to have been contemporary only yesterday, but were treated by the critics in the manner adopted by fashionable shops to the dress styles of a year ago. *A Farewell To Arms*, a novel which seemed to me to have been written only yesterday, was playing in a movie at the Roxy, and one of the Whale's special correspondents found it interesting because it demonstrated how out of touch was the writing of the early 1930s with the reality of Now. "Catherine Barclay," the writer complained, "*used* to be every man's ideal girl." That other anti-war novel of the Thirties, *Paths of Glory*, was also on display in a movie version and I saw it and found it tremendous. But the Whale's press was uninterested in it, and the taxi-driver James Westerley (his foreign-sounding name attributable to the fact that he was a Negro) had the final word on its importance.

"They don' fight wars that way no more," said Westerley. "No, sir, not any more do they fight wars that way."

The next morning I decided I could put it off no longer and went to see my agent with the manuscript, which I delivered just before lunch. As we sipped our coffee after lunch I asked him a few questions about the book trade and his answers did not sound cheerful. He told me what I knew only too well: that the general market for cloth-covered fiction was away below the level of what it had been a dozen years ago. Paper-backs had changed the entire shape of the market. Television had cut heavily into the time available for reading. Some eighty-five percent of American families now owned television sets and the average burning time of a set in America was more than five hours in twenty-four. According to some fairly reliable opinion-samplers, only one American in five read even one book a year and only seventeen percent of Americans *bought* as many as one book in a lifetime.

I left my good friend feeling that the effort of the last years had probably been wasted, and walked around for a while trying to forget that in my little mind my little bodkin was broken.

My favourite part of Manhattan — I am obvious in my tastes — is the stretch of Fifth Avenue between the Plaza and Forty-eight Street and this stretch I now began to pace. My favourite shop in New York is Scribner's, which has the finest window of any bookshop I have ever seen. Mr. Van Duym, who dresses it, is a famous man in the trade; he loves and understands books, and if he really likes a book he has the art of setting it out in the window in such a way that you realize it is a thing much more precious than the diamond tiara you just looked at in Cartier's. I first saw Scribner's window in 1932 and I have looked into it on every visit to New York since that time. I used to think that if ever a book of mine were given even a modest corner of that window, all the work and strain of half a lifetime would have its reward. So now I spent ten minutes studying the window, went inside and browsed, bought a book and emerged for another walk. Ah well, if not with this novel, perhaps with the next. The Whale had never been interested in anything Canadian, and this novel of mine was set in Montreal.

That night I took my departure with the Whale scintillating as he always does on a clear night, and as I rode to Grand Central and saw the towering television masts on the top of the Empire State and the Chrysler, I asked myself why this place seemed to annihilate the value of everything I had ever learned to do in my entire life. But encouragement came in this dark moment from an unexpected quarter.

"This TeeVee," said Steve Svoboda, "ain't gonna last much longer. People all over is getting very weary indeed of TeeVee."

At a traffic light Svoboda pondered further: "They'll come up with sumpin new. When they gotta, they do."

I paid him off, counted the money remaining in my wallet, discovered as always that the Whale had swallowed more than I had expected that even he would be able to swallow, got into the train and slept well. The white snow of Montreal looked comfortable after the White Whale and I muttered that it would be never before I tempted him again. But I knew I was fooling myself, for I always go back to New York. So does everybody. And this brings me to a postscript to the story of my dealings with the Great White Whale.

My forebodings about the book I had written turned out to be well founded, for six weeks after my return I was informed that the publisher to whom the novel had been sent did not wish to publish it. This was a shock, for it meant that for the first time since I became a professional novelist I was without an American publisher. After a very minor revision, the book was despatched to one of the Whale's most ancient and honourable publishers, and there it reposed while the editor considered it. By this time spring had broken out and when my work in the university ended for the season, I boarded a freighter and sailed to England on the first holiday I had enjoyed in a dozen years. The ship took twelve days getting there, and I reached London on a Saturday night. When I picked up my mail at the bank in Cockspur Street the following Monday morning, the first letter I opened contained the news that the second publisher had also rejected the script, his reason being that the prose was turgid and the characters uninteresting. Prospects now were beginning to look alarming. It is worse than grim, it is like writing on the wall, when an established novelist gets two rejections of a script in succession. It is worse still when this happens to what he believes is his best book, for he has always known that at any moment he may cease to please, and that a time comes in the life of every writer when such talent as he possesses fails. Generally he himself is the last person to understand this, just as a faithful wife is often the last person to know what her husband has really been up to on some of his absences from home. Well, I thought, let's forget it and get on with the vacation. So I spent six weeks in England and Scotland and then flew home.

The first letter I opened on my arrival in Montreal was also from my agent, and it told me that the manuscript, as he had all along predicted, was now in safe hands. Scribner's was going to publish it some time in the course of the next year. The months went by and in a rush of new work I pushed the novel into the back of my mind. Proofs arrived and I corrected them, but I diligently kept away from the Great White Whale and professed incredulity when some interesting rumours about the novel floated north. The book appeared on the luckiest day of the year: Friday, the 13th of February, and still I kept away from New York. I was afraid of spoiling the pitch, for no writer, least of all a foreign one, could possibly have received more generous reviews than I was getting from the Whale's special correspondents at that particular moment. My publishers finally invited me down, and down I went.

My mind was confused in that month and I forgot my dates. When I began walking that Monday morning after breakfast the ghastly thought occurred to me that once again something unaccountable might have happened, for at 10:30 the streets were almost deserted and all of the shops were closed. Had the Whale suffered some unexpected disaster during the night? Had the next depression begun? Had Wall Street collapsed? Was an atomic attack impending? As anything is possible in that city, none of these ideas seemed entirely unreasonable.

Then I began noticing that in window after window there was a picture of George Washington, and at last I understood that this was the man's birthday. It is true that the Whale had done no fighting for Washington during the Revolution; indeed, such effort as he expended in that war was mostly on the side of the King. But when the King lost, the Whale of course contrived to make his arrangements with the new government and now he was celebrating this. The holiday would mean a crowded Metropolitan in the afternoon, but it would also mean fairly empty streets. The air was brisk and I continued walking down Fifth until I reached Scribner's window. Honestly I had expected to find nothing there, but what I did find nearly knocked me out.

The entire window had been given over to that little novel of mine, and in my prejudiced eyes Mr. Van Duym had performed the finest work of art in his career. Stacks and stacks of the books were arranged in patterns; in addition there were five large photographs of Montreal, one of Ottawa and another of a Canadian lumber camp. Blown-up photostats of reviews from the *Times* and the *Herald-Tribune* were in the window, and two strangers were bending forward to read them, while every fifth person who walked by stopped to stare.

For myself, I stayed there no longer than fifteen seconds, and when I bolted around the corner I was afraid that I had stayed at least ten seconds too long for my safety. The beastie was at my heels and my father's ghost was on the heels of the beastie. He was reminding me of the winter Sunday years ago when I had come home from a walk and discovered, absolutely out of the blue, that a telegram had arrived informing me that I had won a Rhodes Scholarship months after I had believed that I had lost my last chance of getting one. My father had risen to this occasion in the spirit of his ancestors. "Go out and shovel the snow," he said, and it was the only occasion when he ever ordered me to work on the Sabbath Day. So on that Washington's Birthday, as there was no snow to shovel in New York, I walked and I walked and I walked.

From *Scotchman's Return* (1960) by Hugh MacLennan, born 1907 in Glace Bay, Nova Scotia. A former Rhodes scholar and professor of English at McGill University, MacLennan is one of Canada's most eminent novelists and essayists.

EGYPT
by Ethel Wilson

CLOWN: *What is the opinion of*
         Pythagoras concerning wild
         fowl?
MALVOLIO: *That the soul of our grandam*
         might haply inhabit a bird.

—*Twelfth Night*, Act IV, Scene ii.

"It is airless," said Mrs. Forrester.
"Yes there is no air," said the woman half beside her half in front of her. The mouth of the tomb was no longer visible behind them, but there was light. They stepped carefully downwards. Mrs. Forrester looked behind her at her husband. She was inexcusably nervous and wanted a look or a gleam of reassurance from his face. But he did not appear to see her. He scrutinized the yellow walls which looked as if they were compounded of sandstone and clay. Marcus seemed to be looking for something, but there was nothing on the yellowish walls not even the marks of pick and shovel.

Mrs. Forrester had to watch her steps on the stairs of smoothed and worn pounded sandstone or clay, so she turned again, looking downwards. It did not matter whether she held her head up or down, there was no air. She breathed, or course, but what she breathed was not air but some kind of ancient vacuum. She supposed that this absence of air must affect the noses and mouths and lungs of Marcus and of the woman from Cincinnati and the guide and the soldier and that she need not consider herself to be special. So, although

103

she suffered from the airlessness and a kind of blind something, very old, dead, she knew that she must not give way to her impulse to complain again, saying, "I can't breathe! There is no air!" and certainly she must not turn and stumble up the steps into the blazing heat as she wished to do; neither must she faint. She had never experienced panic before, but she recognized all this for near panic. She stiffened, controlled herself (she thought), then relaxed, breathed the vacuum as naturally as possible, and continued her way down into the earth from small light to light. They reached the first chamber which was partly boarded up.

Looking through the chinks of the planking they seemed to see a long and deep depression which because of its shape indicated that, once, a body had lain there, probably in a vast and ornate coffin constructed so as to magnify the size and great importance of its occupant. The empty depression spoke of a removal of some long object which, Mrs. Forrester knew, had lain there for thousands of years, hidden, sealed, alone, yet existing, in spite of the fact that generations of living men, know-alls, philosophers, scientists, slaves, ordinary people, kings, knew nothing about it. And then it had been suspected, and then discovered, and then taken away somewhere, and now there was only the depression which they saw. All that was mortal of a man or woman who had been all-powerful had lain there, accompanied by treasure hidden and sealed away by a generation from other generations (men do not trust their successors, and rightly), till only this great baked dried yellowish aridity of hills and valleys remained, which was called the Valley of the Kings. And somewhere in the valley were dead kings.

Peering between the boards and moving this way and that so as to obtain a better view, they saw that a frieze of figures ran round the walls above the level of the depression. The figures were all in profile, and although they were only two-dimensional, they had a look of intention and vigour which gave them life and great dignity. There was no corpulence; all were slim, wide of shoulder, narrow of hip. Mostly, Mrs. Forrester thought, they walked very erect. They did not seem to stand, or, if they stood, they stood as if springing already into motion. She thought, peering, that they seemed to walk, all in profile and procession, towards some seated Being, it might be a man, or it might be sexless, or it might be a cat, or even a large bird, no doubt an ibis. The moving figures proceeded either with hieratic gesture or bearing objects. The colours, in which an ochreous sepia predominated, were faintly clear. The airlessness of the chamber nearly overwhelmed her again and she put out her hand to touch her husband's arm. There was not much to see, was there? between these planks, so they proceeded on downwards. The guide, who was unintelligible, went first. The soldier followed them.

If ever I get out of this, thought Mrs. Forrester. The airlessness was only part of an ancientness, a strong persistence of the past into the now and beyond the now which terrified her. It was not the death of the place that so invaded her, although there was death; it was the long persistent life in which her bones and flesh and all the complex joys of her life and her machine-woven clothes and her lipstick that was so important to her were less than the bright armour of a beetle on which she could put her foot. Since all three of the visitors were silent in the tomb, it was impossible to know what the others felt. And anyway, one could not explain; and why explain (all this talk about "feelings"!).

The farther down the steps they went the more the air seemed to expire, until at the foot of the steps it really died. Here was the great chamber of the great king, and a sarcophagus had been left there, instructively, perhaps, so that the public, who came either for pleasure or instruction, should be able to see the sort of sight which the almost intoxicated excavators had seen as they removed the earth and allowed in the desecrating air — or what passed for air.

Since Mrs. Forrester was now occupied in avoiding falling down and thereby creating a small scene beside the sarcophagus which would annoy her and her husband very much indeed and would not help the lady from Cincinnati who had grown pale, none of the guide's talk was heard and no image of the sarcophagus or of the friezes or of the tomb itself remained in her mind. It was as a saved soul that she was aware of the general turning up towards the stairs, up towards the light, and she was not ashamed, now, to lay her hand upon her husband's arm, really for support, in going up the stairs.

They emerged into the sunlight which blinded them and the heat that beat up at them and bore down on them, and all but the two Egyptians fumbled for their dark glasses. The soldier rejoined his comrade at the mouth of the tomb, and the guide seemed to vanish round some cliff or crag. The two soldiers were unsoldierly in appearance although no doubt they would enjoy fighting anyone if it was necessary.

Marcus and Mrs. Forrester and the lady from Cincinnati whose name was Sampson or Samson looked around for a bit of shade. The lion-coloured crags on their left did of course cast a shade, but it was the kind of shade which did not seem to be of much use to them, for they would have to climb onto farther low crags to avail themselves of the shade, and the sun was so cruel in the Valley of the Kings that no European or North American could make shift to move one step unless it was necessary.

"Where's that guide?" said Marcus irritably, of no one, because no one knew. The guide had gone, probably to wave on the motor car which should have been waiting to pick them up. Mrs. Forrester could picture him walking, running, gesticulating, garments flowing, making all kinds of gratuitous movements in the heat. We're differently made, she thought, it's all those centuries.

"I think," said Mrs. Sampson timidly, "that this s-seems to be the best p-place."

"Yes," said Mrs. Forrester who was feeling better though still too hot and starved for air, "that's the best place. There's enough shade there for us all," and they moved to sit down on some yellow rocks which were too hot for comfort. Nobody talked of the tomb which was far below the ground on their right.

Mrs. Forrester spoke to her husband who did not answer. He looked morose. His dark brows were concentrated in a frown and it was obvious that he did not want to talk to her or to anybody else. Oh dear, she thought. It's the tomb — he's never like this unless it's really something. They sat in silence, waiting for whatever should turn up. The two soldiers smoked at some distance.

This is very uncomfortable, this heat, thought Mrs. Forrester, and the tomb has affected us unpleasantly. She reflected on Lord Carnarvon who had sought with diligence, worked ardently, superintended excavation, urged on discovery, was bitten by an insect — or so they said — and had died. She thought of a co-worker of his who lay ill with some fever in the small clay-built house past which they had driven that morning. Why do they do those things, these men? Why do they do it? They do it because they have to; they come here to be uncomfortable and unlucky and for the greatest fulfilment of their lives; just as men climb mountains; just as Arctic and Antarctic explorers go to the polar regions to be uncomfortable and unlucky and for the greatest fulfilment of their lives. They have to. The thought of the Arctic gave her a pleasant feeling and she determined to lift the pressure that seemed to have settled on all three of them which was partly tomb, no doubt, but chiefly the airlessness to which their lungs were not accustomed, and, of course, this heat.

She said with a sort of imbecile cheerfulness, "How about an ice-cream cone?"

Mrs. Sampson looked up at her with a pale smile and Marcus did not answer. No, she was not funny, and she subsided. Out of the rocks flew two great burnished-winged insects and attacked them like bombers. All three ducked and threw up their arms to protect their faces.

"Oh . . ." and "oh . . " cried the women and forgot about the heat while the two vicious bright-winged insects charged them, one here, one there, with a clattering hiss. Mrs. Forrester did not know whether one of the insects had hit and bitten Marcus or Mrs. Sampson. She had driven them away, she thought, and as she looked around and her companions looked up and around, she saw that the insects, which had swiftly retired, now dived down upon them again.

The car came round a corner and stopped beside them. There was only the driver. The guide had departed and would no doubt greet them at the hotel with accusations and expostulations. They climbed into the car, the two women at the back and Marcus — still morose — in front with the driver. The car started. The visit to the tomb had not been a success, but at all events the two insects did not accompany them any farther.

They jolted along very fast in the dust which covered them and left a rolling column behind. At intervals the driver honked the horn because he liked doing it. In the empty desert he honked for pleasure. They had not yet reached the trail in the wide sown green belt that bordered the Nile.

The driver gave a last honk and drew up. As the dust settled, they saw, on their right, set back in the dead hills, a row of arches, not a colonnade but a row of similar arches separated laterally a little from each other and leading, evidently, into the hills. They must be tombs, or caves. These arches were black against the dusty yellow of the rock. Mrs. Forrester was forced to admit to herself that the row of arches into the hills was beautiful. There seemed to be about twenty or thirty arches, she estimated when she thought about it later.

There they sat.

"Well, what are we waiting for?" Marcus asked the driver.

The driver became voluble and then he turned to the women behind, as Marcus, who was impatient to get on, did not seem to co-operate.

"I think he has to w-wait a few minutes for someone who m-may be there. He has to pick someone up unless they've already gone," said Mrs. Sampson. "He has to w-wait."

The driver then signified that if they wished they could go up to the tombs within the arches. Without consultation together they all immediately said no. They sat back and waited. Can Marcus be ill? Mrs. Forrester wondered. He is too quiet.

Someone stood at the side of the car, at Mrs. Forrester's elbow. This was an aged bearded man clothed in a long ragged garment and a head-furnishing which was neither skull cap nor tarboosh. His face was mendicant but not crafty. He was too remote in being, Mrs. Forrester thought, but he was too close in space.

"Lady," he said, "I show you something," ("Go away," said Mrs. Forrester) and he produced a small object from the folds of his garment. He held it up, between finger and thumb, about a foot from Mrs. Forrester's face.

The object on which the two women looked was a small human hand, cut off below the wrist. The little hand was wrapped in grave-clothes, and the small fingers emerged from the wrapping, neat, gray, precise. The fingers were close together, with what appeared to be nails or the places for nails upon them. A tatter of grave-clothes curled and fluttered down from the chopped-off wrist.

"Nice hand. Buy a little hand, lady. Very good very old very cheap. Nice mummy hand."

"Oh g-go away!" cried Mrs. Sampson, and both women averted their faces because they did not like looking at the small mummy's hand.

The aged man gave up, and moving on with the persistence of the East he held the little hand in front of Marcus.

"Buy a mummy hand, gentleman sir. Very old very nice very cheap, sir. Buy a little hand."

Marcus did not even look at him.

"NIMSHI," he roared. Marcus had been in Egypt in the last war.

He roared so loud that the mendicant started back. He rearranged his features into an expression of terror. He shambled clumsily away with a gait which was neither running nor walking, but both. Before him he held in the air the neat little hand, the little wrapped hand, with the tatter of grave-clothes fluttering behind it. The driver, for whom the incident held no interest, honked his horn, threw his hands about to indicate that he would wait no longer, and then drove on.

When they had taken their places in the boat with large sails which carried them across the Nile to the Luxor side, Mrs. Forrester, completely aware of her husband's malaise but asking no questions, saw that this river and these banks and these tombs and temples and these strange agile people to whom she was alien and who were alien to her had not — at four o'clock in the afternoon — the charm that had surprised her in the lily green and pearly cool scene at six o'clock that morning. The sun was high and hot, the men were noisy, the Nile was just water, and she wished to get Marcus back to the hotel.

When they reached the hotel Marcus took off his outer clothes and lay on the bed.

"What is it, Marc?"

"Got a headache."

It was plain to see, now, that he was ill. Mrs. Forrester rang for cold bottled water for Marcus to drink and for ice for compresses. She rummaged in her toilet case and found that she had put in a thermometer as a sort of charm against disease. That was in Vancouver, and how brash, kind, happy, and desirable Vancouver seemed now. Marcus had a temperature of 104°.

There were windows on each side wall of the room. They were well screened and no flies could, one thought, get in; so, by having the windows open, the ghost of the breeze that blew off the Nile River entered and passed out of the room but did not touch Marcus. There was, however, one fly in the room, nearly as dangerous as a snake. Mrs. Forrester took the elegant little ivory-handled fly switch that she had used in Cairo and, sitting beside her husband, flicked gently when the fly buzzed near him.

"Don't."

"All right, dear," she said with the maddening indulgence of the well to the sick. She went downstairs.

"Is that compartment still available on the Cairo train tonight?" she asked.

"*Sì*, madame."

"We will take it. My husband is not well."

"Not well! That is unfortunate, madame," said the official at the desk languidly. "I will arrange at once."

It was clear that the management did not sympathize with illness and would prefer to get rid of sick travellers immediately.

Mrs. Forrester went upstairs and changed the compress. She then went and sat by the window overlooking the Nile. She reflected again that this country, where insects carried curses in their wings, made her uneasy. It was too old and strange. She had said as much to Marcus who felt nothing of the kind. He liked the country. But then, she thought, I am far too susceptible to the power of Place, and Marcus is more sensible; these things do not affect him in this way, and, anyway, he knows Egypt. However high the trees and mountains of her native British Columbia, they were native to her. However wide the prairies, she was part of them. However fey the moors of Devon, however ancient Glastonbury or London, they were part of her. Greece was young and she was at home there. The Parthenon in ruins of glory was fresh and fair. And Socrates, drinking the hemlock among his friends as the evening sun smote Hymettus . . . was that last week . . . was he indeed dead? But now . . . let us go away from here.

Below the window, between a low wall and the river, knots of men stood, chattering loudly — Egyptians, Arabs, Abyssinians, and an old man with two donkeys. The air was full of shouting. They never ceased. They shouted, they laughed, they slapped their thighs, they quarrelled. No one could sleep. The sickest man could not sleep in the bright hot loud afternoon. This was their pleasure, cheaper than eating, drinking, or lust. But she could do nothing. The uproar went on. She changed the compress, bending over her husband's dark face and closed eyes and withdrawn look.

It's odd (and she returned to the thought of this country which in spite of its brightness and darkness and vigour was fearful to her), that I am Canadian and am fair, and have my roots in that part of England which was ravaged and settled by blond Norsemen; and Marcus is Canadian and is dark, and before generations of being Canadian he was Irish, and before generations of being Irish — did the dark Phoenicians come? — and he finds no strangeness here and I do.

In the late evening Marcus walked weakly onto the Cairo train. The compartment was close, small, and grimy. The compressed heat of the evening was intense. They breathed dust. Mrs. Forrester gently helped her husband on to the berth. He looked round.

"I can't sleep down here!" he said. "You mustn't go up above in all this heat!" But he could do no other.

"I shan't go up," she said consolingly. "See!" and she took bedclothes from the upper berth and laid them on the floor beside his berth. "I shall be cooler down here." There she lay all night long, breathing a little stale air and grit which entered by a small grid at the bottom of the door. "Oh . . . you sleeping on the floor. . . !" groaned Marcus.

And outside in the dark, she thought, as the train moved north, is that same country that in the early dawning looks so lovely. In the faint pearl of morning, peasants issue from huts far apart. The family — the father, the ox, the brother, the sons, the children, the women in trailing black, the dog, the asses — file to their work between the lines of pale green crops. There again is something hieratic, ageless, in their movements as they file singly one behind the other between the green crops, as the figures on the frieze had filed, one behind the other. Here and there in the morning stand the white ibis, sacred, unmolested, among the delicate green. How beguiling was the unawareness, and the innocency. Then, in that morning hour, and only then, had she felt no fear of Egypt. This scene was universal and unutterably lovely. She . . .

"A LITTLE HAND," said her husband loudly in the dark, and spoke strange words, and then was silent.

Yes, buy a little hand, sir, nice, cheap, very old. Buy a little hand. Whose hand?

When morning came Marcus woke and looked down in surprise.

"Whatever are you doing down there?" he asked in his ordinary voice.

"It was cooler," said his wife. "Did you sleep well?" and she scrambled up.

"Me? Sleep? Oh yes, I think I slept. But there was something . . . a hand . . . I seemed to dream about a hand . . . What hand? . . . Oh yes, that hand . . . I don't quite remember . . . in the tomb . . . you didn't seem to notice the lack of air in that tomb, did you . . . I felt something brushing us in there . . . brushing us all day. . . That was a heck of a day. . . Where's my tie?"

He stood up weakly. Without speaking, Mrs. Forrester handed her husband his tie.

Marcus, whose was that little hand, she thought and would think . . . whose was it? . . . Did it ever know you . . . did you ever know that hand? . . . Whose hand was it, Marcus? . . . oh let us go away from here!

From *Mrs. Golightly and other stories* (1961) by Ethel Wilson 1890–1980. Born in South Africa, she came to Vancouver, where she taught in public schools 1907–1920. She began publishing stories in 1937, ceasing in the 1960s when she became mentally disabled.

LONDON
by Charles Ritchie

6 November 1940.

Things one will forget when this is over — fumbling in the dark of the black-out for one's front door key while bits of shrapnel fall on the pavement beside one — the way the shrapnel seems to drift — almost like snow-flakes through the air in an aimless, leisurely way and the clink of it landing on the pavement.

9 November 1940.

Dined alone at Brook's off silver plate among the prints of eighteenth-century Whig lords to the sound of German bombers overhead. At the next table the Duke of St. Albans, an old boy in battledress who had spent the day on guard at the Admiralty Arch was saying, 'I hate all the Europeans, except Scandinavians. I have always been for the Scandinavians — of course I loathe all dagoes.'

16 November 1940.

I came back from spending the night at Aldershot to find my flat a heap of rubble from a direct hit, and I have lost everything I own. That is no tragedy but a bore — and doubtless a cash loss, as the Department of External Affairs will never approve replacing suits from Sackville Street at twenty pounds per suit. I am most annoyed at losing my new 'woodsy' tweed suit, the picture of the Rose that Anne gave me, volume two of the book I am reading, my edition of Rimbaud and the little green book of my own chosen quotations. I do not much regret all the pigskin which used to jar on her so much.

I am enjoying the publicity attendant on this disaster, particularly the idea which I have put abroad that if it had not been for a chance

decision to go to Aldershot for the night I should have been killed.
I should probably only have been cut about or bruised. The rest of
the people living in the flats were in the cellar and escaped unhurt.
Hart and I went to see the ruins, and the youth next door was full
of the fact that Lord A and Lady A too had had to be pulled out
of the débris — so had fourteen other people, but what struck him
was that even a lord had not been spared by the bomb. A further
fascinating detail was that Lord A's naval uniform was still hanging
on the hook on the open surviving wall for all the world to see. Now
I know that the *Evening Standard* is right when it prints those items
'Baronet's kinswoman in a bus smash' etc.

I feel like a tramp having only one suit and shirt and in particular
only *one pair of shoes*.

Last week when I wrote this diary I was sitting on my sofa in front
of my electric fire in my perfectly real and solid flat with my books
at arm's length — the furniture had that false air of permanence
which chairs and tables take on so readily — the drawn curtains shut
out the weather. Now all this is a pile of dirty rubble, with bits of
my suits, wet and blackened, visible among the bricks.

On top of the pile my sofa is perched (quite the most uncomfortable and useless article in the flat but it has survived) — this violent,
meaningless gesture like a slap from a drunken giant has smashed
my shell of living into a heap.

17 November 1940. Dorchester Hotel.

It certainly feels safe in this enormous hotel. I simply cannot believe
that bombs would dare to penetrate this privileged enclosure or that
they could touch all these rich people. Cabinet Ministers and Jewish
lords are not killed in air-raids — that is the inevitable illusion that
this place creates. It is a fortress propped up with money-bags. It
will be an effort to go back to an ordinary house which can be blotted
out by one bomb.

I went for a walk in the park with my ballerina. I am trying to
talk her into coming to live with me, but am getting nowhere. She
says her brothers back in Portland always told her it cheapened a
girl in a man's eyes — he never would want to marry a girl who had
done that. We walked round and round the equestrian statue of

William of Orange in St. James's Square arguing the point until an elderly gentleman called out to us, 'I do not want to interrupt you but I feel I should tell you, just in case you did not notice, that there is a police warning on the railings saying that there is an unexploded bomb in the garden!'

17 November 1940.

The ballerina is ridiculous, but I must not begin to think that she is pathetic because she is really very well able to look after herself, and what is more she has succeeded in making me a little bit in love with her.

18 November 1940.

I could have strangled her today while she was eating her chocolate cake, but I was so disagreeable that I do not think she enjoyed it much. Poor little devil — I am sorry for her. She looked so gay and pretty today with her little coloured umbrella in the rainy after-luncheon Jermyn Street. It is rather touching the way she sticks to her American small-town gods in the midst of this London. When I first knew her only a few weeks ago she was excited at being taken to a smart restaurant. Now she thinks it fashionable to complain — 'The smoked-salmon here is not as good as at the Ritz' — 'I like the way they pull the table out for you here' (if the waiter has not pulled the table aside for her to pass).

27 November 1940.

I am living at Brooks's Club, a combination of discomfort and old-fashioned comfort. Magnificent coal fires in the living-rooms, icy bedrooms, the kind of confidential valeting that you get in a good country house, the superb bath towels, yards of them, impossible to manoeuvre — the only thing to do is to wrap yourself up in one and sit down until you dry.

As I write I hear the ever-menacing throb of a bomber coming out of the fog. Tonight there is an old-fashioned London fog. Fumbling my way along Piccadilly I could hardly — as they say — 'see my hand before me.' I hear the hall porter saying in a grieved tone, 'There is no air-raid warning gone.' This is one of the nights when I feel interested in life, when I should much resent a bomb removing me from the scene. There are other nights when I feel it could not matter less.

Came back last night in the tube from Earl's Court. I hear that the drunks quite often fight it out by throwing each other on to the live wire, which contrary to superstition does not always kill you. If the toughs in the shelter tube do not like a chap they wait for him and throw him on to the wire. I must say that I saw nothing of this — just people sleeping, and not the poorest of the poor. They were all fully dressed and looked cleaned and quite prosperous, some pretty girls who might be serving in a big store, quite a lot of men and children. I have never seen so many different ages and types of people asleep before. Their sprawled attitudes, arms flung out, etc. made me think of photographs of the dead in battlefields — their stark and simplified faces. What one misses in the sleeping and the dead are the facial posturings prompted by perpetual vanity.

I am off the ballerina — she is rude to waiters who cannot answer back.

3 December 1940.

If that bloody ballerina does not come across tomorrow I am through with her. She gave me a model of Our Lady of Lourdes today, but she seems positively to be getting colder the fonder she gets of me.

6 December 1940.

Week-end with the Sacheverell Sitwells. He is charming with a sort of gentleness, which is most attractive, and manners that show his delicacy and sensibility. He would disappear after tea with, 'I am going to my room to scribble for a little while' or 'I will withdraw to my apartment.' It was exciting to feel that up there he was distilling another of those magic potions of his. He thinks it is all up with Europe, its culture and vitality exhausted. There I think he is mistaken, although certainly his European tradition — that of the civilised aristocrat — is hard hit. His wife Georgia is a Canadian — a beauty — tall with pale skin and dark eyes. She is amused and amusing and impulsively warm-hearted. I came down on the train with

Princess Callimachi (Anne-Marie), a lively little Romanian with the look of a lizard, who lives with the Sitwells at present.

21 December 1940.

Evening with the ballerina — some progress to report. We dined, thank God without music and away from the frowsy hotel atmosphere at a small but expensive restaurant in Shepherd Market. She felt, I think, that we were rather slumming. As usual she talked an immense amount about 'Mommy and Daddy,' and at one stage of dinner I was sunk in such a stupor of boredom that even she noticed it and I had to pull myself together and begin talking rapidly, desperately and at random. The night was cold and starry outside, with quite a heavy blitz. We walked back to the flat. She has more sense and feeling than one would give her credit for at first. What is shocking about her is the contrast between her romantic looks and her flat commonplace mind. Her mainspring in life appears to be an intense desire to show that she comes from the right side of the railroad tracks. Like many completely uninhibited bores she wins in the end by sheer persistence. She has talked to me so much about people I do not know or care about, her family, the members of the ballet company, etc., that I am beginning to feel I do know them and find myself taking an interest in their doings. Later in the evening we went out to Lyons' Corner House where we were joined by two R.A.F. pilots, both D.F.C.s, one drunk, Irish and very funny. The R.A.F. have a line laid down for them — the gay, brave young pilot with a joke on his lips, irresponsible, living to the full because they may die any day.

22 December 1940.

Dined with Alastair Buchan at Pratt's Club — the best sole in London, that is to say in the world. I always enjoy Pratt's, the atmosphere of open fires and easy unbuttoned chat, the equality where cabinet ministers sit around the table and argue with subalterns — the decor of red curtains and the stuffed salmon caught by His Royal Highness the Duke of Edinburgh in 1886. The other night a rather tight, junior lieutenant back from the Middle East was dining there. Anthony Eden began holding forth at length on the Mediterranean situation. This youth, after listening for some time, turned to a friend and said, 'I do not know who that man is but he is talking awful balls.' Immense satisfaction of all members.

25 December 1940.

Spent Christmas Eve in the country, came back on the morning train to London on Christmas Day — waited of course for nearly an hour at Horsley Station for the train. How well I know those English country stations in the morning after a weekend when you have tipped the chauffeur and told him not to wait and you walk up and down the station platform in the raw air that smells of babies' diapers, with a little view of the railway line and fields and a couple of cows, fields rough-surfaced and untidy seen at close range, although a billiard board of green if you flashed over them in a plane; or a flooded meadow, mist hanging about the trees. Two porters whistling and stamping, a lady in a fur coat taking leave of her rosy-cheeked niece, who wears tweeds and no hat — 'My dear, remember when you come to London there is always a roof.' Then the soldiers — bold-eyed Canadians with a slouch and a swagger, New Zealanders with overcoats hanging untidily, Australians often with girls, and English soldiers going back to London saying good-bye to plain, sensible, loyal wives wearing spectacles and sometimes carrying babies. The soldiers from the Dominions are invading armies of irresponsible younger brothers. The English soldiers look at them not unkindly but with a sober ironic air — puppies and old hound dogs. London was deserted.

29 December 1940.

Walked home tonight by the pink light of an enormous fire somewhere in the City. Heavy blitz. I dined alone at Brooks's. Read R.G. Collingwood's book on Roman Britain — sandy but with oases. I also tried unsuccessfully to put into despatch form some intuitions of how things may develop in this country after the war, provided, of course, that we win it. Funny, though reason may tell me that that is open to doubt, I never really contemplate our not winning. It is eerie tonight, the streets are so light from the fires and so completely deserted and silent now that the planes seem to have passed. Was that a distant barrage or somebody moving furniture upstairs?

No, the only sound is the tinkle of ambulance bells in the empty street. This is not very pleasant. I think I will have a whisky and soda. Supposing that some day one of these days I just was not there to meet Billy for lunch at the R.A.C. The others were there — Billy and Margery and Hart but not me. Now — that was the barrage, and I can hear a plane right overhead. The man at the Club said that a lot of our fighters were up tonight. That was a bomb that time. When the building shakes from the floor upwards it is a bomb.

Spent last night at Stansted. We went to church that morning. Lord Bessborough reading the lessons — 'The flesh is as grass and like grass shall wither away.' He read it well — the rustic choir boys piped up 'Come All Ye Faithful' — clear voices like a running stream. The clergyman ranged from arrangements for the local paper chase to God's purpose. An iconoclast — he announced that God had other preoccupations in addition to the defence of the British Empire. We should will victory — call on the power of thought — pause for a minute every day before the B.B.C. announced the news. It bothers me this talk about calling on the power of thought and willing things to happen to our advantage, as if we were trying to force a lock when, had we the key, it would open itself.

10 January 1941.

The ballerina was rather sweet really. We had breakfast in the Mayfair Hotel — rashers of bacon and great cups of American coffee. She did look beautiful this morning. People turned around in the street to look at her.

12 January 1941.

Reading Gide — the best antidote possible to the triumphant commonplace of an English Sunday. Not even the Blitzkrieg has been able to break the spell which the Sabbath casts over the land. One could not fail by just putting one's hand out of the window and smelling and looking and listening for two minutes to recognise that this is Sunday. In my mind's eye I can see the weary wastes of the Cromwell Road beneath a sullen sky where a few depressed pedestrians straggle as though lost in an endless desert. One's soul shrinks from the spectacle.

Symptoms of Sexual Happiness

1. I look at people, men and women, from the physical point of view, not by class or taste but in terms of the senses. Which ones are out of the stream of sex? (How easy it is to see these!) And why? 2. I am temporarily cured of my mania for seeing things in a straight line. I admit and enjoy confusion. The relief is enormous. 3. Time no longer seems to be slipping away from me. I am happy to spend it carelessly. 4. Other people do not seem worth the usual effort. I cannot help treating them casually, often interrupting them and not listening to what they say. 5. I definitely am very much less amusing. The ballerina leaves today with the ballet company on tour. I am looking forward to early and varied infidelities during her absence.

27 November 1942.

Went to a party at Nancy Mitford's — I had a long conversation with Unity Mitford. She started the conversation by saying, 'I have just hit my left breast against a lamp-post as I was bicycling here.' She said, 'I tried to commit suicide when I was in Germany but now I am a Christian Scientist — not that I believe a word of it, but they saved my life so I feel I owe it to them to be one.' 'I hate the Czechs,' she said suddenly in a loud, emphatic voice, 'but that is natural — they tried to arrest me and I had not done anything. I did not even have the Fuhrer's picture in my suitcase as they said I had.' She has just recently returned to England where her role as Hitler's English friend does not make her popular. I must say I liked her better than anyone else at the party. She has something hoydenish and rustic about her.

Great discussion with George Ignatieff about the future of Europe. He sees the great age of the Slav people dawning. I see our being drawn gradually into supporting every and any regime in Europe that offers a bulwark against communism, i.e., in terms of power politics against a triumphant Russia with overwhelming influence at least as far as the Rhine. Of course we shall try to get rid of the more stinking quislings and put in progressive governments, but above all, we must hold the *cordon sanitaire* against Bolshevism. Could there be two worlds after the war — the Atlantic and the Middle European plus the Balkans — the former dominated by Anglo-Germany — the one democratic and semi-capitalist, the other communist?

What will our relations with Russia be after the war if they win against Germany? As long as they remain behind the Curzon Line and busy themselves with reconstruction we might get along all right, but Russia will inevitably be on the side of every revolutionary government in Europe. We shall become suspicious of her and will tend, for the sake of balance, to back anti-revolutionary forces. Thus a new war will be prepared. Indeed we can see the forces that are already preparing it.

23 December 1942.

Went down to spend last week-end — Elizabeth and I — with Stephen Tennant. It was a dreamlike and unrepeatable occasion. From the moment of coming out of the rainy December countryside into his apartment all was under a magician's spell. It was partly the sense of being picked up on a magic carpet out of the prosaic into the midst of everything that is extravagant and strange. In one wing of what was formerly his country-house and is now a Red Cross Hospital he has furnished a set of rooms to suit his own fantastic taste. Such huge white velvet sofas, piles of cushions and artificial flowers, chandeliers, such a disorder of perfumes, rouge pots and pomades, such orchid satin sheets and pink fur rugs, toy dogs and flounced silk curtains, mirrors at angles, shaded lights and scented fires. But the unreality of it attained to an intensity which was pure artistic illusion — too fantastic to be vulgar or funny and with a strange honesty as a natural mask for Stephen's high-strung, high-coloured but never vulgar nature.

On the train down we found ourselves sitting opposite Augustus John wearing a tweed cap which he removed to reveal that noble head of a moth-eaten lion. Fixing us with his unfocussed gaze he made an effort to assemble meaning and made charming light conversation, full of malice and fun. At intervals he dozed off — his beautiful hands in his lap.

At Salisbury Stephen met us coiffed in a blue knitted helmet — his too-golden hair arranged in a becoming crest. Through the driving rain under a gun-metal sky with sodden leaves piled high in the ditches we drove to Wilsford and were wafted up into the pink rococo of his apartment. 'Rich stains of former orgies,' he said giggling at the spots on the silver-satin cushion covers; but he is not a comic.

121

His drawings are brilliant evocations of the Marseilles underworld. His note-books are full of them and all the same characters reappear — *matelots* and tarts, procurers and pimps — faces which have obsessed him. Perhaps he is too undisciplined to express his obsessions in terms of writing.

Elizabeth talked to Stephen of dialogue in the novel — of how every sentence must bear directly or indirectly on the theme — must be a clue or the counter-point to a clue. In that sense how 'every novel is a detective novel.' It does no harm to linger in places where one has pleasure in writing provided one makes it up by skimming quickly elsewhere so that the tempo of the whole is not slowed up. How a phrase should be written down when it occurs because it may be fruitful of unexpected developments; may contain seeds which would only come to life when it is on paper.

Then they talked about the sticky passages that haunt writers. Whether it was best to make a frontal attack on such difficulties and never rest until they were overcome or, as Elizabeth said, to sidestep the dragon in the path and to go on to what one wanted to write and return to the difficulty later, perhaps from a different angle or aspect. She told us how Virginia Woolf when writing her last book *Between the Acts* was heard to say, 'For six weeks I have been trying to get the characters from the dining-room into the drawing-room and they are still in the dining-room.'

Virginia Woolf haunts the lives of all who knew her. Almost every day something is added to my knowledge of her — that she was a snob — that she could be cruel, as when one lovely May evening a young, shy girl came into her drawing-room in Bloomsbury to be greeted with the overwhelming question from Virginia, 'What does it feel like to be young in May?' The girl stood shambling in silent consternation in the doorway. But how they revolved around Virginia Woolf, how much she must have done to liberate them all, to give them weapons of coolness and wit, and how often they say, 'Virginia would have enjoyed it' or 'she would have enhanced it.' But to me her reflected atmosphere is rather alarming — the exquisite politeness — but an eye that misses nothing and a power to puncture gracefully, opportunely and mercilessly if occasion arises or the mood changes.

28 December 1942.

To have heard (as I did the other night) T.S. Eliot on the subject of Charles Morgan was to be entertained at a most delicate feast of malice — the sidelong, half-pitying, good-natured, kindly approach — ('Poor old Morgan, etc.') the closing in on the prey, the kill, so neat and so final and then the picking of the bones, the faint sound of licking of lips and the feast is over.

From *The Siren Years* (1974) by Charles Ritchie, born in Halifax, 1906. Ritchie was a distinguished Canadian ambassador before retiring and publishing his witty, candid journals, unique in Canadian letters.

CASABLANCA
by A.M. Klein

Whatever the motives were that impelled Uncle Melech toward Casablanca, his instincts were sound. I, too, that first day, fell in love with this beautiful city of the Moghreb el Aksa which, arrayed in all the colours of Islam, stands mirroring itself in the mirror of the Atlantic. As upon some Circean strand magical with voices, I could have halted my travels there; indeed, it was music, a singing that issued like silken coloured thread from the door of a café hard by the Hôtel des Ambassadeurs, where I had just registered for my initial Arabian night, that first snared me, enchanted me to enter, and there held me entangled in the nostalgia of its distant Oriental evocations.

The words of the young Arab's song I could not make out at all, save here and there a few Semitic vocables that spoke to me as through a latticed window — *ward* for flower, *hawah* for love. It was the music, however, its minor key, its gesticulative cadence, that bowed to me, that touched lips and forehead to me, that greeted me with salaam-shalom, that with cantorial trills and tremolos self-infatuated made holiday for me, rising, as the singer swooned, to paradisiac fields, falling, descending, lingering recitative upon a middle path, and finally with meditative mournfulness coming to rest, with sob, with sigh. I recognized in that singing the accents of forgotten kinship and was through it transported back to ancient star-canopied desert camp-fires about which there sat, their faces firelit, my ancestors and that Arab's.

The singer was followed by a storyteller, a bearded wrinkled man, cowled in his burnous, an ape's mischief twinkling from his eyes, who, speaking a strange sun-baked French, regaled his audience with tales of wonder and innuendo. The story of *The Seven Angles of the Yashmak*, whose telling was accompanied by much coy pantomime, set the café roaring; *The Stutterer's Parrot*, too, was a kind of *tour de force* in which Arabic, Berberi, and French stumbled over one another to the great delight of his listeners, whose appreciation was obviously profounder than mine; but it was his *Tale of the Ethiopian Who Did Change His Skin* that was most seriously received and most loudly applauded. This was a fable of an unlucky-lucky Negro whose skin changed with the changing of the seasons: in the summer he was black, black as coal; in the autumn he turned brown, henna-brown; in winter he was yellow; and in the spring he blossomed white. Summer he was black again. It was an engaging anecdote pointing many a moral, and suffused throughout with a sense of the possible-marvellous. The storyteller, moreover, exploited to the full the absurdities of the fourfold dilemma, telling of the Ethiopian's troubles with his wife, who one spring day found that her husband had faded, of the confusion he caused to functionaries who as they registered him brown looked up to see him yellow, and of the pied and mea-sled aspect that was the Ethiopian's one June day when it hailed.

I fell asleep that night to the singing of the young Arab, wafted across the street to the open balcony of my room; but I slept fitfully — it was hot, the very pillows seemed to sweat — and when I did fall off in sleep, I tossed and tossed, disturbed, I think, by the call of old-new affinities, nightmared by the tall Sudanese who paced my dreams, veiled in a yashmak, stuttering.

When I had arrived at Casa it had been too late to go to the office of the JDC, but on the following morning I was there early. It was closed: *fête nationale*. Well, I had waited thirty years to see Uncle Melech; I could wait one day more.

So I spent the rest of that day renewing my courtship of the city which, despite its imposed Gallic quiddities, shimmered of the East, and whose minarets, like flutes, charmed away all that of the Occident still clung to me. Wandering along boulevards named after French marshals and along side streets that remembered quietly mullahs and sultans dethroned, I mingled with the crowd. Everything was a fascination, rich, crayoned. After the drabness and austerity of the Italian camp, after the wan bleached faces among whom I had spent my life up to now, this was cornucopia and these people an arc of the rainbow of race. I lingered in the markets and souks, my eyes luxuriating upon each opulent still life displayed on barrow or heaped up behind the windows of the cool marble-slabbed arcades — the golden oranges of Tetuán, pyramided; navelled the pomegranates of Marrakech; Meknes quince; the sun sweet inside their little globes, and upon their skins the mist of unforgotten dawns, the royal grapes of Rabat. Even the sheathed onions, mauve, violet, pink, polltufted like the warriors of the Atlas, seemed fruit that I had never seen before. And dominating — whether in the cool smooth round or, sliced, as crimson little scimitars adorning the Negro smile — were watermelons, miniature Africas, jungle-green without, and within peopled by pygmy blacks set sweetly in their world of flesh.

The morning passed as upon a flowered dial, and at noon, what with the irresistible fruit, and the lemonade sipped under awnings, there was no desire in me for food. I had been sustained by the richness of scene, by sound, by the pollen of perfume, for in this realm he is a great man, the apothecary, raising with powdered thumb, summoning through the triturated drop the ghosts of roses, the seven-veiled shadows of the jasmine. When I did pause before the entrance of a restaurant — not so much to read the menu as to admire the magnificence of the Senegalese doorman, tall obelisk in basalt, his cheeks with concentric carmine scars carved — the odour of oil and the gorging at all tables, a rite of grossness and plump-fingered delicacy, stifled whatever appetite I had had. Upon another occasion and in a more ascetic environment I might have been tempted by these succulent chickenwings that here made dripping moustaches for the round Levantine in a fez, or by the mounds of saffron and rice, or even the cubed sheep's meat glistening fat. There were too, the classics of the French cuisine, to whose napoleonic strategy my palate had ever surrendered — but the gourmandizers repelled me. They lived well, these Moors; but too well: the thigh-filled pantaloons that waddled along the street; the Negress with scarves, striped as with the lines of latitude, knotted about her large hips, gripping a sausage in her inkish-pink palm; the paunch-proud merchant seating his buttock and belly on his chair — these spoke eloquently of past banquets, of many-coursed meals digested reposeful upon soft pillows and divans beneath the gauze of golden slumber, the brocade of the gold snore.

I ordered some white sugarcakes, drank my little cups of Turkish, and was once again among the gaunt-faced Berbers in bright caftans, the French bureaucrats colonial-correct, the linen tunics, the calico, and the muslin.

It was, however, the everywhere-encountered art of smiths, builders, and craftsmen that won back my admiration and in its shapes and forms dovetailed and mortised into the welcoming hollows of my heart. Like the music I had heard the night before, this was an art of traceries and fretwork where both space and space filled, combined and embraced, interlaced, wove out of iron or the inscribed stone their flowing arabesques: *Neskhi*, the calligraphy of growing things, pattern of shoot and tendril and climbing vine: a virtuosity it was of curlecue and flourish curving gracefully in the tall arched portal or delicately run to shape the cinctured dome: an art of alternations and changes where the white marble gave way to black, the black to white, twins of symmetry in polite accommodating dance; a discipline of design, yet a playfulness, the artist abstracting — may his shadow never diminish! — abstracting the beauty of the world to its planes and lines, rolling in intimate involvement the intertangled triangles, the paired squares; eschewing image, delighting in form; *Kufi*, the very pilgrims of the script, staff-bearing, marching; and everywhere, whether through the cursive, which is like a sultan at ease, or through the angular, which is like a sultan in state, filling my soul with remoteness, with remoteness made familiar and near.

It was not difficult for me to understand, stirred as I was by these inarticulate nostalgias, the sense of at-homeness that in past centuries entire communities of Jews — scholars, goldsmiths, potters, silk-weavers, sandal-makers, minters, poets — had felt dwelling here in the domain of the maariv. I, too, found myself as in some palmet-toed atrium to the Holy Land. But all that day, among faces that continually suggested but never asserted their Semitism, I did not meet a Jew.

My visit the next morning to the rue Gallieni was again a frustration. *Monsieur le Directeur*, I was informed, was away at Oujda and might perhaps be back the next day.

"Can I do anything for you?" The matronly person in charge of the office put into her question both the natural politesse of her French speech and the proverbial hospitality of her Sephardic origin.

127

"I am looking for a Melech Davidson."

"Monsieur Davidson?" She regarded me suspiciously. Her cordiality of the moment before vanished; she turned back to her fellow employees, staring at us, attentive, and I got the impression of a secret shared.

"Monsieur Davidson is parted. He's not here anymore." She looked finality.

"Do you know where I could reach him?"

"He's not here, he's not more at Casablanca."

"But —"

"He was here, but he's been expulsed" — she hadn't intended to say it — "he's been expulsed from the region."

"What for?"

"I believe, monsieur, that you had better speak to Monsieur le Directeur. This is not our department. Moreover, we do not know who you are. We have had enough trouble. Truly, we do not care to discuss the *affaire* of — of the mullah of the mellah?"

The girls tittered.

"I beg your pardon?"

"Monsieur le Directeur will be able to give you all the informations you search. I am not informed. . . . I am not authorized."

There was no point in pressing the conversation further. I would not let go, however, of the last word of hers. Tourist-like I asked:

"Is there a mellah here?"

"*Mais, oui!* And what a mellah! *Le mellah des mellahs!* Would you care" — guide-like she volunteered — "to visit it? Our chauffeur, Monsieur Dauphin, will be pleased to direct you."

She sent a young doe-eyed stenographer to go look for him.

"And ah, yes, we can oblige you. A photograph of your Monsieur Davidson — to solace your disappointment, and" — she smiled — "to atone for our reticence. Not a very good one, but something so that from our office you go not away empty-handed."

All my life I had waited for this picture, and now at last I was to see him, Uncle Melech plain!

She handed me the snapshot.

It showed a man standing in the midst of a group of barefooted boys. But his face — Uncle Melech had again eluded me. It was a double, a multiple exposure!

As I slid the snapshot into my wallet, M. Dauphin appeared. The chauffeur — may Allah be praised for the world's chauffeurs, they preserve the art of conversation — was an extrovert, and loquacity itself. Sitting in the jeep that was to take us the half-dozen blocks to the ghetto, he was at once autobiographical. historical, critical, geographical, and wise. His ancestral name had originally been *Dalfen*, but disliking the connotations of penury that flowed from the Hebrew word, he had had it changed to Dauphin, and felt consequently more French if not more princely. His grandfather, he recalled, had dwelt in the mellah, but through a series of fortunate events had lifted himself in the social scale, and now the grandson could serve a great organization like the Zhaydaysay and live in Casablanca proper, which vaunted these charming esplanades and these hotels ten stages high and the American movies (I had sat in one of them the night before, the film had been of the issue of 1945, and the newsreel had shown Churchill still poising the world upon forked fingers) and all modern conveniences, perhaps almost like New York.

Suddenly across a boulevard upon which there fronted a most impressive hotel — the Dauphin's pride — suddenly against walls such as those upon which circus posters are posted, we came upon the mellah.

"With a car it is impossible to traverse. Too straight."

We parked off the boulevard and proceeded on foot. We entered, we slid into the mellah; literally: for the narrow lane which gaped through the gateway at the clean world was thick with offal and slime and the oozing of manifold sun-stirred putrescences; metaphorically: for in a moment we knew that the twentieth century (with all its modern conveniences) had forsaken us, and we were descending into the sixteenth, the fifteenth, twelfth, eleventh centuries. The streets, narrow and mounting, mazed, descending and serpentine, formicated with life. Everywhere poverty wore its hundred costumes, tatters of red and tatters of yellow, rags shredded and rags pieced, a raiment of patches, makeshifts, and holes through which the naked skin showed, a kind of human badge. Brightness, however, fell only from rags; if a garment was whole, it was black, the sombre ghetto gaberdine.

Most of the people who lived in these labyrinthine hutches and warrens were out in the open: the tailor sitting upon the cobblestones, his feet under him; the housewife caressing a vegetable; the aged, murmuring; and the blind — upon so sunny a day so many blind! — reclining against a wall waiting for tomorrow against a wall to recline. At one strategic corner eighteen of these heaps of helplessness, wrapped in rags and white-pupilled blindness, were counted.

Up and down the streets, a water-carrier, panniered like a beast of burden, walked with a singular air of self-importance.

As we made our way with difficulty through the congested lanes, avoiding a body here, evading a donkey there, we were everywhere beset — by hands! Wherever we turned — hands! I was reminded of those drawings illustrative of Dante's *Inferno* in which the despair of its denizens is shown rising from the depths in a digitation and frenzy of hands, hands snatching at straw, at air, at hands. This was a population of beggars greeting me with outstretched palms, with five-fingered plea. I was making acquaintance with the civic gesture of the mellah of Casablanca.

Over the protest of my guide, who informed me that if I began this thing there would be no end to it — there were twenty-five thousand who lived here — I distributed the largesse of my Moroccan small change and made to go on my way. It was impossible; I was prevented; for there at my feet was the grateful recipient blessing me with all the blessings that the richness of his imagination and the poverty of his state could command, salaaming before me, and finally, prostrate, smiting his forehead thrice upon the ground. I had not realized the intent of these abasements until they were over. Embarrassed, ashamed, yet angry for the innocence of my shame, I hastened forward.

It is a figure of speech, this hastening: for here one cannot hasten. One battles one's way through the ambush of petition, one pushes cruelly forward. At the same time one must be careful of one's footing; there is commerce here! and the refuse of commerce. Here, behind his veil of flies, is a butcher; he has for sale one pendulous hooked piece of liver; he stands before it, fanning it; the flies would bankrupt him. Yonder his competitor does better, he sells tripe; and for tripe there are customers. Fish are for sale today, too; the guts of fish, blood and pale balloon, lie in the roadway alongside which the seven-scummed runnels slowly flow in filthy arabesque. Upon the cobbles of the streets, everywhere, the marks of trade-rubbish, rottenness, the signs of a donkey's passage.

In their booths, standing dark and aesthetic behind their coloured quantums of spice, the spice-venders. Puzzled, I asked M. Dauphin who were the customers who bought these luxuries.

"It is not of luxe at all," he said. "Spice is a great stifler of hunger. It deceives the stomach; it induces a belief that a banquet has been had when only a morsel has been eaten. The spice-venders, these *bnaiattar*, are here a venerable guild."

We came upon another group of beggars, idols in the sun, dreaming of the vizier's ingots.

"You see that mendicant over there?" asked M. Dauphin pointing to a blind, filthily draped, bag-o'-bones hag. "She is unique in the mellah. Not unique in that she is blind and deaf-mute, there are many of such; not even unique in that she has an assistant, the blindness often compels such organization; but unique in the place she inhabits. She has no home, not even one of these hovels; but there at the side of that house is a kennel. Into it her assistant pushes her and, as circumstances require, withdraws."

Now, not even in Canada is poverty mythical, but such wretchedness — I could not believe it real. Some magician out of the *Arabian Nights*, I thought, had cast upon me a spell and conjured up with sinister open-sesame this melodramatic illusion. Or perhaps it was a desert mirage that was playing tricks with my vision. Or I was dreaming, I was imagining. Or some Hollywood producer had come here to stage a frightful scene.

But it was real. There was an element that confirmed reality.

The stench!

The odour of the centuries hovers over the mellah and will not dissipate. Not all the breezes of the Atlantic, less than a mile away, have yet effected a purification. It is an odour palpable and pervasive. Escape therefrom there is not; flight into a side alley but changes its intensity, not its nature or gust. It is, at times, an odour of nuances; an odour, also, of thick heavy undertones. Only occasionally, as when upon the air there are wafted some few motes of the pulver of spice, only then are there subtleties for the nostrils; all, otherwise, is miasma and reek. The fish-heads scattered beneath the booths give off their peculiar smell; the viands, too, send up their intimations of ptomaine;

131

there is a touch of the rancidity of dairies; garbage and refuse steam mephitic on the ground. Through the fanfare of stenches it is only the very sensitive who can distinguish the special contribution of the cat carcass drying in the sun. Yet it is not a composition without a theme; again and again, in the intervals between the abatement of one rankness and the rise of another, there is sensed the presence of the major offensiveness. It is that of ordure and dregs. Decades of digestion raise their disgust through the streets. There is no water in the mellah. The mellah's alleys are its cloaca.

Squeamish Westerner, I had to stop in my tracks. I could not proceed farther through this worst of augean stables, one which mangered humans. I turned aside and, feigning the necessity of a handkerchief, sought refuge in its clean laundered smell.

As I stood there trying to control a hypercritical gorge, M. Dauphin found my plight very amusing. "This is nothing," he said; "you should consider the condition of Jews in those Moslem countries which are unimproved by our civilization."

At that word, it almost came up. "Isn't there a place around here where I can breathe? A public building? A synagogue?"

"But certainly."

"Then let's go."

M. Dauphin turned up a side street and we passed through an open courtyard where a woman was emptying slops. "The water's last waterfall," said M. Dauphin. "First it is used for drinking, then for washing the fingers before eating, then for dishes, then for clothes, then for flushing."

"But there is plenty of water in Casablanca, is there not? Across the boulevard in the hotel there is hot and cold running water, all the time, and to spare. Why does the flow of civilization stop here at the gates of the mellah?"

"I do not know, monsieur. Perhaps it is too costly to bring water here. Perhaps it is necessary that there should be three categories of convenience: one for the metropole where live the French functionaries, one for the medina, the Arab slum, and one for the mellah where live the Jews. The French Government has much trouble often to keep the Arabs and Berbers pleased with the benefits which it has brought them; I am told that the fact that there are Jews who are very much in worse condition than they are helps toward their contentment. I do not know. But this at least is true: Jews are much better off here than among other Moslem populations — there are, you know, almost a million Jews living under Moslem rule — and better off now than when I was a little boy. Then no Jew was allowed to walk on the sidewalk as an Arab passed; no Jew was permitted to mount a horse — a horse, it is an animal noble — no Jew was permitted to mount a donkey, for then he would have been looking down on the Arab. And plus, it was prohibited that he wear white; black he had to wear, the colour of indignity, and even to this day you can distinguish, despite their common swarthiness, Arab from Jew by their headgear: a black skullcap is a Jew. It was bad. I mention only the outer signs of discrimination, the mood of the country, its atmosphere. When a Moslem had to bring the word *Jew* into his conversation, he would apologize, as for a pornography; I do not detail the actual injustice and oppression. Some of the disabilities still remain, but the French have effected veritable progress. Moreover, monsieur, these people do not feel as sad about their condition as you do. The evil has also brought its own alleviation — they, too, have been infected by Islam's submissiveness. Ask one of them how he stands it and he will no doubt answer: *Katoob*! It is written. It is written; he accepts."

We had reached the synagogue, and here, too, there were the usual paupers, lying on the steps, intoxicated with the hashish of *katoob*. The synagogue was cool and airy and afforded a pleasant relief from the swarming, stifling out-of-doors. There adorned it the customary Judaic symbols. Hanging from the base of the menorah, however, was a shaped metal hand; the design recurred throughout the synagogal ornamentation. I pointed to it, inquiringly.

"The hand of Fatima," said M. Dauphin. "For good luck."

M. Dauphin, apparently, was not pleased with my reaction to this novel ecclesiastic appurtenance. "You remind me," he said, "you remind me very much of the last man I guided through the mellah. He wasn't precisely a visitor, he came from arriving to Casa to take up his duties with our organization and I was instructed to conduct him through the mellah. He, too, was nauseated, he actually rejected. And you should have heard him on Fatima, on the water question, on *katoob*. He moved even me, truly. When he came back to the office he was practically in tears, clutching at his bearded jowls, pacing up and down, forgetting altogether that he was a subordinate. To think of it, he kept exclaiming: 'These are Jews! Jews whose forefathers were once the dons and hidalgos of the golden age of Spain! Jews whose ancestors were once counsellors and advisers to caliphs, to kings, whose writ ran current through the land, who are of the true blood, the unbroken lineage! Go see them now! Once their sires sat in the seats of justice, judging, whose scions now stand at the gates of the mellah begging! Impossible! Impossible! Morocco, Fez, Tetuán — these were names once glorious in our annals, seats of learning, sanctuaries of Torah! Now they are the prisons of untouchables. Casablanca, Casablanca, beautiful Casablanca, where Churchill and Roosevelt planned the triumph of our civilization — I spit!' M. Davidson was a very hysterical man."

"But not a man in error."

I tried to be as casual as I could, I remembered the taciturnity of the office. "Surely his anger was justified."

"Perhaps, but he caused us much trouble. We have to be cooperative with authority. We could not get very far with critique. Monsieur le Directeur, I can assure you, feels just as sensitively about the whole thing as did this Davidson. But to make scenes! That only makes us retrogress. . . . We sent him into the mellah to gather up statistics for us. He was in fact very efficient and brought us back the calculations. He showed, for example, that the death rate was among males fifty per cent in thirteen years; there are no official records, but Monsieur Davidson compared the names in the book of circumcision with the names in the book of *bar mitzvahs* and found half missing. He brought us statistics on blindness, on trachoma, on ringworm of the scalp, on itches, scabs, and young boys' baldness. He made us a graph of the incidence of tuberculosis, a tall black chart. All this was very useful, it helped us make our plans, settle our appropriations. But then what do you think he did? He sat down and wrote a letter to the editor of *Le Maroc* in which he made public all the facts and figures he had collected and ironized about the triple slogan of the French revolution!"

"That didn't bring any reforms?"

"That didn't bring any reforms. The letter wasn't even published! The editor telephoned the *directeur* and we had to make explanations and apologies. For in all our efforts the Government is very helpful. It facilitates our good works. It does not even hinder our program of emigration to Israel, which is assuming greater proportions every day. As much as possible, the Government is very sympathetic. Naturally, it does not want to chicane with the natives. Our Monsieur Davidson, of course, was reprimanded. But that didn't stop him. Oh no, not him. He created yet another incident. The authorities, you will understand, are very concerned over the good repute of Casa, it is a modern French city, they do not wish begging in the streets. They pass, therefore, very severe ordinances to suppress the mendicancy. Anyone convicted of begging in the streets is sent for eight days to the pond — an open enclosure in the desert without shelter from the sun. Very uncomfortable. Now one day a group of them, Jews, are sent away. They are there three days, four days, five days. Monsieur Davidson then commences organizations. He is very popular in the mellah, the beggars have faith in him, they follow his counsel; so in the dead of night he leads a whole company of them, armed with sticks, stones, and other weapons, out into the desert. *Le Maroc* described it the next day: 'a horde of beggars, the halt, the crippled, the dumb, the blind, led by the blind, led by the maimed, and Davidson at their head!' The pond has only one guard, a Negro who, catching sight of the grotesque and threatening crew, runs away. The freed beggars are brought back to the mellah. . . . Naturally Davidson is arrested."

"And sent to the pond?"

"Almost. It was an affair of scandal — in our office we do not care to talk about it — but Monsieur le Directeur interceded for him, and we succeeded in having the accusation broken. He was, however, demissioned from his post. He was, in fact, sent with our last boatload to Marseilles, from there they proceed, or already have proceeded, to Israel."

We had reached the gate of the mellah and the long, broad palm-sentinelled boulevard. One could breathe again.

I did not go back the next day to the rue Gallieni. I knew what I had wanted to know. I was eager to leave the city where the word Jew was a term of pornography, eager to leave it and its false music, its hollow art, eager to shake from my feet the dust of this city of the teated domes and the phalloi of minarets.

From *The Second Scroll* (1951) by A.M. Klein, 1909–1972. Born in Montreal, he became a lawyer, editor of *The Canadian Jewish Chronicle* and an active Zionist. In Casablanca in 1952, he asked the characteristic question: was it good for the Jews? One of Canada's finest poets, he broke down in the mid-1950s and wrote no more.

PARIS
by Mordecai Richler

In the summer of 1967, our very golden EXPO summer, I was
drinking with an old and cherished friend at Montreal airport,
waiting for my flight to London, when all at once he said, "You know,
I'm going to be forty soon."

At the time, I was still a smug thirty-six.

"Hell," he added, whacking his glass against the table, outraged,
"it's utterly ridiculous. Me, forty? My father's forty!"

Though we were both Montrealers, we had first met in Paris in
1951, and we warmed over those days now, *our* movable feast, until
my flight was called.

A few days later, back in London, where I had been rooted for
more than ten years, I sat sipping coffee on the King's Road, Chelsea,
brooding about Paris and watching the girls pass in their minis and
high suede boots. Suddenly, hatefully, it struck me that there was
a generation younger than mine. Another bunch. And so we were
no longer licenced to idle at cafés, to be merely promising as we were
in Paris, but were regularly expected to deliver the goods, books and
movies to be judged by others. At my age, appointments must be
kept, I thought, searching for a taxi.

Time counts.

As it happened, my appointment was with a Star at the Dorchester.
The Star, internationally-known, obscenely overpaid, was attended
in his suite by a bitch-mother private secretary, a soothing queer
architect to keep everybody's glasses filled with chilled Chevalier Mon-
trachet, and, kneeling by the hassock on which big bare feet rested,
a chiropodist. The chiropodist, black leather tool box open before
him, scissor-filled drawers protruding, black-bowler lying alongside

137

on the rug, was kneading the Star's feet, pausing to reverently snip a nail or caress a big toe, lingering whenever he provoked an involuntary little yelp of pleasure.

"I am ever so worried," the chiropodist said, "about your returning to Hollywood, Sir."

"Mmmnnn." This delivered with eyes squeezed ecstatically shut.

"Who will look after your feet there?"

The Star had summoned me because he wanted to do a picture about the assassination of Leon Trotsky. Trotsky, my hero. "The way I see it," he said, "Trotsky was one of the last really, really great men. Like Louis B. Mayer."

I didn't take on the screenplay. Instead, on bloody-minded impulse, I bought air tickets and announced to my wife, "We're flying to Paris tomorrow."

Back to Paris to be cleansed.

As my original left bank days had been decidedly impecunious, this was something like an act of vengeance. We stayed on the right bank, eating breakfast in bed at the Georges V, dropping into the Dior boutique, doing the galleries, stopping for a fin de maison here and a Perrier there, window-shopping on the rue du Rivoli, dining at Lapérouse, le Tour d'Argent, and le Méditerranée.

Fifteen years had not only made for changes in me.

The seedy Café Royale, on Boul. St. Germain, the terrace once spilling over with rambunctious friends until two in the morning, when the action drifted on to the Mabillion and from there to the notorious Pergola, had been displaced by the sickeningly mod, affluent le Drugstore. In Montparnasse, the Dôme was out of favour again, everybody now gathering at the barn-like La Coupole. Strolling past the Café le Tournot, I no longer recognized the abundantly confident *Paris Review* bunch (the loping Plimpton in his snapbrim fedora, Eugene Walter, Peter Mathiessen) either conferring on the pavement or sprawled on the terrace, dunking croissants into the morning café au lait, always and enviably surrounded by the most appetizing college girls in town. Neither was the affable Richard Wright to be seen any more, working on the pinball machine.

Others, alas, were still drifting from café to café, cruelly winded now, grubbiness no longer redeemed by youth, bald, twitchy, defensive, and embittered. To a man, they had all the faults of genius. They were alienated, of course, as well as being bad credit risks, rent-skippers, prodigious drinkers or junkies, and reprobates, and yet — and yet — they had been left behind, unlucky or not sufficiently talented. They made me exceedingly nervous, for now they appeared embarrassing, like fat bachelors of fifty tooling about in fire-engine red MGs or women in their forties flouncing their mini-skirts.

The shrill, hysterical editor of one of the little magazines of the Fifties caught up with me. "I want you to know," he said, "that I rejected all that crap Terry Southern is publishing in America now."

Gently I let on that Terry and I were old friends.

"Jimmy Baldwin," he said, "has copied all my gestures. If you see him on TV, it's me," he shrieked. "It's me."

On balance, our weekend in Paris was more unsettling than satisfying. Seated at the Dôme, well-dressed, consuming double scotches rather than nursing a solitary beer on the lookout for somebody who had just cashed his GI cheque on the black market, I realized I appeared just the sort of tourist who would have aroused the unfeeling scorn of the boy I had been in 1951. A scruffy boy with easy, bigoted attitudes, encouraging a beard, addicted to t-shirts, the obligatory blue jeans and, naturally, sandals. Absorbed by the Tarot and trying to write in the manner of Céline. Given to wild pronouncements about Coca-Cola culture and late nights listening to Sydney Bechet at the Vieux Colombier. We had not yet been labelled beats, certainly not hippies. Rather, we were taken for existentialists by *Life,* if not by Jean-Paul Sartre, who had a sign posted in a jazz cellar warning he had nothing whatsoever to do with these children and that they hardly represented his ideas.

I frequently feel I've lost something somewhere. Spontaneity maybe, or honest appetite. In Paris all I ever craved for was to be accepted as a serious novelist one day, seemingly an impossible dream. Now I'm harnessed to this ritual of being a writer, shaking out the morning mail for cheque-size envelopes — scanning the newspapers — breakfast — then upstairs to work. To try to work.

If I get stuck, if it turns out an especially sour, unyielding morning, I will recite a lecture to myself that begins, Your father had to be out at six every morning, driving to the junk yard in the sub-zero dark, through Montreal blizzards. You work at home, never at your desk before nine, earning more for a day's remembered insults than your father ever made, hustling scrap, in a week.

Or I return, in my mind's eye, to Paris.

Paris, the dividing line. Before Paris, experience could be savoured for its own immediate satisfactions. It was total. Afterwards, I became cunning, a writer, somebody with a use for everything, even intimacies.

I was only a callow kid of nineteen when I arrived in Paris in 1951, and so it was, in the truest sense, my university. St. Germain des Prés was my campus, Montparnasse my frat house, and my two years there are a sweetness I retain, as others do wistful memories of McGill or Oxford. Even now, I tend to measure my present conduct against the rules I made for myself in Paris.

The first declaration to make about Paris is that we young Americans, and this Canadian, didn't go there so much to discover Europe as to find and reassure each other, who were separated by such vast distances at home. Among the as yet unknown young writers in Paris at the time, either friends or nodding café acquaintances, there were Terry Southern, Alan Temko, Alfred Chester, Herbert Gold, David Burnett, Mavis Gallant, Alexander Trocchi, Christopher Logue, Mason Hoffenberg, James Baldwin, and the late David Stacton.

About reputations.

A few years ago, after I had spoken at one of those vast synagogue-cum-community plants that have supplanted the pokey little *shuls* of my Montreal boyhood, all-pervasive deodorant displacing the smell of pickled herring, a lady shot indignantly out of her seat to say, "I'm sure you don't remember me, but we were at school together. Even then you had filthy opinions, but who took you seriously? Nobody. *Can you please tell me,*" she demanded, "*why on earth anybody takes you seriously now?*"

Why indeed? If only she knew how profoundly I agreed with her. For I, too, am totally unable to make that imaginative leap that would enable me to accept that anybody I grew up with — or, in this case, cracked peanuts with at the Mabillion — or puffed pot with at the Old Navy — could now be mistaken for a writer. A reputation.

In 1965, when Alexander Trocchi enjoyed a season in England as a sort of Dr. Spock of pot, pontificating about how good it was for you on one in-depth TV discussion after another, I was hard put to suppress an incredulous giggle each time his intelligent, craggy face filled the screen. I am equally unconvinced, stunned even, when I see Terry Southern's or Herb Gold's picture in *Time*.

I also find it disheartening that, in the end, writers are no less status-conscious than the middle-class they — we, I should say — excoriate with such appetite. As my high school friends, the old Sunday morning scrub team, has been split by economics, this taxi driver's boy now a fat suburban cat, that tailor's son still ducking bailiffs in a one-man basement factory, so we, who pretended to transcend such matters, have, over the demanding years, been divided by reputations. If our yardstick is more exacting, it still measures without mercy, coarsening the happy time we once shared.

Paris.

It would be nice, it would be tidy, to say with hindsight that we were a group, knit by political anger or a literary policy or even an aesthetic revulsion for all things American, but the truth was we recognized each other by no more than a shared sense of the ridiculous. And so we passed many a languorous, pot-filled afternoon on the terrace of the Dôme or the Sélect, improvising, not unlike jazz groups, on the hot news from America, where Truman was yielding to Eisenhower. We bounced an inanity to and fro, until, magnified through bizarre extension, we had disposed of it as an absurdity. We invented obscene quiz shows for television, and ad-libbed sexual outrages that could be interpolated into a John Marquand novel, a Norman Rockwell *Post* cover, or a June Allyson movie. The most original innovator and wit amongst us was easily the deceptively gentle Mason Hoffenberg, and one way or another we all remain indebted to him.

Oddly, I cannot recall that we ever discussed "our stuff" with each other. In fact, a stranger noting our cultivated indifference, the cool café posture, could never have guessed that when we weren't shuffling from café to café, in search of girls — a party — any diversion — we were actually labouring hard and long at typewriters in cramped, squalid hotel rooms, sending off stories to America, stories that rebounded with a sickening whack. The indifference to success was feigned, our café cool was false, for the truth is we were real Americans, hungering for recognition and its rewards, terrified of failure.

The rules of behaviour, unwritten, were nevertheless, rigid. It was not considered corrupt to take a thousand dollars from Girodias to write a pornographic novel under a pseudonym for the tourist trade, but anybody who went home to commit a thesis was automatically out. We weighed one another not by our backgrounds or prospects, but by taste, the books we kept by our bedside. Above all, we cherished the unrehearsed response, the zany personality, and so we prized many a bohemian dolt or exhibitionist, the girl who dyed her hair orange or kept a monkey for a pet, the most defiant queen, or the sub-Kerouac who wouldn't read anything because it might influence his style. Looked at another way, you were sure to know somebody who would happily bring on an abortion with a hat pin or turn you on heroin or peddle your passport, but nobody at all you could count on to behave decently if you were stuck with your Uncle Irv and Aunt Sophie, who were "doing Europe" this summer.

Each group its own conventions, which is to say we were not so much non-conformists as subject to our own peculiar conformities or, if you like, anti-bourgeois inversions. And so, if you were going to read a fat Irwin Shaw, a lousy best-seller, you were safest concealing it under a Marquis de Sade jacket. What I personally found most trying was the necessity to choke enthusiasm, never to reveal elation, when the truth was I was out of my mind with joy to be living in Paris, acutally living in Paris, France.

My room at the Grand Hotel Excelsior, off the Boul' Mich, was filled with rats, rats and a gratifying depraved past, for the hotel had once functioned as a brothel for the Wehrmacht. Before entering my room, I hollered, and whacked on the door, hoping to scatter the repulsive little beasts. Before putting on my sweater, I shook it out for rat droppings. But lying on my lumpy bed, ghetto-liberated, a real expatriate, I could read the forbidden, outspoken Henry Miller, skipping the windy cosmic passages, warming to the hot stuff. Paris in the fabled twenties, when luscious slavering American school teachers came over to seek out artists like me, begging for it. Waylaying randy old Henry in public toilets, seizing him by the cock. Scratching on his hotel room door, entering to gobble him. *Wherever I travel I'm too late. The orgy has moved elsewhere.*

My father wrote, grabbing for me across the seas to remind me of my heritage. He enclosed a Jewish calendar, warning me that Rosh Hashonnah came early this year, even for me who smoked hashish on the sabbath. Scared even as I smoked it, but more terrified of being put down as chicken-shit. My father wrote to say that the YMHA *Beacon* was sponsoring a short story contest and that the *Reader's Digest* was in the market for 'Unforgettable Characters.' Meanwhile, the *New Yorker* wouldn't have me, neither would the *Partisan Review*.

Moving among us, there was the slippery, eccentric Mr. Soon. He was, he said, the first Citizen of the World. He had anticipated Gary Davis, who was much in the news then. Mussolini had deported Mr. Soon from Italy, even as he had one of our underground heroes, the necromancer Alistair Crowley, The Great Beast 666, but the Swiss had promptly shipped Mr. Soon back again. He had no papers. He had a filthy, knotted beard, a body seemingly fabricated of mecanno parts, the old clothes and cigarettes we gave him for questioning. They wanted to know about drug addiction and foreigners who had been in Paris for more than three months without a *carte d'identité*. Mr. Soon became an informer.

"And what," he'd ask, "do you think of the poetry of Mao Tse Tung?"

"Zingy."

"And how," he'd ask, "does one spell your name?"

My American friends were more agitated than I, a non-draftable Canadian, about the Korean War. We sat on the terrace of the Mabillion, drunkenly accumulating beer coasters, on the day General Ridgeway drove into Paris, replacing Eisenhower at SHAPE. Only a thin bored crowd of the curious turned out to look over the general from Korea, yet the gendarmes were everywhere, and the boulevard was black with Gardes Mobiles, their fierce polished helmets catching the sun. All at once, the Place de l'Odeon was clotted with communist demonstrators, men, women and boys, squirting out of the backstreets, whipping out broomsticks from inside their shapeless jackets and hoisting anti-American posters on them.

"RIDGEWAY," the men hollered.

"A la porte," the women responded in a piercing squeal.

Instantly the gendarmes penetrated the demonstration, fanning out, swinging the capes that were weighed down with lead, cracking heads, and smashing noses. The once disciplined cry of *Ridgeway, a la porte!* faltered, then broke. Demonstrators retreated, scattering, clutching their bleeding faces.

A German general, summoned by NATO, came to Paris, and French Jews and socialists paraded in sombre silence down the Champs Elysées, wearing striped pyjamas, their former concentration camp uniforms. A Parisian Jewish couple I had befriended informed me at dinner that their new-born boy would not be circumcised, "Just in case." The Algerian troubles had begun. There was a war on in what we then called Indo-China. The gendarmes began to raid left bank hotels one by one, looking for Arabs without papers. Six o'clock in the morning they would pound on your door, open it, and demand to see your passport. "I am a c-c-c-itizen of the world," said Greenblatt, at that time something called a non-figurative poet, now with Desilu Productions.

One night the virulently anti-communist group, Paix et Liberté, pasted up posters everywhere that showed a flag, the Hammer and Sickle, flying from the top of the Eiffel Tower. HOW WOULD YOU LIKE TO SEE THIS ? the caption read. Early the next morning the communists went from poster to poster and pasted the Stars and Stripes over the Russian flag.

With Joe Dughi, a survivor of Normandy and the Battle of the Bulge, who was taking the course on French Civilization at the Sorbonne, I made the long trip to a flaking working-class suburb to see the Russian propaganda feature film, *Meeting on the Elbe.* In the inspiring opening sequence, the Russian army is seen approaching the Elbe, orderly, joyous soldiers mounted on gleaming tanks, each tank carrying a laurel wreath and a portrait of Stalin. Suddenly, we hear the corrupt, jerky strains of Yankee Doodle Dandy, and the camera swoops down on the opposite bank, where the unshaven behemoths who make up the American army are revealed staggering toward the river, soliders stumbling drunkenly into the water. On the symbolically lowered bridge, the white-uniformed Russian colonel, upright as Gary Cooper, says, "It's good to see the American army — even if it's on the last day of the war." Then he passes his binoculars to his American counterpart, a tubby pig-eyed Lou Costello figure. The American colonel scowls, displeased to see his men fraternizing with the Russians. Suddenly, he grins slyly. "You must admit," he says, lowering the binoculars, "that the Germans made excellent optical equipment." The Russian colonel replies: "These binoculars were made in Moscow, comrade."

In the Russian zone, always seen by day, the Gary Cooper colonel has set up his headquarters in a modest farm house. Outside, his adorable orderly, a Ukrainian Andy Devine, cavorts with sandy-haired German kids, reciting Heine to them. But in the American zone, seen only by night, the obese, cigar-chomping American colonel has appropriated a castle. Loutish enlisted men parade enormous oil paintings before him, and the colonel chalks a big X on those he wants shipped home. All the while, I should add, he is on the long distance line to Wall Street, asking for quotations on Bavarian forest.

Recently, I have been reading John Clellon Holmes's *Nothing More To Declare,* a memoir which makes it plain that the ideas and idiom, even some of the people, prevalent in the Village during the Fifties were interchangeable with those in Paris. The truculent Legman, once a *Neurotica* editor, of whom he writes so generously, inevitably turned up in St. Germain des Prés to produce his definitive edition of filthy limericks on rag paper and, incidently, to assure us gruffly that the novel was dead. Absolutely dead.

Even as in the Village, we were obsessed by the shared trivia and pop of our boyhood, seldom arguing about ideas, which would have made us feel self-conscious, stuffy, but instead going on and on about Fibber McGee's closet, Mandrake's enemies, Warner Brothers' character actors like Elisha Cook Jr., the Andrew Sisters, and the Katzenjammer Kids. To read about such sessions now in other people's novels or essays doesn't make for recognition so much as resentment at having one's past broadcast, played back as it were, a ready-to-wear past, which in retrospect was not peculiar to Paris but a Fifties commonplace.

At times it seems to me that what my generation of novelists does best, celebrating itself, is also discrediting. Too often, I think, it is we who are the fumblers, the misfits, *but unmistakably lovable,* intellectual heroes of our very own fictions, triumphant in our vengeful imaginations as we never were in actuality. Only a few contemporaries, say Brian Moore, live up to what I once took to be the novelist's primary moral responsibility, which is to be the loser's advocate. To tell us what it's like to be Judith Hearne. Or a pinched Irish school teacher. The majority tend to compose paeans of disguised praise of people very much like themselves. Taken to an extreme, the fictional guise is dropped and we are revealed cheering ourselves. And so George Plimpton is the pitcher and hero of *Out of My League* by George Plimpton. Norman Podhoretz, in *Making It,* is the protagonist of his own novel. And most recently, in *The Armies of the Night,* Norman Mailer writes about himself in the third person.

This is not to plead for a retreat to social realism or novels of protest, but simply to say that, as novelists, many of us are perhaps too easily bored, too self-regarding, and not sufficiently curious about mean lives, bland people. The unglamorous.

All at once, it was spring.

One day shopkeepers were wretched, waiters surly, concierges mean about taking messages, and the next, the glass windows encasing café terraces were removed everywhere, the Parisians were transmogrified: shopkeepers, waiters, concierges actually spoke in dulcet tones.

Afternoons we took to the Jardins du Luxembourg, lying on the grass and speculating about Duke Snider's arm, the essays in *The God That Failed,* Jersey Joe Walcott's age, whether Salinger's *The Catcher in the Rye* could be good *and* a Book-of-the-Month, how far Senator Joe McCarthy might go, was Calder Willingham overrated, how much it might set us back to motorcycle to Seville, was Alger Hiss lying, why wasn't Nathaniel West more widely read, could Don Newcombe win thirty games, and was it disreputable of Max Brod to withhold Kafka's 'Letter To My Father.'

Piaf was big with us, as was Jacques Prévert's *Paroles,* the song *Les Feuilles mortes,* Trenet, and the films of Simone Signoret. Anything by Genet, or Samual Beckett was passed from hand to hand. I tried to read *La Nausée* in French, but stumbled and gave it up.

Early one Sunday morning in May, laying in a kitbag filled with wine, *paté,* hardboiled eggs, quiches and salamis and cold veal from the charcuterie, cheeses, a bottle of armagnac and baguettes, five of us squeezed into a battered Renault quatre-chevaux and set off for Chartres and the beaches of Normandy. 1952 it was, but we soon discovered that the rocky beaches were still littered with the debris of war. Approaching the coast we bumped drunkenly past shelled-out, crumbling buildings, VERBOTEN printed on one wall and ACHTUNG! on another. This moved us to incredulous laughter, evoking old Warner Brothers films and dimly recalled hit parade tunes. But, once on the beaches, we were sobered and silent. Incredibly thick pill boxes, split and shattered, had yet to be cleared away. Others, barely damaged, clearly showed scorch-marks. Staring into the dark pill boxes, through gun slits that were still intact, was chilling, even though gulls now squawked reassuringly overhead. Barefoot, our trousers rolled to the knees, we roamed the beaches, finding deep pits and empty shell cases here and there. As the tide receded, concrete teeth were revealed still aimed at the incoming tanks and landing craft. I stooped to retrieve a soldier's boot from a garland of sea weed. Slimy, soggy, already sea-green, I could still make out the bullet-hole in the toe.

Ikons.

We were not, it's worth noting, true adventurers, but followers of a romantic convention. A second *Aliyah,* so to speak. "History has not quite repeated itself," Brian Moore wrote in a review of *Exile's Return* for the *Spectator.* "When one reads of the passionate, naive manifestos in Malcolm Cowley's 'literary odyssey of the 1920s,' the high ambitions and the search for artistic values which sent the 'lost generation' to Paris, one cannot help feeling a touch of envy. It would seem that the difference between the American artists' pilgrimage to Europe in the Twenties and in the Sixties is the difference between first love and the obligatory initial visit to a brothel.

"Moneyed by a grant from Fulbright, Guggenheim, or Ford, the American painter now goes to France for a holiday: he knows that the action is all in New York. Similarly, the young American writer abroad shows little interest in the prose experiments of Robbe-Grillet, Sarraute, and Simon; he tends to dismiss Britain's younger novelists and playwrights as boring social realists *(we finished with that stuff twenty years ago),* and as for Sartre, Beckett, Genet, or Ionesco, he

147

has dug them already off-Broadway. It seems that American writers, in three short generations, have moved from the provincial *(we haven't yet produced any writing that could be called major)* to the parochial *(the only stuff worth reading nowadays is coming out of America). "*

Our group, in the Fifties, came sandwiched between, largely unmoneyed, except for those on the GI Bill, and certainly curious about French writing, especially Sartre, Camus, and, above all, Céline. We were also self-consciously aware of the Twenties. We knew the table at the Dôme that had been Hemingway's and made a point of eating at the restaurant on rue Monsieur le Prince where Joyce was reputed to have taken his dinner. Not me, but others regularly sipped tea with Alice Toklas. Raymond Duncan, swirling past in his toga, was a common, if absurd, sight. *Transition* still appeared fitfully.

Other connections with the Twenties were through the second-generation. David Burnett, one of the editors of *New-Story,* was the son of Whit Burnett and Martha Foley, who had brought out the original *Story.* My own first publication was in *Points,* a little magazine that was edited by Sinbad Vail, the son of Lawrence Vail and Peggy Guggenheim. It wasn't much of a magazine, and though Vail printed 4,000 copies of the first issue, he was only able to peddle 400. In the same issue as my original mawkish short story there was a better one by Brendan Behan, who was described as "27, Irish . . . Has been arrested several times for activities in the Irish Republican Army, which he joined in 1937, and in all has been sentenced to 17 years in gaol, has in fact served about 7 years in Borstal and Parkhurst Prison. Disapproves of English prison system. At present working as a housepainter on the State Railways."

Among other little magazines current at the time there were *Id* and *Janus.* ("An aristocrat by his individualism, a revolutionary against all societies," wrote Daniel Mauroc, "the homosexual is both the Jew and the Negro, the precursor and the unassimilable, the terrorist and the *raffiné* . . . .") and *Merlin,* edited by Trocchi, Richard Seaver, Logue, and John Coleman, who is now the *New Statesman's* film critic. *Merlin's* address, incidently, was the English Bookshop, 42 rue de Seine, which had once belonged to Sylvia Beach.

In retrospect, I cannot recall that anybody, except Alan Temko, perhaps, was as yet writing fantasy or satire. Mostly, the stories we published were realistic and about home, be it Texas, Harlem,

Brooklyn, or Denver. Possibly, just possibly, everything can be stripped down to a prosaic explanation. The cult of hashish, for instance, had a simple economic basis. It was easy to come by and cheap, far cheaper than scotch. Similarly, if a decade after our sojourn in Paris a number of us began to write what has since come to be branded black humour, it may well be that we were not so much inspired as driven to it by mechanics. After all, the writer who opts out of the mainstream of American experience, self-indulgently luxuriating in bohemia, the pleasure of like-minded souls, is also cutting himself off from his natural material, sacrificing his sense of social continuity; and so when we swung round to writing about contemporary America, we could only attack obliquely, shrewdly settling on a style that did not betray knowledge gaps of day to day experience.

For the most part, I moved with the *New-Story* bunch, David Burnett, Terry Southern, Mason Hoffenberg, Alan Temko, and others. One afternoon, Burnett told me, a new arrival from the States walked into the office and said, "For ten thousand dollars, I will stop in front of a car on the Place Vendôme and say I did it because *New-Story* rejected one of my stories. Naturally, I'm willing to guarantee coverage in all the American newspapers."

"But what if you're hurt?" he was asked.

"Don't worry about me, I'm a paraphrase artist."

"A what?"

"I can take any story in *Collier's,* rewrite it, and sell it to the *Post.* "

New-Story, beset by financial difficulties from the very first issue, seldom able to fork out the promised two bucks a page to contributors or meet printer's bills, was eventually displaced by the more affluent *Paris Review.* But during its short and turbulent life *New-Story* was, I believe, the first magazine to publish Jean Genet in English. Once, browsing at George Whitman's hole-in-the-wall bookshop near Notre Dame, where Bernard Frechtman's translation of *Our Lady of the Flowers* was prominently displayed, I overheard an exasperated Whitman explain to a camera-laden American matron, "No, no, it's not the same Genet as writes for the *New Yorker.* "

Possibly, the most memorable of all the little magazines was the French publication, *Ur, Cahiers Pour Un Dictat Culturel. Ur* was edited by Jean-Isador Isou, embattled author of *A Reply To Karl Marx,* a slender riposte hawked by gorgeous girls in blue jeans to tourists at right bank cafés — tourists under the tantalizing illusion that they were buying the hot stuff.

Ur was a platform for the Letterists, who believed that all the arts were dead and could only be resurrected by a synthesis of their collective absurdities. This, like anything else that was seemingly new or outrageous, appealed to us. And so Friday nights, our pockets stuffed with oranges and apples, pitching cores into the Seine, scuffling, singing *Adon Olam*, we passed under the shadows of Notre Dame and made our way to a café on the Ile St. Louis to listen to Isador Isou and others read poems composed of grunts and cries, incoherent arrangements of letters, set to an anti-musical background of vacuum cleaners, drills, car horns, and train whistles. We listened, rubbing our jaws, nodding, looking pensive.

— *Ça, alors.*

— *Je m'en fous.*

— *Azoi,* Ginsberg. *Azoi.*

Ginsberg was the first to go home. I asked him to see my father and tell him how hard up I was.

"Sometimes," Ginsberg told him, "your son sits up all night in his cold room, writing."

"And what does he do all day?"

Crack peanuts on the terrace of the Café Royale. Ruminate over the baseball scores in the *Herald-Tribune*.

We were all, as Hemingway once said, at the right age. Everybody was talented. Special. Nobody had money. (Except of course Art Buchwald, the most openly envied ex-GI in Paris. Buchwald, who had not yet emerged as a humourist, had cunningly solved two problems at once, food and money, inaugurating a restaurant column in the *Herald-Tribune*.) We were all trying to write or paint and so there was always the hope, it's true, of a publisher's advance or a contract with a gallery. There was also the national lottery. There was, too, the glorious dream that today you would run into the fabled lady senator from the United States who was reputed to come over every summer and, as she put it, invest in the artistic future of five or six promising, creative youngsters. She would give you a thousand dollars, more sometimes, no strings attached. But I never met her. I was reminded of the days when as a kid in Montreal I was never without a Wrigley's chewing gum wrapper, because of that magic man who could pop up anywhere, stop you, and ask for a wrapper. If you had one with you, he gave you a dollar. Some days, they said, he handed out as much as fifty dollars. I never met him, either.

Immediately before Christmas, however, one of my uncles sent me money. I had written to him, quoting Auden, Kierkegaard, *The Book of Changes,* Maimonides, and Dylan Thomas, explaining we must love one another or die. "I can hear that sort of crap," he wrote back, "any Sunday morning on the Manischewitz Hour," but a cheque for a hundred dollars was enclosed, and I instantly decided to go to Cambridge for the holidays.

Stringent rationing — goose eggs, a toe-nail size chunk of meat a week — was still the depressing rule in England and, as I had old friends in Cambridge, I arrived laden with foodstuffs, my raincoat sagging with contraband steaks and packages of butter. A friend of a friend took me along to sip sherry with E.M. Forster at his rooms in King's College.

Forster immediately unnerved me by asking what I thought of F. Scott Fitzgerald's work.

Feebly, I replied I thought very highly of it indeed.

Forster then remarked that he generally asked visiting young Americans what they felt about Fitzgerald, whose high reputation baffled him. Forster said that though Fitzgerald unfailingly chose the most lyrical titles for his novels, the works themselves seemed to him to be without especial merit.

Unaccustomed to sherry, intimidated by Forster, who in fact couldn't have been more kind or gentle, I stupidly knocked back my sherry in one gulp, like a synagogue schnapps, whilst the others sipped theirs decorously. Forster waved for my glass to be refilled and then inquired without the least condescension about the progress of my work. Embarrassed, I hastily changed the subject.

"And what," he asked, "do you make of Angus's first novel?"

Angus being Angus Wilson and the novel, *Hemlock and After.*

"I haven't read it yet," I lied, terrified lest I make a fool of myself.

I left Forster a copy of Nelson Algren's *The Man With the Golden Arm,* which I had just read and enormously admired. A few days later the novel was returned to me with a note I didn't keep, and so quote from memory. He had only read as far as page 120 in Algren's novel, Forster wrote. It had less vomit than the last American novel he had read, but . . . .

At the time, I was told that the American novel Forster found most interesting was Willard Motley's *Knock On Any Door.*

Cambridge, E.M. Forster, was a mistake; it made me despair for me and my friends and our shared literary pretensions. In the rooms I visited at King's, St. Mary's, and Pembroke, gowned young men were wading through the entire *Faerie Queene,* they had absorbed *Beowulf,* Chaucer, and were clearly heirs to the tradition. All at once, it seemed outlandish, a grandiose *chutzpah,* that we, street corner bohemians, kibbitzers, still swapping horror stories about our abominable Yiddish mommas, should even presume to write. Confirmation, if it were needed, was provided by John Lehmann, who returned my first attempt at a sub-Céline novel with a printed rejection slip.

"Hi, keed," my brother wrote, "How are things in Gay Paree?" and there followed a list of the latest YMHA basketball scores.

Things in Gay Paree were uncommonly lousy. I had contracted scurvy, of all things, from not eating sufficient fruit or vegetables. The money began to run out. Come midnight, come thirst, I used to search for my affluent friend Armstrong, who was then putting me up in his apartment in Étoile. I would seek out Armstrong in the homosexual pits of St. Germain and Montparnasse. The Montana, the Fiacre, l'Abbaye, the Reine Blanche. If Armstrong was sweetening up a butch, I would slip in and out again discreetly, but if Armstrong was alone, alone and sodden, he would comfort me with cognacs and ham rolls and take me home in a taxi.

Enormous, rosycheeked, raisineyed Armstrong was addictd to acquired Yiddishisms. He'd say, "Oy, bless my little. I don't know why I go there, Mottel."

"Uh huh."

"Did you catch the old queen at the bar?"

"I'm still hungry. What about you?"

"*Zut.*"

"You know, I've never eaten at Les Halles. All this time in Paris . . . ."

"I don't care a tit if you ever eat at Les Halles. We're going home, you scheming *yenta.*"

Armstrong and I had sat next to each other in Political Science 101 at Sir George Williams College. SYSTEMS OF GOVERNMENT, the professor wrote on the blackboard,

a. monarchy   c. democracy
b. totalitarianism   d. others

Canada is a _____

Armstrong passed me a note. "A Presbyterian twat."

At Sir George, Armstrong had taken out the most desirable girls, but I could never make out. The girls I longed for longed for the basketball players or charmers like Armstrong and the only one who would tolerate me had been the sort who read Penguins on street-cars or were above using make-up. Or played the accordion at parties, singing about Joe Hill and *Los Quatro Générales.* Or demonstrated. Then, two years ago, Armstrong had tossed up everything to come to Paris and study acting. Now he no longer put up with girls and had become an unstoppable young executive in a major advertising company. "I would only have made a mediocre actor," he was fond of saying to me as I sat amidst my rejection slips.

Once more I was able to wrangle money from home, three hundred dollars and this time I ventured south for the summer, to Haut-de-Cagnes. Here I first encountered American and British expatriates of the Twenties, shadowy remittance men, coupon-clippers, who painted a bit, sculpted some, and wrote from time to time. An instructive but shattering look, I feared, at my future prospects. Above all, the expatriates drank prodigiously. Twenties flotsam, whose languid, self-indulgent, bickering, party-crammed life in the Alpes-Maritimes had been disrupted only by World War II.

Bit players of bygone age, they persisted in continuing as if it were still burgeoning, supplying the *Nice-Matin,* for instance, with guest lists of their lawn parties; and carrying on as if Cyril Connelly's first novel, *The Rockpool,* were a present scandal. "He was only here for three weeks altogether, don't you know," a colonel told me.

"I'm only *very* thinly disguised in it," a lady said haughtily.

Extremely early one morning I rolled out of bed in response to a knock on the door. It was Mr. Soon.

"I have just seen the sun coming up over the Mediterranean," he said.

In spite of the heat, Mr. Soon wore a crushed greasy raincoat. Terry Southern, if I remember correctly, had given it to him. He had also thoughtfully provided him with my address. "Won't you come in?" I asked.

"Not yet. I am going to walk on the Promenade des Anglais."

"You might as well leave your coat here, then."

"But it would be inelegant to walk on the Promenade in Nice without a coat, don't you think?"

Mr. Soon returned late in the afternoon and I took him to Jimmy's Bar, on the brim of the steep grey hill of Haut-de-Cagnes.

"It reminds me most of California here," Mr. Soon said.

"But I had no idea you had ever been to California."

"No. Never. Have you?"

I watched, indeed, soon everyone on the terrace turned to stare, as Mr. Soon, his beard a filthy tangle, reached absently into his pocket for a magnifying glass, held it to the sun, and lit a Gauloise. Mr. Soon, who spoke several languages, including Chinese, imperfectly, was evasive whenever we asked him where he had been born in this his twenty-third reincarnation. We put him down for Russian, but when I brought him along to Marushka's she insisted that he spoke the language ineptly.

Marushka, now in her sixties, had lived in Cagnes for years. Modigliani had written a sonnet to her and she could recall the night Isadora had danced in the square. Marushka was not impressed by Mr. Soon. "He's a German," she said, as if it was quite the nastiest thing she could think of.

I took Mr. Soon home with me and made up a bed for him on the floor, only to be awakened at two a.m. because all the lights had been turned on. Mr. Soon sat at my table, writing, with one of my books, *The Guide For The Perplexed,* by his side. "I am copying out the table of contents," he said.

"But what on earth for?"

"It is a very interesting table of contents, don't you think?"

A week later Mr. Soon was still with me. One afternoon he caught me hunting mosquitoes with a rolled newspaper and subjected me to a long, melancholy lecture on the holy nature of all living things. Infuriated, I said, "Maybe I was a mosquito in a previous incarnation, eh?"

"No. You were a Persian Prince."

"What makes you say that?" I asked, immensely pleased.

"Let us go to Jimmy's. It is so interesting to sit there and contemplate, don't you think?"

I was driven to writing myself a letter and opening it while Mr. Soon and I sat at the breakfast table. "Some friends of mine are coming down from Paris the day after tomorrow. I'd quite forgotten I had invited them to stay with me."

"Very interesting. How long will they be staying?"

"There's no saying."

"I can stay at the Tarzan Camping and return when they are gone."

We began to sell things. Typewriters, books, wristwatches. When we all seemed to have reached bottom, when our credit was no longer good anywhere, something turned up. An ex-GI, Seymour, who ran a tourist office in Nice called SEE-MOR TOURS, became casting director for extra parts in films and we all got jobs for ten dollars a day.

Once more, Armstrong tolerated me in his Paris flat. One night, in the Montana, Armstrong introduced me to an elegant group of people at his table, including the Countess Louise. The next morning he informed me, "Louise, um, thinks you're cute, boychick. She's just dumped Jacques and she's looking for another banana."

Armstrong went on to explain that if I were satisfactory I would have a studio in Louise's flat and an allowance of one hundred thousand francs monthly.

"And what do I have to do to earn all that?"

"Oy-vey. There's nothing like a Jewish childhood. Don't be so provincial."

Louise was a thin wizened lady in her forties. Glittering earrings dripped from her ears and icy rings swelled on the fingers of either hand. "It would only be once a week," Armstrong said. "She'd take you to first nights at the opera and all the best restaurants. Wouldn't you like that?"

"Go to hell."

"You're invited to her place for drinks on Thursday. I'd better buy you some clothes first."

On Thursday I sat in the sun at the Mabillion consuming beer after beer before I risked the trip to the Countess's flat. I hadn't felt as jumpy or been so thoroughly bright and scrubbed from the skin out since my bar-mitzvah. A butler took my coat. The hall walls were painted scarlet and embedded with precious stones. I was led into the drawing room where a nude study of a younger Louise, who had used to be a patroness of surrealists, hung in a lighted alcove. Spiders and bugs fed on the Countess's ash-grey bosom. I heard laughter and voices from another room. Finally a light-footed American in a black antelope jacket drifted into the drawing room. "Louise is receiving in the bedroom," he said.

Possibly, I thought, I'm one of many candidates. I stalked anxiously round an aviary of stuffed tropical fowl. Leaning against the mantelpiece, I knocked over an antique gun.

"Oh, dear." The young American retrieved it gently. "This," he said, "is the gun Verlaine used in his duel with Rimbaud."

At last Louise was washed into the room on a froth of beautiful boys and girls. She took my hand and pressed it. "Well, hullo," I said.

We sped off in two black Jaguars to a private party for Cocteau. All the bright young people, except me, had some accomplishment behind them. They chatted breezily about their publishers and pro-ducers and agents. Eventually one of them turned to me, offering a smile. "You're Louise's little Canadian, aren't you?"

"That's the ticket."

Louise asked me about Montreal.

"After Paris," I said, swaying drunkenly, "it's the world's largest French-speaking city."

The American in the black antelope jacket joined me at the bar, clapping me on the shoulder. "Louise will be very good to you," he said.

Azoi.

"We all adore her."

Suddenly Louise was with us. "But you must meet Cocteau," she said.

I was directed to a queue awaiting presentation. Cocteau wore a suede windbreaker. The three young men ahead of me, one of them a sailor kissed him on both cheeks as they were introduced. Feeling foolish, I offered him my hand then returned to the bar and had another whisky, and yet another, before I noticed that all my group, including my Countess, had gone, leaving me behind.

Armstrong was not pleased with me, but then he was a troubled man. His secretary, a randy little bit from Guildford, an ex-India Army man's daughter, was eager for him, and Armstrong, intimidated, had gone so far as to fondle her breasts at the office. "If I don't screw the bitch," he said to me, "she'll say I'm queer. Oy, my poor *tuchus.*"

Armstrong's day-to-day existence was fraught with horrors. Obese, he remained a compulsive eater. Terrified of blackmailers and police *provocateurs,* he was still driven to cruising Piccadilly and Leicester Square on trips to London. Every day he met with accountants and salesmen, pinched men in shiny office suits who delighted in vicious jokes about queers, and Armstrong felt compelled to prove himself the most ferocious queer-baiter of them all.

"Maybe I should marry Betty. She wants to. Well, boychick?"

In the bathroom, I looked up to see black net bikini underwear dripping from a line over the tub. Armstrong pounded on the door.

"We could have kids," he said.

The medicine cabinet was laden with deodorants and sweetening sprays and rolls of absorbent cotton and vaseline jars.

"I'm capable, you know."

A few nights later Armstrong brought a British boy home. A painter, a taschist. "Oy, Mottel," he said, easing me out of the flat. *"Gevalt,* old chap."

The next morning I stumbled into the bathroom, coming sharply awake when I saw a red rose floating in the toilet bowl.

After Armstrong had left for work, the painter, a tall fastidious boy with flaxen hair, joined me at the breakfast table. He misunderstood my frostiness. "I wouldn't be staying here," he assured me, "but Richard said your relationship is platonic."

I looked up indignantly from my newspaper, briefly startled, then smiled and said, "Well, you see I could never take him home and introduce him to my family. He's not Jewish."

Two weeks later my father sent me enough money for a ticket home and, regretfully, I went to the steamship office at l'Opéra. An advertisement in the window read:

"liked Lisbon, loved Tahiti. But when it comes to
getting the feel of the sea . . ."
give me the crashing waves and rugged rocks
give me the gulls and nets and men and boats
give me the harbours and homes and spires and quays
GIVE ME NEW BRUNSWICK
CANADA.

I had been away two years.

From *Shovelling Trouble* (1972) by Mordecai Richler, born in Montreal, 1931. As a comic novelist he is probably Canada's most widely acclaimed writer. He spent two years in Europe before he was 20, afterwards living for many years in England.

TANGANYIKA
By J.C. Cairns

October has passed. The *Boma* was deluged with problems. The little rains were due, but they did not come, and the whole district burned and fried under the sun. There was dust everywhere; in the houses, on my shoes, on the dried withered grass, on the leaves of trees. Along the road, when I drove, a long wake of fine red dust billowed like powder, rose in the air, then slowly settled. On *safari* a film of dust coated my shirt and shorts; my throat was dry and gritty and I had a thirst that was unquenchable. I dreamed of ice cold beer, foaming and frosty, in limitless amounts. This is a dream of all dry *safaris,* the compensation for heat, and dirt, and sand; the compensation for drinking water from village wells that is muddy and silt filled, like warm black soup.

In the south the hunger continued, like a bad play that would not end. I made more *safaris,* this time with dried cassava. Dried cassava comes in chunks the size of a potato, sometimes bigger. At its best it is sweet and nutty and filling, but at its worst chalky, bitter and crumbly as ashes. We gave it free mainly to the old and sick and women with children, for now the able-bodied men were at work on relief projects and earning food of their own.

The projects were organized by the D.C., who has worked incessantly on anti-famine plans, and they will be paid for by the Native Authority. The N.A. is poor, for this is a poor district. Its main source of revenue is ten shillings per year per tax-payer, plus a varying amount from licence fees and market dues. The N.A. in a sense is like a needy father, who, when he helps his hungry children, must do so carefully, without waste. For this reason it cannot issue food too freely. This, which seems strange, was widely agreed. The headmen said, 'If food were given free when people asked, who would ever work?'

So in the hunger area plans were made for road building and repairs. Men would work and with their labour cards get food at the village shops. The shops would turn the cards in to the Native Authority, who would pay. There were also huge communal *shambas,* which would give food and profit for next year; special seed distribution; and lorry loads of cassava cuttings for planting.

The clerk Yusuf was involved in these arrangements, and he, too, came on *safari* often, with the D.C. and myself. In the *dukas* in Kilwa there was food to buy, so he was never hungry. But he was angry about the famine. More angry than the people concerned, who were inured to sickness and famine and death. He was as worried as the D.C. or myself, for he was no longer a fatalist, and he looked on hunger with European eyes.

'It is an enemy,' he said. 'Like sickness and disease. Something to be conquered.'

The little rains came late and scattered, and all through the area the peasants planted short term crops. In two or three months these should mature and relieve the famine.

In the villages and *shambas* people said, '*Al-hamdulilahi,* God has sent the rains.' They watched the sky, where clouds had gathered. All through their lives they had looked at the sky and the clouds, for they had always depended on the rains. Without them nothing grew; the earth lay dead, barren, fruitless. The rains determined everything.

But this time, when they were most needed, the rains betrayed them. They stopped. The clouds passed, the drought continued, and the newly planted crops withered and died in the ground.

There were other problems.

By great efforts seed was imported into the district. It was rushed to the hunger area and distributed for planting, so much to each cultivator.

This alone was an enormous job, for it was necessary to ensure that each *shamba* owner was given his share and that nobody was left out. It required *safaris,* meetings, arrangements with headmen, and porterage of food into roadless, almost inaccessible areas.

But the seed was ill-omened, for much was planted and lost in the false little rains. The rest lay in people's huts, awaiting the heavy rains.

Yusuf, who was watching these arrangements, warned, 'There will be trouble with the seed.'

I asked, 'What kind of trouble?'

'The people want food,' Yusuf said pointedly. 'The seed is in their huts.'

'But they must save the seed, or they will starve next year as well.'

Yusuf shrugged and said, 'They are not thinking of next year. They are hungry now.'

I felt Yusuf was exaggerating, but I did not know Africa yet, although I was learning.

A few weeks passed, and then, from all over the hunger area, reports arrived that the people were eating the seed.

Cassava is grown from cuttings, and thousands of new cuttings would be needed for the coming season. These were available in the north of the district, and people there were urged to contribute. This would cost them nothing, for who is so poor he cannot spare cassava cuttings?

But in the north, in the good areas, the Africans were suspicious. The famine was in their district, true, but it was far away, among another tribe.

Men asked, 'Why should one tribe help another?'

I was disgusted at this, and said, "They are suffering. It costs nothing to help.'

'Nothing? Ehhh, *bwana*. Is it nothing to work in the sun and cut cassava?'

'Men must help their brothers.'

"How can they be our brothers, *bwana,* when they are four days' walk away?'

I said, 'I am ashamed to hear this. In my country we help people who suffer.'

'We are Africans. What do we know of your country? Each place has its own customs.'

Finally there was a response, but it came slowly and reluctantly, after pleadings and urging. For loyalties here were still at the village level, and each man's horizon was limited to his own area, to places he knew and villages he had seen.

The last great difficulty was to get food into the hunger area. This was a physical problem, involving roads, lorries and communications. It was especially hard since the only lorry directly available, the one from the Native Authority, could never transport the food required, and it was necessary to hire lorries from the traders.

In the Asian shops in Nanjirinji, in the famine zone, there were already stocks of cassava, but insufficient to last until the new crops were ready. A further eighty or ninety tons were needed, and these must come from Lindi, the neighbouring district to the south.

At this stage meetings were held with the D.C. and the Asian traders over transport. But the traders could help little, for throughout the district, their own up-country shops needed supplies before the rains set in. Their lorries were tied up.

Arrangements were then made to use lorries from Lindi District, and food moved in slowly from Lindi by road. But this was only a trickle, like water from a nearly corked bottle. There were continual delays, peculiarly African; and day after day I had maddening, depressing, sometimes ludicrous conversations with the trader responsible for the transport.

'How much food has gone today?' I would ask.

'Today? The big lorry could not go, sir. The driver is sick. He has fever.'

'What about the other lorries?'

'One has a broken spring. We are looking for a spare. Perhaps God will send a spare soon.'

'You mean there are no lorries on the road?'

'There is one, sir. It started two days ago. That is the new lorry.'

'Well, where is it now? Has it arrived?'

'How can it arrive, sir? It has broken down in the bush. The food is being stolen.'

These problems were not occasional, but constant, so that each day's work became a half-comic, half-tragic battle.

162

By now the famine had exhausted me, as it had Yusuf and many of the headmen and clerks. At night I dreamed of hunger and starvation and gaunt, emaciated people. And each day, in the office or on *safari,* I was overwhelmed by innumerable frustrations and problems. Things that at home would have taken a day took weeks. The inertia of the district, the bad roads, the isolation, lack of staff, lack of money, all these made the simplest job difficult and sometimes impossible.

Yusuf, who was with me continually, was worn out but cheerful. He worked with a dogged determination.

'We will win,' he said repeatedly. 'We will defeat the famine.'

In December, after protracted efforts, a large shipment of cassava arrived by coastal steamer. It was stored in the Customs shed, and the N.A. lorry, with the driver and the *turni* boy, began shuttling it into the famine area a load at a time.

When a third of the cassava had been moved, the rains broke in the south. They came spasmodically, and the roads stayed open. But now my worries became acute, for it was essential to stock the famine area before the roads were washed out. The alternative would be head porters, carrying food from the coast.

I discussed this with Yusuf, for the D.C. was temporarily absent from the district. I said, 'We would need two thousand porters at least. Where would we get them?'

'It is impossible,' Yusuf said, and he took a piece of paper and began jotting notes on it. 'If we got them, who would watch them on *safari?* How could we stop them eating the food themselves? None of the food would reach the famine area, sir.'

This was my own opinion, and I knew there could be no solution by head porters.

As a last resort, a final meeting was held with the Asian traders. We sat in the immense old *Boma* in Kilwa Kivinje. The walls were cracked and dingy, of enormous thickness. The room where we met was big and dark, a room where long ago German officers sat, where many *shauris* had been heard. Beyond the parapet we could see the beach littered with rotting dhows.

163

This time the mood was auspicious, for the up-country shops were now stocked, the lorries of the traders were free, and they were eager to help.

Next day in the early morning thirteen lorries arrived at Masoko to collect the food. They loaded and pulled out in convoy on the long *safari* to the far end of the district. With them went the N.A. lorry.

That afternoon and until long after dark they unloaded in the *dukas* of Nanjirinji. Next day, empty, they returned, and I knew that the worst of our problems and fears were ended.

The *turni* boy, tired and dirty, reported triumphantly:

'God has helped us. The food is there. We have conquered.'

February. The weather is hot and steamy. The heavy rains have begun and suddenly tapered off. In the afternoon thick clouds pile up and sometimes there is intermittent thunder and lightning in the distance. The Africans look at the sky and talk continually about rain, as farmers do at home.

In the famine area the road work and food distribution continues.

March. We are surprised and a little disappointed, for we have been transferred to another district. My work on food distribution, seed, N.A. projects, the continuing difficulties of the famine, all these will be taken over by another D.O. To me, this seems odd, and I ask myself, can anybody else be as concerned over these things as I have been? Yet in the district I am posted to, the D.O. I am replacing will surely feel like this about me.

The new station is Mikindani, a few hundred miles to the south and the last district in Tanganyika north of Portuguese East Africa. It is undeveloped, an agricultural district like Kilwa, but smaller.

Now, before us, we have the work of packing the house and the problems of moving.

Leaving a station like Kilwa is hard to describe, for many emotions are involved. When we first came a year ago, the district was as it is now, primitive, isolated, and forbidding. People, customs, traditions, environment, all these were strange, and the villages and the life of the Africans seemed far away and unapproachable.

Now in a year all this has changed. The Africans are familiar, for I have been caught up and absorbed in their life. In the most isolated villages I know clerks and elders, teachers and hunters. I worry about headmen with sick wives and children with yaws. All through the district people have told me their problems about crops and children, money and seed and illness. Hundreds of Africans have looked at me, as they do at all District Officers, and said:

'We are in trouble. You must help. You are our father and mother.'

In a few years much of this will fade from memory, but much will remain. In twenty or thirty years, scenes from Kilwa will come back to me. I will think of Yusuf, the famine, the *safari* across the dried-up river bed, the problems of the *turni* boy.

Perhaps in the bush villages people will remember me and talk of me occasionally.

They will say, 'He was the *bwana* with the strange accent. The tall one we called *Bwana Okay*. The *bwana* of the big famine.'

In our last week in Kilwa there was a continuous round of parties. A few days before we left the Indian merchants held one, followed by the African Association and the merchant Habib.

There was also a gala affair arranged by the Liwali of Kivinje in the Customs shed. We arrived to find the place decked with streamers, flags, and palm leaves, a band playing furiously, and a general air of festivity. We ate cakes, drank tea, and chewed small hard biscuits. The market master, Mohamed Jabiri, made a flowery speech, and Beverley was then presented with an Arab silver chain necklace. The presentation was made by the Liwali, and the matter was handled properly, in true Moslem style. The Liwali is an old man, dignified, and corpulent. He advanced to our table, bearing the necklace, and Beverley inclined her head, to allow the necklace to be slipped over her neck. The Liwali demurred. Beverley inclined her head again, but the Liwali still refused. We were now puzzled, for something was clearly wrong. The Liwali, however, solved the difficulty. He motioned to me and gravely placed the necklace over my head instead.

After the party Yusuf said, 'The Liwali was embarrassed, just as you were. But he is a strict Moslem. He knows women are not important. Not like men. It would be against custom to hand such a gift to a woman.'

From *Bush and Boma* (1959) by J.C. Cairns. Born in Galt, Ontario, 1921, Cairns was a district officer in Tanganyika, East Africa, a British trust territory, in the late 1950s. This was a most unusual post for a Canadian. After its independence and union with Zanzibar, Tanganyika became Tanzania.

MEXICO
by Malcolm Lowry

T he bus journey from Mexico City to Cuernavaca was deceptive, as Sigbjørn knew of old. Although it was only forty or fifty miles, this gives little idea of its nature. A long, dreary, dusty road leads out of Mexico City itself, and then, half an hour later, the long circuitous climb to Tres Marias begins. Having started at an altitude of eight thousand feet you ascend to an altitude of ten thousand. At the highest point of the route, a desolate clapboard of decaying huts named Tres Cumbres in the Tres Marias, where you may encounter a blizzard, you begin to descend, unwinding, by a similar circuitous road, until, in Cuernavaca, you find yourself at an altitude of some three thousand feet, that is at a point rather lower than the one in which you have started; in this regard the journey had always struck Sigbjørn as rather like life itself. Repeat the journey many times and you have the eerie sense of repeating an existence over and over again, which, although perhaps true of any journey, seems for some reason particularly true of this one. One is liable because of the altitude and abrupt change of temperature, to feel exhausted, and when one arrives finally in Cuernavaca, quite worn out. But Primrose and Sigbjørn, if not for travel, shared, other things being equal, a love of bus journeys, which was all to the good.

And Sigbjørn could feel Primrose was enjoying herself, taking in the beautiful scenery, the flowers, the straggling adobe villages, the little pigs, the delicate ankles of the Mexican women. A vast shrouded slope loomed before them, the Tres Marias. They reached Tres Cumbres, where they stopped briefly and Sigbjørn without any haggling at all, of which he was beginning to have a dread, to her delight secured her a torta, through the window from a scolding old woman.

This, for him, was a feat as well as being unselfish: for there was something in his nature that loathed to break the rhythm; only more than stopping at all did he hate to move on, lulled into a certain mood. To the right there was a signpost pointing down a windy road: *A Zampoala*. It was a lake, very high in the mountains, which Sigbjørn remembered he had never seen and he made up his mind to take her there. It was a possible happiness for Primrose over there, lakes, heights, choices, superterrestrial or sublacustrine.

As they rolled forward again, Sigbjørn remembered the visit they had made to the basilica at Guadalupe a few days earlier. They had taken the bus by Bellas Artes, and at the basilica Sigbjørn had been delighted by the sideshow: *La Maldición de Dios. . . ¡ No deje de ver este asombroso aparato de óptica! La cabeza que habla su cuerpo fue devorado por las ratas.* The malediction of God! Step up ladies and gents and see the spectacle of the head who has his body devoured by rats. Primrose had been enchanted with the women, however poor, who wore exquisite silver earrings, and had lovely ankles and hands and often gorgeous rebozos, and carried themselves like queens, and the dancers: one man in fringes of scarlet with feathers two feet high on his head, the other wearing a horrible grinning mask on the back of his head.

They drank marvelous beer in a little booth at one side facing the basilica: the figurine of the Virgin looked like a model in an American department store window of 1917 or so, dressed in bright print and carrying in one hand a lamp — a boy of sixteen or so stood by her, leaning on her shoulder. They watched the little families sitting under trees with their sweet quick smiles, and then they wandered through the basilica of Guadalupe — they who had not been in a church in twenty years. Sigbjørn felt the sense of complete faith when Primrose knelt and prayed at the altar, and he watched the expression of passionate sincerity on people's faces, the father with the little girl, showing her how to cross herself, the old woman touching the glass case and rubbing the baby's face with it, Mexican babies, aware of man's tragic end, do not cry: "I slept here once," Sigbjørn did not say, meaning on the floor of the basilica itself, tight, in a borrowed mackintosh, in December, 1936. They smelt the smell of Mexico City, the familiar smell, to him, of gasoline, excrement, and oranges, and drank beautiful Saturno for forty-five centavos.

Then something happened, or nearly went wrong, wrong enough at all events, wrong enough, so that, had he been writing about it, he would have preserved it as the "first bass chord." They were wandering, mingling with the crowd at Guadalupe, scarcely knowing where they were going; such a crowd indeed that unable to make any progress they turned into a little tiendita in which as in many such, they sold beer and spirits. People were drinking and talking at the counter, but way was courteously made for them. They ordered Carta Blanca and were drinking happily but watching the scene outside, rather than inside. A blind woman tottered past carrying a dead dog. A borracho, in a state of drunkenness almost unique, carrying a stick, and so far as Sigbjørn could see without the slightest provocation suddenly began striking her brutally with the stick and then struck the dead dog, which fell to the pavement with a horrible smack. The blind woman, furious, with obscene grief, groped, felt for the dead dog, and finding it, clutched it to her bosom again. Meantime the crowd had turned as a body from the counter and pressed toward the open doorway to watch what was happening, in the course of which Primrose's bottle of Carta Blanca, which had been standing on the counter, was knocked over by a whiskerando Indian and smashed. This Indian generously apologized and began to pick up the pieces, Sigbjørn helping him, and then, because of the chaos, thought that for Primrose's sake it was time to pay the bill.

"Nosotros no somos americanos ricos," Sigbjørn began, since by the price list on the wall they were being charged a peso a bottle more for seventy-five-cent beer. This, however, was the signal for the borracho to turn on Primrose and him. The broken bottle etc., they must pay. Americanos! Abajo los tiránicos americanos! Sigbjørn refused but seeing that the whiskerando was offering to pay, offered to pay himself. But now, the borracho insisted that five extra pesos be paid, and there were cries of "Policía!" The police already had arrived for that matter and were talking angrily to the blind woman. And while everyone was arguing they made their escape as best they could.

"It's our fault," Primrose said. "The Americans come down here and throw their money around. What can you expect?"

"Pero nosotros no somos americanos," Sigbjørn said gently, at which moment also noticing he had been robbed of his tobacco, someone doubtless having mistaken it for his notecase. "Nosotros somos cana-

169

dianos *pobres*." In spite of his calm however, now they were safe, even if in another tiendita, the cruel and bestial little scene had made a fearful impression on him. He knew only too well to what such things could lead in Mexico. And their crime would have been that they were not being muy correcto, and behaving like Americans, in drinking at a lowly cantina. In fact, in a subtle manner, they had not even any right to have a look at the image of the Virgin of Guadalupe at all. Sigbjørn didn't like the dead dog any better, which itself seemed exhumed out of *The Valley of the Shadow of Death*. It was an incident at least such as he might have used and perhaps it was not too late to use it.

The tumultuous scene about the basilica was very curious: the merry-go-rounds and obscene or gruesome sideshows, and yet tents of shade in the tremendous heat (he had only visited the basilica before at night) with the shouts of "Step up ladies and gentlemen and see the amazing spectacle of the head that has his body devoured by rats," the wild pagan dances, the sense of freedom and confinement at once, and the feeling of definite *pilgrimage* toward the basilica, and yet the virtual impossibility of moving a step, or one found that one was only going round and round the square, the sense of sacred miracle preserved in the midst of all this chaos, the contrast of the bishop speaking, or rather mutely opening and closing his mouth, so that he might have been Mynheer Peeperkorn prior to his suicide making his final speech before the clamour of the waterfall in *The Magic Mountain* for all one heard, and yet pronouncing in the midst of all this his benediction, almost as if it were his encyclical to a closed order, on all present, even Sigbjørn and Primrose, as the yelling jukeboxes shrieked and whinnied in English louder and louder, "I'm dreaming of a white Christmas" — all this had an absurdity and horror, would have been justified as an experience simply by its overwhelming effect of absurdity and ugliness, but for the equally overwhelming sense of something sublime everywhere present, of faith.

You could not say it was a simple faith, omnipresent as the jukeboxes and a curious sign that he had observed, *Kilroy was here*; you could not pin it down at all. For that matter even a devout Catholic — Primrose was descended from a Catholic-burning bishop and Sigbjørn from practicing Manx sorceresses — of the usual Western type would have been equally disgusted, and have been far more critical than he of the tasteless votive symbols of that belief, while in Sigbjørn himself — probably far more highly superstitious and less skeptical a person, and yet reluctant to submit himself to the discipline of any church, disbelieving indeed in public worship — he might have detected an element of pride, in many respects humble indeed as Uriah Heep, humble though he was, that would have immediately placed him among the damned. And yet again, there was the overpowering sense of something irrefutably sublime, of faith, or a complex faith.

Now as they commenced the unwinding descent to Cuernavaca, Sigbjørn could not help reflecting on the strange vagueness of their plans. They had, in fact, no plans at all, unless Sigbjørn's to have a drink as soon as possible could be called such; perhaps Primrose imagined that he had, but he had not thought of where to put up in Cuernavaca and for all he knew all the hotels would be full, or prohibitively expensive. They were drawn on as by an invisible cord. But these thoughts were held in abeyance for the moment by the wild excitement at seeing the volcanoes again, for Primrose loyally wanted to see them exactly as they appeared in his book. If this feeling were indeed to be compared to anything whatever, Sigbjørn thought, it would strangely be to reading a book. Yes, precisely a book that, while the terrain is so vividly communicated that it seems familiar, that indeed has become, even as we read, familiar, is exasperating in that we are being held up continually by the notion (conviction) that we can do it better ourselves. In this case, he supposed, it was, if inexactly, as though in part this book were his own, and the passages in question equivalent to that village here, or that mountain peak there, were conjured up by either a sense of their omission or ineptitude, or even a phrase of the flowers, a straggling village, the novelty of the tortas, a little pig. I didn't get that! Damn it, how could I have missed that? If he felt at this moment any clear belief that he would write again, he would have spoilt his enjoyment by making notes in the margin, or in the notebook that, alas, he carried no longer.

On the other hand, and far more powerfully, this book that he was reading was like a book that, paradoxically, had not yet been wholly written, and probably never would be, but that was, in some transcendental manner, *being* written as they went along. Viewed in this light by Sigbjørn what he read was more enthralling still. The temptation here, however, was, due to the anxiety as to what was going to happen to the protagonists, to skip ahead and see. Since this was impossible, and at least in part up to fate, and since they themselves were the protagonists, although self-absorption could perhaps not go much further, what actually seemed to happen was that from time to time they seemed on the point of disappearing altogether, a sensation so pleasurable that one forgot that one had a hangover and wished to protract it forever.

Coming back to earth at this moment with the realization however of this hangover, with which simultaneously came, once more, terror (perhaps one deliberately courted hangovers because it was the closest analogy of the feeling inspired by helpless love), it was to realize that a drink at the earliest possible moment was the best manner to protract this sensation. More or less in this way, at all events, just as he could explain his reluctance at making any move at Tres Cumbres, even to buy a sandwich for Primrose, Sigbjørn could explain to himself the vagueness of his plans. On the most obvious level of thinking anyhow it certainly was extremely odd to be going back to this town, so odd that Sigbjørn would have been quite at a loss to interpret these thoughts logically, which perhaps were so weird indeed that Sigbjørn began to find that the drink was their only essential feature. But those thoughts were held in abeyance anyhow for the moment by Primrose's loyal yet genuine wild excitement at the prospect of seeing the volcanoes again in what Sigbjørn had assured her was their most admirable setting, exactly that was, as they had appeared in his book. "Look, no, there, no there," she was searching as excitedly as she had done in the plane. They were hidden, however. It perhaps, he thought, emphasized the shadow-line quality in both their lives: both were leaving their youth behind. Nothing, however, could be more deceptive than this gloomy and logical notion, because just as in the song in *The Maid of the Mountains*, it is at this moment that perhaps your youth opens up before you all its possibilities that you were not mature enough to see before. Far more often is it than in adolescence we experience the stultifications we associate with old age. And in old age itself recapture the wonder that is popularly supposed to be correlative of childhood, when in fact we often, still as blind as starved kittens and still as unwanted, are in danger of being sent down to the bottom of the ocean with a stone in the sack. It was hard to explain this to Primrose. How often do you read: "She was a woman of middle age" or approximately forty. Have we noticed this, the more often perhaps as approaching forty, ourselves, and never without a shudder. Take heart! It is not true, for this at least is one way in which the world has advanced. Ten years ago it was sufficient for a protagonist to be approaching thirty. With the Victorians "She would never see twenty-five again" was sufficient to suggest that the apple was about to fall off the tree. As for himself, in his mid-thirties, Sigbjørn thought: if ever he should write an autobiographical novel he would begin it: "I was now approaching the critical age of five."

Although Cuernavaca itself was now clearly to be seen far down below them at regular intervals as they rounded the corners, a sort of violet haze hanging over the whole valley obscured the volcanoes from sight, and although it was a fine hot day, becoming ever hotter as they descended, it did not seem to Sigbjørn from what he could remember of the climate that this haze would lift in time for them to see the mountains before sunset. Still it was not far from the full moon, and perhaps Primrose would see them tonight by moonlight, which would be still better. To Sigbjørn's eye a suggestion of bulk in the distance, an inkling of a sloping shape within the haze, gave a hint as of some great presence there, rendered them to him even more impressive in their defection.

Now the road straightened out and they began to pass through the outskirts of Cuernavaca itself and a little later, opposite a large barracks that had not been there before, appeared a sign *Quauhnahuac*, Cuernavaca's Aztec name, with its translation in Spanish, Near the Wood. This was an innovation. Nine years ago Sigbjørn, who had not then read Prescott, had been at pains to discover what this Aztec name was and had thought, by using it, that the fact that the scene of his book was largely in Cuernavaca would be thereby disguised. Now in the event of that book coming out, and in spite of the delay in his hearing from England, and the disappointing reports from America, his hopes were not yet altogether dashed, anyone who had visited Cuernavaca recently would know. They would suppose too that he had got the geography wrong due to his lack of observation, whereas in truth this was because that part of his terrain that was not wholly imaginative was equally based upon the city of Oaxaca and sus anexas. The bus passed, still going down, the Cuernavaca Inn, to which they were making certain obscure additions. Yet hideous buildings were going up everywhere, Bebe Coca-Cola, the huge stone statue; the new bus stop — his old Terminal Cantina was no more; and where would Señora Gregorio be? — was below Cortez Palace, so that almost immediately on getting out, they were confronted with a view of the Rivera murals that he had described in his Chapter VII of *The Valley*. The wall below Cortez Palace was being reinforced, however, and the path that the Consul and Yvonne had taken when she returned to him through the rubbish heap was no more; they would now have had to come down some stone steps.

After some difficulty they checked their bags at the bus stop, with the exception of Primrose's fur coat, and on Sigbjørn's suggestion strolled up to the square. They paused by Cortez Palace to look once more in vain for the volcanoes. He guided their steps to a cantina called La Universal, which he had immediately noticed was still there, and where he once knew the proprietor, a Spaniard with whom he played dice and who always "bumped the dice" on his head. Jukeboxes, at least twenty of them apparently, kept up an endless caterwauling. La Universal was where, inside, he had obtained some of the dialogue that he had put in his Chapter XII, which he made actually take place in an awful place called the Farolito in Oaxaca — it was partly the Farolito and partly another place in the city of Oaxaca called El Bosque, that also meant The Wood.

The Universal always had been a sidewalk café and it was still. They sat down, tired, at a round table, and Sigbjørn having ordered two beers draped Primrose's coat upon a neighbouring chair. With the forethought that had often been lacking during the many years he had not been drinking, he had insisted that she bring it, for it had struck him that it might be some time before they left the Universal, and the nights were cold, and the checking room at the bus station might be shut. The beer was black and delicious; they toasted each other, and ordered another one. Every now and then the cathedral let loose a jangling gaggle of bells. "I wish Juan Fernando would just happen by." He had meant to add, then we wouldn't have to go to Oaxaca, but refrained for that would hurt Primrose, who said something of the sort and Sigbjørn said, "Well, we'd go to Oaxaca anyhow. Perhaps with Fernando."

In a square, as Primrose pointed out, there was even a Ferris wheel and a few roundabouts not in use, to welcome him; although this Ferris wheel had the air of a permanent feature rather than an appurtenance, as it was in his book of a fiesta, it was swarming with Americans, in every kind of costume and all with the air of having great deal of money. Many were in uniform. Many, however, paused at the Universal; they seemed to favour it and another little sidewalk café between theirs and the Hotel Bella Vista. Luxurious American cars made their way slowly past and occasionally an isolated tourist, or a couple, in shorts, with packs upon the backs and looks of wonder: if he could only be like that, Sigbjørn thought. Still, perhaps, why not, since doubtless he had more wondrous things to look upon than any tourist. The jukeboxes bellowed.

The second beer arrived and they waited for fate to step in. Meantime, however, the aspect of things seemed to change for Sigbjørn. He began to feel excited. How on earth could one communicate — or for that matter, excommunicate — the extraordinary drama of all this to him? There must be some way: but how to do it. Then again, perhaps it was not interesting, save to him. All these thoughts that had been amorphously in his mind before now, with the proximity of their realization, took concrete shape. Every now and then the little Chapultepec bus drove up, stopped, drove away. That was the bus in his book that went to Tomalín. Before him, on that park bench, was where the Consul had sat. And down beyond Cortez Palace, in a direction that he scarcely had let himself think about, down that street at the end, lay, would it be there, that madhouse of M. Laruelle's, which even Yvonne actually *forgot* was there when Sigbjørn had caused her to return? Would it still be there? And would the writing on the wall still be there, *No se puede vivir sin amar*? And would the Calle Humboldt be the same as Yvonne had found it? And would the Consul's house at number 65, which had once been his, Sigbjørn's and Ruth's, still be there? Good God! Laruelle's house, where the Consul had made his act of will.

Sigbjørn went inside to find out what the price of beer was — Nosotros no somos americanos ricos — and when he returned, it was to find the marmalade-haired Spanish woman and her man seated with Primrose. They had seen the Wildernesses deceived in the Plaza Netzalcuayatl. "We are ashamed of my country."

They began to have a party and the day became triumphant. Señor Kent, the proprietor of the café, came by and was introduced. "Haven't I seen you before?"

Sigbjørn had stood up politely. "Why yes . . ."

"Don't you remember me?" Señor Kent gave him his card, but at the moment simultaneously his attention was called by someone in the road and Sigbjørn, catching the table in imbalance, spilled the tequila in the Mexican's lap, and the next moment, he dropped the card. They were helped by a rather slovenly waitress, who later charged them too much. Quite apart from anything else, what was continental in Sigbjørn required, even as Don Quixote, a café of some sort as a center of his circle, this was a necessity of travel to him, if he must travel, and La Universal — which so to speak was a divided character leading a double life, Dr. Jekyll outside and Mr. Hyde within while sometimes at night the two would mix, clearly would not do. Things began now to happen very swiftly in Sigbjørn's mind.

"Do you know what, Sigbjørn," Primrose said excitedly, "he says he thinks he knows of an apartment to let in the Calle Nicarague — I mean the Calle Humboldt."

"In the where!" Sigbjørn's heart began to thump loudly.

"Good heavens. Well, there usen't to be any apartments there in my day. They're all private houses." Sigbjørn was feeling very strange indeed.

Primrose went off and returned, enchanted with everything she had seen, the masses of flowers, the men on horses and burros, the terrific loads that they carried.

And then, Primrose was saying even more excitedly, "I've been to the Calle Humboldt and it's still just like you describe it. . . . And do you know what, Mr. Laruelle's tower's still there — it's just like you say only there's not so many gewgaws on it, and there's no writing outside on the wall. But it's wonderful inside."

"I've never been inside. I made it all up."

"And do you know, I was so excited I almost forgot to tell you. It's been turned into apartments and we can have one there. There's a swimming pool and an enormous garden and it's called the Quinta Dolores."

"Are you quite sure?"

"Sure about what?"

"Sure that there's no writing on the wall."

"Perfectly sure."

"It's all right. It's only my joke."

But Sigbjørn had never been inside it. Good heavens, what a thought! What if he were, after living in it, so to speak, so long, to go inside it, to live inside the tower, now, if this tower should become, for a while, their home, and this again, by simply what was known as coincidence, for he had not moved a muscle in that direction, had not, apart from vaguely having moved them — the most obvious, the most logical, the, indeed, almost inevitable move to anyone who is acquainted with Mexico at all and cannot bear the city and does not have the most specific plans — toward Cuernavaca itself made any more at all. What if this were to happen? What would that be like? Surely it bankrupted the imagination, or at least invested it with powers that were normally held to be beyond it, unless they were in truth so far below it and behind it, that it had the same effect: it was enough to drive you crazy, or make you think that you were on the track of some new truth that everyone had somehow overlooked and yet was somehow bound up with some fundamental law of human destiny.

The Quinta Dolores itself was largely a garden that stretched right down from the Calle Humboldt to the barranca. It was uncultivated on the slope and where the declivity began, on level ground, was a swimming pool. The nearest approximate to the establishment in America or Canada was indeed one of those "drive-ins" or "auto camps of the better class" that had threatened and were threatening Primrose and Sigbjørn's existence in Eridanus. This however was unfair to the Quinta Dolores. Grotesque in design, as it was deficient in plumbing, roomy yet uncomfortable at the same time, the whole place nonetheless had a beauty, not to say splendour, usually quite lacking in its more efficient American counterpart.

They settled for one hundred and five pesos a week, and afterward Sigbjørn took Primrose for a walk up the Calle Morelos, down which they had come early that afternoon on the bus: the glimpse through the archway of the old man and the boy on the bench, the cobbled court and stone building at right, then rolling hills and fields and sense of light and space with low afternoon sun and marvelous piles of clouds: later, the black horses running across the tilted fields,

Popo in magnificent form, a cloud like a hat turning into a cloud streaming off the top as though erupting, then the barranca! — *the* barranca: just as he had described it.

Primrose said, "Is it? I must know."

"It's not *the* place, of course."

Though this was not *the* place, it was vast, threatening, gloomy, dark, frightening: the terrific drop, the darkness below. They lingered long on the scene, and Primrose beautifully remarked: roads that are laid straight east and west, those get the sun all day, but roads that go north and south get the sun later, and lose it by three o'clock in the afternoon. It was like a poem. It was difficult to see how any happiness could come — for the Consul, his hero, it would not — out of this but so it did, floating like an essence. It was the happiness engendered, strangely enough, by work itself, by the transformation of the nefarious poetic pit into sober or upright prose, even if jostled occasionally by Calderon, or it was the happiness engendered by the memory of work finished, of happy days, other evening walks, or rather, more accurately, of the memory of their escape — from some or other part of that transformation, after tea, when they discussed it to some sort of conclusion, and in this respect purposely of turning evil into good — to see Mauger, the fisherman with his tales of salmon drowning eagles, or of how the wind blowing wildly seemed to keep the tide high up a whole day, or of beaked fish with green bones.

And of other walks in Eridanus, the time they had called on old William Blake, for instance, an Englishman too, who was making a garden by the forest. His house was very clean, with fresh shingles and scarlet sills. "It is the best built house on the beach," he said proudly. "Aye, and the inside's good too. On the shore," he added, "'ave you seen them? They're *crabs wot jump!*" His speech was such, or so he persuaded himself, as Wordsworth dreamed to record, humble and good as plates on a farmhouse shelf. He fed the chipmunks, then showed them the spring where the deer came down to drink. "The deer come right down to the lighthouse, swimming right across the sound." In winter time they were tame, you could feed them. Then, because it was the beginning of their life in Eridanus, and Primrose and he did not know the way well, he showed them their trail, the trail now widened by loutish loggers, loutish not for being loggers, but because they practiced high rig logging, who had left nothing but a vicious slash behind. "Keep to the left," he said, "and you can tell when you are almost home, because the trail bends, and where you look out to sea the trees are thinner, where you can see the light in the sky." Then there was the time, long before their own fire, and there was even happiness in this memory, because it *was* at that time, when they stumbled on a burned house in the wood. The eaves lay to one side: a smashed barrel-tree the owners had planted, and smashed pint bottles in a pool, limp dungarees, the washing pole overgrown with vine. Thus was disaster's message without word.

Now they walked higher up into the town for a view of moonrise over the volcanoes, meaning to drop in afterward to the Cuernavaca Inn, which was kept by a Señor Pepe, who should have known Sigbjørn of old. As they approached the inn the full moon, seen over an orange junkyard filled with broken and rusted tin cans, was already rising above Ixtaccihuatl. At her summit a veil of cloud was billowing in the moonlight. Entering the inn, Sigbjørn said:

"This is the place where Hugh really used to offer the Consul strychnine. However that's a long story, I don't know if I've ever told you."

But all Don Pepe could say was "Mucho tiempo, mucho tiempo"; he didn't really remember after eight years and Sigbjørn was more than half relieved. The inn was much changed, the old swimming pool now hidden by a huge wall, no one lived in the ramshackle old building.

When Sigbjørn and Primrose came out, it was to see an extra-ordinary sight. Over Ixtaccihuatl the moon was in eclipse, which, as they walked to the Quinta Dolores, catching strange glimpses of the ever-increasing horrendous shadow of Tellus, the earth, on the moon between houses, became total. They had mysterious glimpses of it down narrow streets, and as they walked watching, little by little the shadow of the old earth drew across the moon; everybody else ignored it save one Chinese boy in the zócalo with opera glasses and a man carrying a baby down the Calle Humboldt, which was his old Calle Nicaragua. How sinister and yet exciting in this shadow blacker than night had Laruelle's house, had the Quinta Dolores seemed then. What sinister omen did it hold for them, going groping into the grounds of this house on this day, and afterward what glorious silver portent? They heard the pure voice of a Mexican singing somewhere

179

on a balcony, as if rejoicing that the world had relinquished its shadow and the moon was with them again. And after the eclipse, standing on the roof balcony, the sense of space and light, of being almost up in the sky. Long vines were waving and making shadows on sun blinds. Stars were winking like jewels out of white fleecy clouds, silver clouds; and the wide *near* sapphire-and-white sky, a white ocean of fleece, and the brilliant full moon sliding down the sapphire sky.

From *Dark as the Grave Wherein my Friend is Laid* (1968) by Malcolm Lowry, 1909–1957. Born in England, Lowry lived from 1940–1949 at Dollarton, B.C., and afterwards in Ontario. His life, a typical boozer's hard-luck story, was redeemed by his majestic novel *Under the Volcano* (1945), to which allusion is made above under the title, *The Valley of the Shadow of Death*.

LENINGRAD
by Diana Goldsborough

The name doesn't fit. Originally it commemorated the saint with the keys, and a king who wished his city to be a key to unlock the secrets of the West. The progress of events dictated the dropping of the Germanized 'burg' (what had foreign ways done for us?) and the 'Saint' (what had foreign saints done for us?) and finally achieved a new name altogether. It seems a pity. It would have been more tasteful, to both the old and new hero, to name a new city after Vladimir Ilyitch. One of the manifestations of the revolutionary fervour is the urge to re-name. Perhaps the future will bring another reassessment, and a deleninization will return St. Petersburg to its legend.

Nothing prepares you for its beauty. The ideal approach of course, would be by sea, and that was the common one till 1917. Then the splendour would burst on you all at once — the river, the harbour, the islands, the barges, the bridges, the dream palaces on the embankment, the fortress, and the golden spire of Peter and Paul topping all. Now you arrive at the dreary Finland Station (still haunted by Lenin; his enormous figure greets the trains as the welcoming Petersburgers on a famous occasion once greeted him), and the miles-long drive down Nevsky Prospect reveals little of the city's charm and magnificence. That breaks upon you with every successive walk and ramble.

Leningrad is a planned city on the lines of Washington or modern Paris, and older than either. And as the prized pet city of a succession of despots, some rarely gifted, it exhibits a multitude of treasures — palaces, royal and noble, theatres, churches, cathedrals, bridges, statues, parks, promenades, vistas — all results of the powers' love and care and unchecked and uncensured flow of wealth. And most of all, the city, like Venice or Amsterdam or Bangkok, exudes the special grace and charm of a settlement wrested by man's almost incredible labours from hostile terrain.

For there is water, water everywhere. Here the Neva met the Gulf in a marshy wide-spreading delta. From here in 1703 Peter the Great finally drove out the aggressive Swedes. (Interesting to remember that the Swedes were once very aggressive, with the reputation throughout northern Europe of enjoying slaughterous strife as their chief entertainment. It is only in the last 100 years that they have gone in for happy remoteness from the maelstroms around them.) To clinch his victory and drive a nail into his acquisition of the area, Peter wanted a great city, a new capital, a 'window on Europe.' Dutch engineers were summoned for their advice and assistance in conjuring a city from a bog. Piles were driven into the marshes (the city is literally on stilts) and canals were dug to channel the ooze in clean-running lines. Impelled by the great one's driving will, the work progressed apace. Shocking numbers of workmen were killed by the miasmic vapours. The Peter and Paul fortress went up, originally intended as defence against the Swedes, but becoming almost at once what it was to remain — a political prison. Before the last pile was driven it had found its first inhabitant. The Neva banks were shored up. Later, at a certain spot near the embankment, 1200 piles were driven in to support the granite and marble immensity of St. Isaac's, the great cathedral desired by Peter, but unseen by him, to commemorate Poltava.

Now three major canals — the Moika, the Fontanka, and the Caterina — concentrically semicircle the embankment, and a multitude of lesser runlets criss-cross the city. Peter's great avenue, the Nevsky Prospect, 120 feet wide and remarkable for its time, intersects the three, running straight as an arrow from the seat of government on the embankment right through the city to Znamensky Square, where it angles and runs straight again out to the Alexander Nevsky Monastery. This monastery was founded by Peter to harbour the bones of the ancient hero which he ravished from another order and imported to give cachet and historical interest to his new city. The original owners pardonably were appalled at the loss, and secretly and at great risk the monks had the bones removed and stolen back to their old resting place. Then they loudly proclaimed Miracle! The saint obviously wished to remain where he was. Peter briskly returned the bones to their new setting and let it be known that any further miracles would remove the monks summarily to a sphere where they could take the matter up with the saint himself. So runs the story.

The eighteenth century was the great era of building when successive monarchs, especially the empresses Anna and Catherine, hired foreign architects, artists, and craftsmen to beautify their capital and make it resplendent. How much Leningrad owes the foreigners! Leblond, Monferrand, Rastrelli, Rossi, de la Mothe, Vitali, Guarenghi, Grimm — these are the real creators of Petersburg, who gave it the outline that became the admiration of an age and which it still possesses today. A French visitor of the late *dix-huitième*, arriving at long last after the wearisome overland journey through barrens and plains, marvelled 'Ville superbe, que fais-tu là?' and gave voice to a lasting wonder.

Now the elegant palaces of the nobles, pale rose and green and blue, that line the canals and are reflected in them, are faded and decayed. The churches are museums, or under *remont*, an excuse given universally, and it is true. Everything is either under repair or in immediate need of it. Constant reconstruction was always necessary here, where marsh and flood undermined. In the days of the czars and nobles fortunes were sunk every year in the greedy bogs; and now, after decades of neglect and wartime dilapidation, and with private ownership dead, the government finds it a herculean task to keep the buildings in working order. Work is always going forward on the main treasures (I think the powers have some inkling of what a potential tourist jackpot they have on their hands) but the decay runs ahead of them and they are finding it impossible to catch up. Walking about, you feel as if the whole fabulous city is crumbling before your eyes and will return to powder in the marshes. This communication of transient beauty is part of the enchantment the city weaves, and it is not wholly sad. The citizens of Leningrad must be unique in northern Europe in growing up and living with the eighteenth century. (Though perhaps Dubliners do too. Dublin also has the air of a superseded city unduly full of the ghosts of departed grandeur.) The older and newer capital, Moscow, whose splendours, and uglinesses, are purely Russian, was always jealous of the upstart rival, the czars' pet. Now the Muscovites can triumph. 'Leningrad is so dull,' they say. 'Nothing happens there.' And it's true. The worst has happened: Peter's town has become provincial. The window to the West is shuttered.

A first walk, down the Prospect (unmissable because of width and its street signs beginning with HEB. The second word looks vaguely like PROSPEKT — having the same number of letters, anyway) to the embankment and Winter Palace, was very rewarding. I crossed the Fontanka by the Anichkov Bridge, with its statues of the horse-tamers, reminiscent of the *chevaux de Marly* in Paris, and sauntered along, looking in the shop windows. In the days of the czars the Prospect used to be an ultra-fashionable promenade, its lavish display and luxury shops rivalling those of London or Paris and providing memorable contrast to the wretchedness of the mass of the populace. It is hard to remember, looking at the eighteenth-century elegance of the centre, that the city has been an industrial town since its inception, when Peter imported the cloth-workers, and that even now, with the mannered facade of the famous part of the town looking untouched, Leningrad is a great industrial city, the second in the Soviet Union. The factories are built far out in the suburbs where the ground is solider, and the centre is left with its past intact. Here was the contrast between the miserable majority and the high-living, free-spending minority at its most striking. There were always outbreaks of unrest in Petersburg, continuing until the final great one.

Now the great stores contain nothing of interest. Block upon block stretches with no window to claim the attention even of a Russian. Entertainment must be found elsewhere. On almost all corners are ice-cream vendors, the *morozhenoye*, and fruit-drink sellers. These are old landmarks, if you consult the old guide-books. A late nineteenth-century book I found invaluable, far more useful than the modern Intourist guides or the Russian-in-the-street, who give a different answer every time you ask. We learned to be wary of statistics that flowed fluently out but were apt to vary extraordinarily from person to person or even from time to time with the same person. This, I am sure, was not from any desire to mislead, but merely because when a stranger is interested enough to ask, it is considered very rude to respond, as a Westerner would, with 'I don't know' or

'Look it up.' A prim English guide-book of the eighties warns: 'A Russian is the most fluent of liars, and from the most amiable of motives.' My guide-books comment on the ice-cream and fruit-drink sellers everywhere, and also on vendors of salmon, perch, mushrooms, oranges, lemons, and strawberries, now impossible to get. Oh, delightful Petersburg in the eighties (if you were a wealthy tourist). We saw no fresh fruit the whole time we were in Russia — yes, once we did. At a maternity hospital beside a new mother's bed there was a pineapple. We eyed it with the fixed stares of incipient scurvy, and had it not been so bulky and prickly and difficult to make off with, I think the young mother would have been bereft.

Now on the left the Kazan cathedral, brick and stucco, with its two ranges of crescent arcades, like a little St. Peter's. Here Catherine the Second was crowned and General Kutuzov prayed before marching against Napoleon. It is now a museum. Not far away, on the other side of the street, is a beautiful crumbling building with an exquisite baroque facade, *putti* with garlands over the boarded windows, looking over the heads of the Soviet populace below with seraphically remote expressions. Scaffolding fills the interior and even it is decaying. Over the door is written DOMUS MEUS, DOMUS ORATIONIS and the pigeons perch on the bosses above and fly up with a flap of wings. 'The Polish Church,' a guide surmised later in answer to my question. It was probably St. Catherine's for the colony of Roman Catholic Poles in Petersburg.

On, and a brief shudder at the gigantic horror of the Resurrection Cathedral down a street to the right, a nineteenth-century aberration. Somebody thought Petersburg should have a St. Basil's, and here it is, vivid brick, with nine nightmare domes and rich in mosaic and enamel on a par with the Albert Memorial's. In smoothly dignified Leningrad it stands out like a Brighton Pavilion in St. Peter's Square. In Moscow it would look fine.

Now the Moika Canal, with the Police Bridge, and overlooking it one of the most bewitching palaces in the city. This building was the home of the Stroganovs, and a plate over the door tells us it was the work of Rastrelli. It is perfectly proportioned baroque, pale green like a little Winter Palace but with the royal extravagance disciplined down to a graceful lightheartedness. The coat of arms, with two ermine, stands over the door. There is an inner courtyard where anyone can come in and sit down — at least I hope so, because I did. The eighteenth-century lamps still hang, and the coach houses are there, and the cobblestones seem to echo the sound of the wheels of arriving guests.

The bridge's hanging lamps are like modern copies of the Stroganovs'; it is a charming bridge, one that invites leaning over and gazing, which many people do. You see Soviet sailors in their loose blouses and long streamers, looking like a chorus from HMS *Pinafore*. Couples like to saunter here. I am surprised at how young the sexes start pairing off. Multitudes of 12- and 13-year-olds walk along two by two, hand in hand. (They may, of course, be sets of brothers and sisters.)

At last the Admiralty looms over me. I have been seeing its bright gold spire (1735; one of the works ordered by the Empress Anna) for the last mile. From here the Prospect and two other main streets radiate out over the whole city. Then under the beautiful archway into enormous Palace Square. The spaces in Russian cities are immense. The average square is eight times the size of an English or French market square. I am convinced that in this one four Grey Cup games could be played simultaneously. The Alexander Column, generally called the Peace Pillar, stands here, and the angel on top has the best view in Leningrad, one of the most satisfying in the world.

Here is the embankment, and the Neva, and the famous palace dominating the waterfront. It is really several palaces, and the facades, looking from right to left, are marvellous in summing up national styles. First we have the Italian Rastrelli, resplendent in green and cream; a high crescendo of ornate baroque. (Strange that I should have to wait till Russia to become fond of baroque. The masculine forceful extravagance seems to be what is wanted in this northern scene.) Then de la Mothe's Hermitage, a model of tasteful moderation — nothing extreme, nothing to exclaim over, everything just as it should be, sublimely French. Then the extension to the Hermitage by Felten, the Russianized German. This makes an effort to live up to its companions, but has a heavy blankness, a Teutonic thud. This was the palace of great Catherine and of successive emperors and empresses until the end. Now it is all museum (entrance: two roubles).

The buildings are connected by inside passageways and you can pass from the splendour of Catherine's day to the no less splendid unfurnished galleries where are the acquisitions of two centuries — one of the four greatest art collections in Europe. Two half-day visits cannot absorb more than a fraction of it. I headed purposefully for the French Impressionist galleries. Here are rooms of Van Gogh, Gauguin, Matisse, Picasso, in bursting richness. The rest of the museum was crowded to the windows; these rooms were deserted. The biggest crowds we found were in the rooms below devoted to Pushkin, the Byronic idol of Soviet youth, and in the great chamber with the map of the USSR done in semi-precious stones.

Peter the Great rears his charger in Decembrists' Square — another re-name, after the unfortunate heroes of an early abortive revolution — on the embankment behind St. Isaac's. Catherine had Falconet design it, and on the base rock, shaped like a French cap of liberty (a conscious irony on the part of the French designer?) is inscribed 'To Peter, from Catherine' appealingly, like a birthday present. The horse rears, and since the hind legs alone were not sufficient to bear the weight of the barrel-body, a great serpent was added, rising from under the hoofs to the horse's rump. It is supposed to have great symbolic value, representing evil crushed under Peter's hoofs, but the effect is rather unfortunate. A visitor remarked once: 'A fine animal. What a pity it should have worms!'

This statue shares the honour, along with the Commandatore in *Don Giovanni*, of playing a main part in a work of art. The ballet from Pushkin's *Bronze Horseman* was being staged by the Leningrad Ballet while I was there, and I lost no time in getting a ticket. I had heard so much about this ballet, which is renowned for the spectacular stage effects so beloved by the Russians and well produced by them. It seemed a great piece of luck that it should be playing, and at the Kirov theatre, the *ci-devant* Marynsky, theatre of the Imperial Ballet School where Nijinsky trained and Pavlova danced. It's a beauty — not large, but exquisitely proportioned and perfectly maintained, its gilt gleaming and its red velvet sumptuous. The Imperial boxes, at this time containing visiting Chinese delegations, were splendid, and the pale green ceiling was lovely, with angels radiating out from the central chandelier.

The ballet concerns a pair of lovers who are in the habit of meeting by the great bronze horseman. One of the periodic floods that so devastated Petersburg sweeps over the town; the hero turns up at the rendezvous but she does not. The waters rise and rage and lo, a piece of her house floats by. He is rescued as the torrent laps his chin, but he gives himself up to despair. In an abandoned *pas seul* he seems to see the bronze horseman come to life and pursue him, hounding him to death.

This tale, as you may imagine, strains the stage-effect people to the utmost. The big *pièce de résistance* is the flood, and realism is such that the fans are hard put to it not to draw up their feet under them. First little trickles and wavelets creep across the stage in the wake of the driving rain. (The storm was something too, only it tends to be erased from the mind by what follows.) Then the water rises apace, and heaves and billows (wind blown under canvas?). The hero climbs on the plinth, and finally the back, of a handy stone lion. He is rescued in the nick by a rowboat that follows shrubs, branches, pieces of tree, corpses, and as aforesaid, part of a house, all tossing across the stage. He plunges into the billows and is picked up by the boatmen who then row sturdily off, rising on crests and plunging into troughs all the way from the right-centre to off-left. In the mad sequence Peter's great horse rears still more and drops shudderingly, then falls into an eerie gallop (rather rocking: I think the experts had exhausted themselves on the flood — it could have been better done with shadows) and bounds about to drive the young man out of his mind. There is also some ballet tucked in here and there.

But the chief applause is reserved for the stage effects, and each new one gets its clap, like a star turn. Obviously the audience knows the piece well and loves every wave of it. Part of its charm for me was seeing it in the city of its setting and recognizing the buildings of the backdrop, just as Prokoviev's opera *War and Peace* gained from being staged in Moscow. In that piece too, stage effects bulked large. Moscow burned before your eyes, and the pall of the battlefield practically hooded you. In the ballet *The Twelve Months*, season blended into season as you watched; trees budded, burst into leaf, were bronzed, gilded, and fell bare all in a matter of minutes, and while the audience clapped. It is spellbinding, and I don't know how it's done. In a way it reminded me of what I've read of the Victorian theatre when bare stages first gave way to elaborate realism and audiences were enthralled by waterfalls and real rabbits on stage in *A Midsummer Night's Dream*. Part of it was the realization of what science could do for the stage and part of it was the public's love of the spectacular, which social history dictated at that time.

Indeed, so many things in Russia give the visitor the feeling of being transported backwards in time, although not always to the eighteenth and nineteenth centuries. Some things are of this century — just — such as modern Russian art and architecture, and hotel decor. The hotel our tour was in was more Diamond Jim Brady-Lillian Russell vintage — red plush, ball fringe, marble statuary, gigantic urns, potted palms, and enormous oil paintings of stags at bay — but the band was modern, 1920s, and would have been snapped up by an alert Hollywood director instantly for one of those flapper musicals. The bands they hire at present don't give the quality at all — they haven't that tinny sound. Our hotel group had it and a connoisseur could have listened for hours to its renditions of 'Tippy Tippy Tin' and 'Charmaine.'

I was very fortunate in having a Russian-speaking room-mate — a Latvian woman who had left as a young girl to study in Vienna and had eventually settled down in England. Her brother came up from Riga to see her for the first time since she was in her teens, and the tour saw little of her. But she was invaluable to me, finding out from the girls at the desk why there were no plugs in the basins (Russian basins never have plugs) and where was the telephone book (Russian cities have no telephone books). I remember too that she managed to have a bath, which the rest of us didn't. (Russians share the Eastern prejudice against bathtubs, thinking it piggish to bathe in one's own dirt. Showers are the thing.) She related to me, in her charming borscht accent, her struggles to achieve the bathtub:

'First I talk to the girl at the desk on our floor. I have to say three times. She cannot understand why a Russian woman wants a bass. "Why is this? There are showers." I say no, I must have bass. She is very cross, and I sink oh dear, I will not have bass. And tomorrow I cannot walk. Then she says: "But perhaps is rizzins of hels you must having bass?" And I say: "Yes, yes, rizzins of hels." And is true. If I do not have bass, tomorrow I am a dead woman. Then she is all smiles, very kind, and say on next floor is bass. I must get the key from the girl on the desk there. And she puts me in the lift to ride one floor (I am a sick woman who needs bass). Then all over again with the girl on the next floor who has never heard of the key. "What is this? What key? There is no key!" And the girl on the desk on our floor hears her and shouts up: "The key to bass, great stupid!" And the second girl says: "It is you who are stupid!" Then they are quoiling up and down the stairs, very angry, until at last the first girl comes up and says: "Stupid and uncultured! This lady for rizzins of hels must having a bass!" Then the second girl is very sorry and says: "Oh. I know now where is the key. Come." And we all go down the hall and find a little man, a janitor, and at last he has the key. Then to the other end of the hall, all four of us — the girls helping me, the sick lady — and the man takes out the key with a great smile, and they all smile, and he opens the door, and zere at last I am alone in a room with a very old, very yellow bass.'

These triumphs were beyond me. I know no Russian and used about ten Russian words while I was there, the most recurrent being 'Please,' 'Thank you,' 'Will you tell me when we get there?' (the first phrase I learn in any language), 'tea' (this was an English tour), and 'chess stamp.' This last I shouted into wickets wherever stamps were sold in Leningrad and Moscow. Most Russian stamps are rather boringly designed colour ones of biologists or of Stalin greeting heroes of the collectives; but I saw a charming brown-and-white one celebrating some event in the chess world. I wanted some badly and tried everywhere, hoping 'shakmati marok' would do the trick. It didn't. I doubt if a Russian would meet success either, haring round Toronto post-offices bleating 'Kanustomp' appealingly to the people behind the wicket.

I didn't even know the Cyrillic alphabet. I was just catching on to it by the time I left. Quite often, after a word is spelled out laboriously, it turns out to be one you know, like *buffet* or *toilet* or *étage*. So many French and German words turn up in Russian, dating from the eighteenth-century importation of Western ways. English has contributed to the industrial and sport vocabulary. I was a while recognizing *lift* (pronounced 'leevt') in its Cyrillic disguise over the elevator, and *res* and *futbol* and *sport* came as surprises too. The most baffling one was *cheslongov* which could be hired by the hour, according to a signboard at the gate of Leningrad's Park of Rest and Culture. My Russian-reading companion was also puzzled. 'It's plural, but what is it? Since *my* day, I suppose.' We sounded it out several times and light dawned: *Chaise longue*. They turned out to be folding chairs. In the end, what helped most with the alphabet was visiting the art galleries. All foreign names are spelled phonetically, a great boon, and Gogē, Tifan, Kalo, and Pusē helped to put the alphabet in its place for me. Of course you have to recognize the paintings, for often as not the Roman spelling is not bothered with. We met with our embarrassments, spending far too much time trying to figure out what artist Keto (no, not Vato) could be who had perpetrated a shoddy horror of a man clawing his belly in anguish. Finally distant memories of second-year Latin sidled to the rescue. The painting showed the suicide of Cato, and who the artist was we never could decipher. It was far too bad a painting anyway, we consoled ourselves, to be in the Hermitage. A Rembrandt exhibit cleared a lot of ground. Besides the Hermitage Rembrandts there were reproductions shown of all the other most famous ones, with owner cities printed underneath. Kopengagen, Vafinton, Glasgo, and London presented no problems; Gaga was with little difficulty interpreted as The Hague; but then there was the place we figured out slowly as Sofra. So many Rembrandts were there and never to have heard of it! Some distant spot in Russia? A Russian gallery-goer, unable to bear it any longer, hissed 'Parees.' We'd flubbed a letter in the Louvre. Phonetic spelling is an enormous help to the Russian masses too. Theirs is not the stupefaction that is the lot of the Anglo-Saxon when presented with an unfamiliar name. Barely literate remote Uzhbeks or Kazhaks can pronounce all foreign names correctly, or at least uniformly.

I was forever being impressed with Russian linguistic talent. Students are learning French and English. Whenever more than one of us went out and talked together, we were approached by young people saying: 'Please. We are learning English and would like to speak with you.' Their English always seemed to be accentless. I wonder to what extent phonetic spelling is responsible for Russian excellence in languages. You would be mistaken, though, to rely on much English being spoken. As throughout northern Europe, German is the second language. Whenever I was lost, or got off the wrong stop in the subway (a frequent occurrence with me), I addressed a group in German and there was always a response. The conversations were interesting to me, but not very useful in forming those deep generalizations and deductions of *weltpolitik* that I envy other travellers to the Soviet Union. Here runs a typical one.

Two of us were headed for the Leningrad Museum from a starting point in a distant suburb and we had lost the way. As we debated the streets, two young girls approached us and offered to accompany us there. They were students, one of English, one of French. Since my companion spoke no French, I left the English student for her. The other girl had been studying French for seven years, and had never met a Frenchman.

'Will you go to Paris to study?' I asked. 'C'est mon rêve,' she answered solemnly. She had seen the occasional French film, and Paris looked so beautiful. Films as a subject always interest me. I admired the actor Nikolai Cherkassov in *Ivan the Terrible* and *Alexander Nevsky* and wondered what he was appearing in now. 'I do not think he acts any more,' she said vaguely. 'I think he has not good health.' A movie that she liked tremendously was *Pont de Waterloo*, apparently just released in Russia. 'So sad,' she said. 'Such a good tragedy.' She had seen Chaplin films, and we exclaimed together over *Temps Moderne, Lumières de Ville*, and *Fièvre d'Or*. I went into a brown study trying to think of the French for *Limelight*, discarding 'Lumière de Citron' and several others. I emerged in vain (what is French for limelight?) to hear her saying: 'But who I really admire is the actor Flun — do you know his work?' She seemed very much struck that I didn't, and went on: 'He is such a good actor, so *athlète*; we see him now in 'Robin Good' and admire him very much.' 'Oh, Flun!' I cried, thunderstruck. 'Yes, I know him.' 'Tell me then about him. I admire so much the little moustache. I have a picture of one of my uncles when he was young. He was an officer, and had a moustache, but bigger than Flun's. I like it, and now you never see them any more; the Russian men no longer have the moustache.' (I had a vision of the modern Soviet banning the moustache, as Peter had once chopped the boyars' beards.) I summoned up what I could of the less picaresque data on Mr. Flynn. She seemed surprised that the picture was not new. 'I don't think he is so *athlète* any more,' I said, 'and I don't think he still wears the moustache.' 'Just like the Russian men,' she mourned. 'It is the same everywhere.'

By the time we were at the doors of the Leningrad Museum. My English companion and I went into a huddle, thinking it would be a grateful gesture on our part to buy the girls tickets into the museum, but the rouble situation being what it was, we regretfully decided we couldn't swing it. The students were whispering together too, and I became instantly convinced that they had had the wish to buy ours, but were forced to give up the idea for the same reason. We parted with a slight mutual embarrassment.

This money difficulty was the chief handicap in Russia. For we could wander at will wherever we liked, hampered only by no language, no maps, and no money. The language problem wasn't insuperable, as I have discussed, and Leningrad is such a beautifully laid out, orderly city that a map wasn't missed. (It was different in mazy Moscow. There I remember a guide in the Lenin Museum halting the tour in front of a map of the city to show us where street fighting went on in the early days of the revolution, and looking so pleased and surprised when we all whipped out pads and pencils — it was the first map we'd seen, and forty years old or not, we were getting down the details.) But ready cash, at four roubles to the dollar, was in short supply indeed. This cruel, completely unnatural rate of exchange meant that we paid a quarter for a cup of tea, or a postcard, or an ice cream ('Sounds like France,' a soured tourist commented to me later), and we were continually poor. We had to count every kopeck (100 to the rouble), whereas to a Russian they mattered so little that when he dropped a handful he didn't bother to pick them up. We saw this happen in the subway; our eyes followed every rolling coin and it was all we could do not to scramble for them on our hands and knees, like Ulysses' men, recently pigs, when Circe dropped the acorns. If we got fifteen kopecks' change instead of twenty, we tended to make a big scene, leaving the shopkeeper or ice-cream vendor thinking probably, 'These Westerners — they must be just as impoverished as we are told.' Now the exchange rate is ten to the dollar (I knew this would happen as soon as my trip was over) and tourists will not suffer so.

Several members of the tour supplemented their allowances by selling clothes on the black market. This can't be too much frowned on by the authorities because little men openly clustered round the doors of hotels harbouring Westerners; and they approached Western men in the streets or parks, fingering their jackets and saying: 'Business? Dollars?' I suppose there aren't so many tourists as to constitute a real threat. If the Western influx increased, the government would crack down. Men's clothing is chiefly in demand. One man with us went out with an old jacket, a couple of shirts, and a pair of pyjamas, and came back with 400 roubles, and presumably the marketeer made a large profit. Pop records too fetch huge sums. Louis Armstrong and Stan Kenton are popular with the *cognoscenti*, but you can get still more for a Doris Day or a Frank Sinatra record. Plain ordinary postcards of London or Paris or Rome will sell. The tourist is apt to think wistfully of all the everyday things he could have stocked up on and unloaded to eke out his few roubles. But men's clothing is the best bet. Women's clothing should be but isn't. There has never been much of a market anywhere for second-hand women's clothes. Whether it's that fashion changes so, or that they don't have the wearing qualities, or what, the market is small.

An Australian (male) tour member, walking down Nevsky Prospect, remarked meditatively: 'I don't see them all looking enviously at you women because you're better dressed.' I hadn't been watching, but then I started to notice all the stares, the critical appraisal from head to foot, the glances lingering especially on hair and shoes. We were cased thoroughly everywhere — we stuck out like sore thumbs. After a couple of days we too could spot a Westerner a block away — a Western tie, Western trousers or haircut instantly exposed either a tourist or high-up Party member. Russian clothes aren't cut properly, and they don't hang properly, and apparently there is an electrical shortage because they are never ironed. Skirts and dresses all seem to be cut on the bias; the men's trousers are all bell-bottomed. Very few men wear ties. Popular women's shoes are the wedge sandal, as worn in the early days of the war, and open-toe strap pumps with heavy heels, and these are always worn with ankle socks, never stockings. I defy any woman to present a good leg when she is wearing pumps and ankle socks. The summer dress is the cheap cotton print, and it never is sleeveless, frontless, or backless. The Western female tourist's scanty garb causes a good deal of comment. We had an English tour member, a ravishing blonde, an ex-model, and a good dresser. When she wore one of her clinging sleeveless numbers she was forbidden entrance to the Hermitage, much to her husband's rage. His Communist sympathies suffered a setback. (The only other museum I have known to be so exigent is the Vatican Museum. The two extremes have more in common than they realize.) I loved to walk a little behind her and drink in the sensation she caused, for she always drew a train of Russians after her, like the Pied Piper. Wife called to husband, 'Vassily, come here,' and damsel to her girl friend. 'What are they saying?' I asked my Latvian room-mate. 'They're wondering, "Isn't she cold?"' she answered shortly. Why should they look envious indeed? Would we look envious if we were suddenly shown fashions of 1980? We would think: 'What curious clothes! How can women bear to go round looking such freaks?' The Russian women's clothes you see in the shops look right out of the prop box of an amateur dramatic society — one that is preparing for *The Boy Friend* — and against the windowpanes are pressed noses of women wishing those visions could be theirs. When that is what they are used to, how could they like ours? They do look enviously at shoes and hair — the appraisal always lingers longest at the two terminal points. Western shoes are of good material and wear longer, they can see that; hair is skilfully cut and the wave can look natural. Russian women, if they are smart, leave their hair in long braids or bound into a bun at the back; the unwise go to the hairdressers who cut and set it into those rigid waves, like a ploughed field, that were prevalent here when permanents first came in.

The Australian, who had been unnaturally silent some minutes, suddenly broke out: 'You know, this is a revelation. This is what women really look like. Take away your cosmetics, your nylons, your styles, your corsets, brassieres, depilatories, deodorants, and this is what you are. I can never look at any of you with the same eyes again. This is basic woman, and it's terrifying.'

'I don't think you should know such words,' I said primly. I would have liked to have some snappy rejoinder, but there was none. It's true, men aren't so dependent on fashion. Russian men have a generally unkempt look, and I think there must be a shortage of razors or shaving brushes, and their trousers may be bell-bottomed, but they don't look creatures from another era like the women. Of course so many of them are in uniform. (A Petersburg guide-book of 1860 comments on the number of uniforms even then, and says that one-tenth of the males are in uniform. Every service had its own livery, from

195

diplomatic to engineering.) The higher the rank, the better the material for the outfit and the smarter the cut. The only well-dressed males you see are officers — a considerable incentive to progressing in the army, you would think.

As a matter of fact, I thought Russian men were rather sweet. They offer women their seats on the subway. It's very agreeable to enter a crowded subway and have a line of Soviet males spring up, and I often think of it as I sway up Yonge Street at five o'clock. Male acquaintances don't respond at all well to hearing about it. 'Whatsamater? You one of these commies or something?' they inquire nastily. We all know that the more legal rights women have, the less likely they are to be offered seats. In Spain and Portugal I was always given a seat; in Italy usually; in Germany sometimes; and in France, Britain, Scandinavia, and at home, never. I had expected that in Russia, the land of complete equality, courtesies between the sexes would have disappeared completely, but not so. It was always the man who opened the door, carried the parcels, the baby, and the umbrella. I saw an impeccably dressed officer standing in the subway, his Ivor Novello profile turned away remotely. Clutched to his bosom was an enormous pink paper parcel bound in string. No Guardsmen's rules here. It may not always be so, and it may not be so outside the cities. In the Park of Rest and Culture I saw among the cartoons put up to inculcate manners and morals in the citizenry one showing a subway car's population of males all buried in their papers on the entrance of a parcel-laden woman. My visit may have coincided with a courtesy campaign at its height. If so, I am very grateful.

And whatever the Soviet women may look like, they always seem to be knee-deep in men. ('Sex is a wonderful thing,' commented the Australian.) I kept thinking repeatedly of all the intensified press agentry directed at the North American female drumming the cult of attractiveness; of all the teen and pre-teen advice columns that swamp her from the time she is old enough to read: 'Use this shampoo, this nail polish, or you'll never get a date. Wear this off-the-shoulder, learn to dance the mambo, smile, smile, take an interest in football or you'll never, etc.' The great Or Else hangs over our girls like a cloud of Mum mist. How rewarding if Elizabeth Arden et al, were all dumped in Russia to be shown than even when their products are taken away, it all goes on just the same. How relaxing to see that all you really need is to be female.

Since a Soviet girl has to work all her adult life at a job outside the home, it is hard to see why she should rush into marriage. The Western girl always has before her the fond hope that after the wedding she can retire from the office and sleep in for a change, but a Russian girl knows that she is only adding housekeeping and childbearing to her chores. A husband no longer represents economic security. Perhaps under these circumstances the Russian male has to hump himself to gain her favour, and if anyone has to fret about attractiveness, it is he. Some of the tour's women and myself, with an interpreter, visited a hospital in Leningrad. There were only two males on the medical staff (over sixty per cent of Russia's doctors are women; men right now are channelled into more 'essential' professions, engineering and technology) and we enjoyed ourselves talking to the women, many of them married and with children. One of our Englishwomen, a trained economist, said 'We envy you,' and went on to explain the obstacles in the path of a woman in her country who wished to advance in her profession, though married and with a family. She herself had had to give up working, though she hoped to go back to it when the children were grown. 'But what do you do, then?' asked a doctor when this had been translated. 'Oh, stay at home. Play with the children. Take them to the parks. Make their clothes; put up curtains. Go shopping . . .' our woman answered apologetically. After the interpreter did her work there was a silence. I never saw two groups of women look at each other with such mutual envy.

I had read about the Soviet Union before I came that there were never any evidences of the tender passion to be observed. I knew this would be nonsense when I read it, and so it proved to be. I'm sure if we arrived on Mars and there were any sort of animate life on that planet, there would be mating couples lining those canals. Reporters who talk about the cold, dour, sexless life of the Russians must be wearing blinkers or travelling about in the dead of winter. A second thought would reveal how absurd such statements are anyhow. Where do they think all that increasing population is coming from? Leningrad in the summer is a city of lovers, rivalling Paris. The city is con-

structed for it, with the river, the embankments that have been promenaded grounds for centuries, the many canals, the bridges to lean
over, the fifty-some parks (we were told), and the broad tree-lined
avenues. The parks have double lines of thigh-high hedges ideal for
the purpose. I can't see park commissioners here getting away with
it. As in a southern city, the populace is in the streets all night, prom-
enading up and down the Prospect, talking and sometimes singing.
At this time of year there is only an hour's dark, and about the time
the sun comes up again everyone drifts home to bed. This is a short
and lovely season and no-one wants to miss any of it: they can sleep
in the winter. I was astounded at the difference of Leningrad's way
of life from that of Helsinki, at the same latitude. The Finnish capital
drops dead at ten, and the streets are deserted. This has always been
Petersburg's way: the late supper, from ten o'clock on, and then the
fashionable promenade down the street and out to the harbour or
the Strelka on Vasilevsky Island to watch the long sunset, richly
beautiful at this time, when the sun's dying rays fill all space with
subtle gradations of light, bringing out the pale green of the Winter
Palace and then eclipsing it; turning the waves black and then light
and then black; flashing into piercing life the gilded spires of the
Admiralty and Peter and Paul. Ways of life change very little and
successive governments fail appreciably to alter the pattern. Now the
aristocratic carriages no longer set the pace and the court coachmen
in scarlet liveries do not inject colour into the mass of uniforms. Some
parks that were private are now public, but the same entertainments
proceed. In the big Leningrad Park of Rest and Culture, much more
attractive than the Gorky Park in Moscow, there are expanses of winding water filled with rowboats (girls energetically rowing, and beam-
ing men sitting back — saving their strength, no doubt, for later on).
There are courts for tennis and volleyball, a stage for singing or folk
dancing, and a soccer field, but the most popular sport is the age-
old one of strolling round with the girl friend. After nine o'clock you
see little rest and, I assure you, absolutely no culture.

Generalizations are always entertaining, and I had read a great
many before coming to Russia, some of which incline me to think
that the writer has never read a word on Russia's part or that he has
never been to any other country. So many of the things reported as

typically Soviet, and probably sinister, are typically northern, or typically eastern, or typically Russian since the dawn of recorded time. The following observations, for instance, I seem to have seen repeatedly:

Russians in the streets always look dour and unhappy.

When they travel, reporters look at people in the streets; when they're at home they don't. Street crowds in any northern city look dour and unhappy. Look at the faces around you when next you go out — ninety per cent look newly emerged from the nether regions. As a matter of fact, Leningrad crowds in the summer look much more animated and effervescent than Toronto crowds.

You hardly ever see children in the city streets.

No, you don't. Westerners are so used to seeing mothers shopping with a small whiner dragging on each arm, or growing boys and girls taking up all the seats in the public transport, that they miss their absence. Modern commentators report that, with all the women working, Soviet children are looked after in state schools from infancy up. I only add that all guide-books on Russian cities, dating back to the 1820s, also remark on the absence of children from the streets. It looks as if Russians just don't approve of children in the streets, and I for one am all for it.

Russians are very silent and secretive and never talk to strangers.

Russians don't talk to strangers who address them in a language they don't know, and neither would you. Also, they won't talk to strangers who start off a conversation by asking them leading political questions that they would be fools to answer.

Russians are very garrulous, especially after dinner.

Russians love after-dinner speech-making, and so do Finns, Swedes, and Norwegians. Finns — my word. I was present at a Finnish end-of-cruise dinner on which occasion the after-dinner speeches took almost three times as long as the dinner. Throughout the north hardly a family meal can take place without every member's standing up and sounding off. It is something that has evolved, I think, to while away the long northern winter.

Russian cities are full of drunks.

I didn't see a single drunk, night or day, in Leningrad, and I was watching keenly. There were one or two in Moscow who might have been drunk, but might equally have been not. A far cry from the hordes that assail the eye and nose in Stockholm, Oslo, Stavanger, London, Glasgow, Belfast, or any other northern city with puritanical liquor laws. To come right down to it, I have never, in any city in Europe or North America, encountered the quantity of drunks I have in Toronto. I have yet to be in Toronto public transport — bus, subway, or street-car — after eight o'clock at night that does not contain at least one drunk. If you don't credit this, start taking count yourself, you Torontonians.

Russian women are dour, hard, and sexless as worker ants.

After I'd been in Russia a week or so, I found myself jotting down: 'Russian men are sweet lambs, kind and helpful and go miles out of their way to show you the place you're headed for. Russian women are hard-faced shrews, narrow-minded, and suspicious of the female stranger.' This sounds like a good generalization, just what is wanted, until I remember that this was exactly my opinion of men and women respectively in Sweden, Norway, Ireland, Scotland, Holland, Germany, Austria, Switzerland, Yugoslavia, Greece, etc. When I recited my jotting to the Australian (male) he was staggered. 'What are you talking about?' he said. 'The men are stolid-faced impassive clots who could watch me sink under the Neva without lifting a finger to help. In any crisis it is a Russian woman who comes to the rescue. They are alert, intelligent, all smiles, and know the answers to whatever questions you ask. You know,' he added dreamily, 'they're beginning to grow on me.' I add also the opinion of a Swede I encountered later who had lived in the Soviet Union for several years. 'A Russian woman has such enthusiasm, loves with such enthusiasm. She holds nothing back; she gives with her whole soul. There is no self-consciousness. After you have been loved by a Russian, all other women seem tame. This was interesting, but I add the rider that I have never known a Swede who was not a pushover for any woman who was not a Swede.

Among those, find the generalization that suits you, and happy hunting.

From *The Tamarack Review* (No: 4, Summer, 1957). Diana Goldsborough, born in Toronto, 1927, is a scholar and traveller who has worked in advertising and publishing.

RIO DE JANEIRO
by Garry Marchant

The Brazil *Herald* was something of a runt of a newspaper: small (16 to 20 pages a day), imperfect, troublesome, sometimes obscene. But it was, after all, the second-largest English language daily in South America (after the venerable Buenos Aires *Herald*, no relation), speaking to and for a thriving, influential English speaking community in the continent's largest, richest country. And we never missed an issue, despite expensive new typesetting computers that didn't work, a semi-literate editorial staff and a Brazilian production staff with the irrepressible irresponsibility of that zany race of people. Every morning, except Monday, the slim tabloid rolled off the presses at 65 Rua do Resende, Rio de Janeiro, sometimes 12 hours late, usually full of errors, often deliberately smutty, but *there*, in its own way a journalistic achievement. I was its editor for close to a year, and I loved it.

It is a typical evening in the *Herald's* seedy editorial office. John, the assistant editor, a mad mystic recently released from the Georgia state prison after serving two years on a drug conviction, is hiding somewhere, smoking a joint. The social editor, Laura, is drunk again, gleefully cursing me from across the desk, rejoicing in her multilingual command of the invective. The Latin American editor, a tall, pale, bland Canadian girl, appropriately named Pamela, is in a tearful tizzy because she has lost all her wire stories. Walter, our sports editor, a large, shaggy American college student, is, as usual, brooding about the true spiritual meaning of life ("I mean, what does it all boil down to?") instead of writing headlines. And business editor Betty, an executive-wife newspaper groupy, is urging my meagre staff to "Screw the paper. Let's go downstairs and get drunk."

The production staff is huddled around a radio in the corner, refusing to work until the Brazilian national soccer team's exhibition game in Europe is over. Two typesetters burst from the computer room to demand, in screaming, rapid-fire Portuguese (a language that I do not understand), that I referee their latest squabble. Government goons hold up production anyway while they censor *Opinião*, a satirical weekly printed at our plant. The computer typesetting machines are spewing gibberish. The rain has put out the connection with UPI, our only source of news. And in a few hours, we have to have a paper out, bringing news, gossip, sports and stock market reports to more than 17,000 tourists and businessmen in Rio, São Paulo, Brasilia and across Brazil. Nine months as a reporter-photographer on small British Columbia weeklies had not prepared me for this.

One year earlier, in 1972, I had returned to Canada after four years of wandering and working around the world. Approaching 30, broke and untrained for anything useful, I took the traditional way out. I became a journalist, the only trade requiring no degree, papers or evidence of experience or ability. If you can do the job, you are a journalist. If you can't, you are fired.

On the basis of an article I wrote for the Vancouver *Sun* about my experience as a malaria control district officer in New Guinea, I got a job on the Powell River *News*. Three months each on the *News*, the Comox District *Free Press* and as Port Alberni bureau man for the Nanaimo *Free Press*, and I felt ready for foreign lands. My wife Janet and I headed south, overland to South America by bus, train, boat and thumb, up the Andes, down the Amazon and across the pampas, stopping for a brief rest in Rio de Janeiro.

Rio is seductive, the beaches inviting, the pace easy, the weather warm, the prices low. We have seen the *Herald* on the newsstands, and decide that it might be good for a job for a few months, giving us the chance to linger in *o cidade maravilhosa* (the marvelous city).

The Brazil *Herald's* editorial office is on the second floor of an old brick building, near the centre of the city. This area, neither classy nor run down, is noted only for the nearby Atlantica brewery and the transvestites who hang around the street corner, bait for rich kids who cruise by in their expensive cars.

And this is a real newspaper office. None of that modern, sissy stuff found in most Canadian newspaper offices now: the carpets, fluorescent lighting and video display terminals, like TV sets, replacing an honest working newsman's typewriter surrounded by mountains of crumpled paper. Old wooden desks form a rough horseshoe at the end of a large, unpartitioned room. A few antiquated Underwoods share desk tops with full ashtrays and empty beer bottles. Torn newspapers and lengths of teletype paper litter the floor, making walking difficult. Ceiling fans shift scraps of copy paper around, but do nothing to cool the stifling evening air. The silence is broken only by an old UPI teletype machine chattering in a corner. Quiet, ashen-faced young people hunch over wire stories or lean back in swivel chairs, feet on desks, reading the day's paper. You just *know* there is a bottle of rye and paper cups in the editor's drawer.

In the centre of the paper junk heap, a long-haired, pale-faced boy of about 20 sits reading wire service dispatches and wiping the sweat from his face with sheets of newsprint. Eric Hippeau, at 21, claimed to be the youngest daily newspaper editor in the world. The son of UPI's vice-president in charge of South America, Eric, a French-man raised in England, speaks French, English and Portuguese. He entered journalism early, worked for the *Herald* for a time, and when the previous editor returned home to Lebanon, Eric stepped in.

Now, he has to abandon career and girlfriend in defense of the dwindling French empire. He has been drafted into the French overseas army in Devil's Island, French Guiana. Eric has the pasty, mushroom-man appearance of one kept too long out of the sun (this in Rio in mid-summer), and I should take the warning right now. I try to picture him, a hirsute legionnaire in kepi and red pantaloons. I sympathize. But about that reporter's job . . .

"We don't have any jobs for reporters. We don't even have reporters. Could you be editor?"

Editor? My brain switches reels from *Beau Geste* to *Front Page*. Green eye shades, fedoras with PRESS cards in the hatband, scurrying copy boys, screams of "Stop the presses," blazing headlines, all-night sessions with the boys at the press club, trading lies about great scoops over large glasses of whiskey and water (no ice). I am hooked. After a lifetime of fighting a successful rearguard action against incipient maturity and responsibility, I grab at the bait like a reporter at a free drink. In a month, I will be managing editor of the second-largest English language daily in South America.

I couldn't speak Portuguese, the only language of all but a few on the paper. I had never written a headline or laid out a news page. I had no real idea how a newspaper worked. Back in B.C., I was the guy who chased ambulances, photographed little league hockey games and covered school board meetings. My takeover would coincide with the paper switching from linotype to cold (computer) type. The paper was constantly short staffed. And what a staff. I was the only one who had ever worked on another newspaper. That qualified me as editor.

For a month, I learned the workings of the paper as assistant editor. Then, to the stirring sounds of *La Marseillaise*, Eric marched off sadly to his year of hell in Cayenne. And I had the *Herald*. January 22, 1973 was an inauspicious start to my career. It was hectic, and there were inevitable foulups, but by 2 a.m., only three hours late (we had worked 12 hours, about a normal day), we were finished. The paper would be on doorsteps and in the newsstands all over Brazil on time later in the day. Except that, while we were sweating out the paper, George Foreman was beating Smokin' Joe Frazier senseless in Kingston, Jamaica, to become the new world heavyweight champion in the second round. And we missed the story.

"It was on television last night," the publisher, Bill Williamson, moaned the next day, with a pained expression that was to become so familiar. "We should have at least mentioned it." My excuse: by the time the fight story was beamed from Kingston to New York (UPI headquarters), then sent back to South America (sports being a low priority item), we were all in the bar downstairs, congratulating ourselves on a job well done. Of course, while we were working on the paper, our building guards and janitors were in the next room, watching the fight on TV. But I am not a sports fan. And nobody told me.

The paper should have been easy to put out. When I started, it was 16 tabloid pages during the week, 20 on Sunday with the *Times of Brazil* supplement. When I left, it had grown to 20 and 24 pages, sometimes more. We carried a lot of canned stuff — comics, Dear Abby, the crossword puzzle (the most popular part of the paper, judging by complaints if we left it out). Since we were forbidden to comment on Brazilian national issues, the editorial page was made up of American columnists — a choice of William F. Buckley Jr., Jack Anderson, Marianne Means or Art Buchwald — and an editorial selected from one of the better Brazilian papers and translated into fractured English by national affairs editor Herbert Zschech, an aged, balding German gnome. A cartoon from Copley, the Californian right-wing news agency, rounded it out. This was the cheapest way to put together an editorial page, and probably suited the biases of most of our readers.

The finance pages had stock market reports and a few stories from UPI. International and sports news came in English, and Latin American news in Spanish over the UPI teletype. Social notes were brought in by a dithery English lady. A gossip column came in Portuguese from another paper, as did most of the classified ads. Other columns arrived in various forms of English. Besides Spanish and Portuguese, we had to translate German English, Hungarian English, Italian English, East Indian English, Brazilian English and English country garden English.

Today, leafing through yellowing copies of that slender journal, I wonder what all the fuss was about. But I remember. There was the staff, a mixture of European refugees, semi-literate North American hitch-hikers, drifters, criminals, dope-smoking misfits, boozers and a few out-of-place college students taking a year off school to travel around South America.

Assistant editor, John, fresh from being a link in a Georgia chain gang, was "into" dope, black magic and an obsessive, and successful pursuit of sex. I had met him earlier, on a banana boat coming down the Amazon, where he was travelling with two Argentinian hippie girls. He was given to posing at dusk, on the roof of the riverboat in his ankle-length *ruana* (Colombian poncho) and leather Brazilian cowboy hat, and to reading Alistair Crowley. John was always excited about the ritual offerings of cigars, liquor and beer, food and burning candles left in Brazil's gutters at night. The story was that no one would dare touch these *condomble* (black magic) sacrifices in this superstitious country for fear of the devil. But they were always gone in the morning so I guess Rio's beggars ate and drank well if hazardously in a cosmic sense.

John couldn't spell, and his English was poor. While he learned eventually the operation of the paper, he had a distressing habit of getting headlines on two stories reversed, so that, for instance, a story on the Miss Universe contest might sit under a head for Disastrous Storm Hits Kansas or Vietnam POW Accord Signed.

Laura, the social editor, was an old-timer on the paper, with almost a year's service. About 20 years old and 90 pounds soaking wet, her pale, beautiful, ascetic face belied a healthy appetite for life's physical pleasures. After a morning of smoking grass at home, Laura would wander into the office with a double cuba libra in hand from the bar downstairs, and drink her way through the night. Chortling and cursing, she would gleefully urge me to partake of porcine fornication. But she was good at her job, so I tolerated her bestial recommendations.

With her strange sense of humour and preoccupation with carnal activities, this delicate English rose caused me constant distress. One of her jobs was to translate the "Rio By Night" column, which came in Portuguese from another paper, into English. The daughter of a high-ranking Reuter executive, Laura spoke Portuguese like a *Carioca* (native of Rio). Rio by Night is typical of the sycophantic rubbish advertising salesmen love, and marginal publications must tolerate to survive. The column blatantly plugged restaurant and nightclub advertisers under the guise of a gossip column. Laura was liberal with her translations, adding low class double entendres, locker room humour, smut and sarcasm. A "Seen dining last night . . ." item came out: "Seen gorging themselves again . . ." The caption "Fill It Up" appeared under a picture of a lady singer clutching a phallic microphone before her large, wide-open mouth. "We are sure she will go down well," the caption added. And, under a picture of a sexy samba chorus line: "Those loin-gyrating mulattas will pop your fly buttons."

Every week or so would find me in Bill, the publisher's, now-familiar office. "Tell Laura to cool it or find somebody else to do Rio By Night. This is a conservative, family newspaper." But the column soon reverted to its style, and I suspect we got away with it only because none of the advertisers or entertainers could read English. Laura is still with the *Herald*, and I see from a recent issue that her style lives on. The caption under a picture of a short man with a big grin, surrounded by tall, voluptuous dancers, reads: "Oba Oba emcee Amador Bendoyan creams gently in the cushiony company of slender mulattas, Beth, Maria Helena and Sandra."

I always suspected that Bill secretly enjoyed the less outrageous columns. He told me once of a furor raised by an earlier contributor to the *Herald*, Dr. Hunter S. Thompson, founder of gonzo journalism. Thompson's snide, insulting report of a speech made by Georgia Senator Herman Talmadge to Rio's American Chamber of Commerce had the business community furious at the *Herald*. "I thought the story was hilarious; luckily I was out of town when it was published," Bill told me. Other early *Herald* staffers included Dawn Addams, who later became an actress, and Tad Szulc, later a New York *Times* correspondent. The *Herald* had no such talent on staff when I was there.

Betty, the stylish, forty-fiveish American executive-wife walked into the *Herald* one day and started working for nothing. Eric hired her; I suffered for it. Betty didn't need the money. She arrived at the office in a chauffeur-driven car, which returned for her in the evening. When we worked late (almost always), the chauffeur would wait, on overtime pay.

Betty wanted to be a journalist. She was, in some ways, intelligent, and wrote a reasonable, housewifey column for the Sunday *Times of Brazil* supplement. She started on the finance pages, mainly a clerical job copying stock market reports from the UPI wire on to a large form for the typesetters. But she had her blind spots, and trying to teach her basic editing consumed many valuable hours. A story date-lined New York, for instance, began: "A freak blizzard here yesterday snarled traffic . . ." So Betty's headline read: "Blizzard Here Snarls Traffic." She would not accept that it was wrong. The headline said the same thing as the story, didn't it?

Besides being a journalist, the big thing in Betty's life was to get a face-lift. (Rio has world renowned plastic surgeons, and friends of our homosexual apartment mate would go in every two years to get their tummies trimmed. It was easier than exercise.) Betty's excitement over her impending rejuvenation was the talk of the female staff for weeks. Unfortunately, like every face-lift I have ever seen, this one failed. Instead of a beautiful, middle-aged face with a few pleasant lines, she ended up with the smooth, shiny skin of a baked apple.

Betty soon turned from journalism to the journalist's disease, alcohol, regularly turning up for work clutching large bottles of Brahma Chopp beer and trying to entice the staff down to the bar for *batidas*. Eventually, she phoned in to say that I was not giving her her big break, and that she quit. I missed Betty. Before the knife job at least, she was a pleasant, pretty face around the office.

Compared to the others, Walter the sports editor was normal, given only to fits of depressed musings over the inner meanings of life. An American college student, he was competent and conscientious, and probably should have been assistant editor. The only other Canadian on the paper, Pamela, the Latin America editor, was a preacher's daughter. Serious, sober and upright, Pamela was out of place in that questionable crew, always losing stories she had translated from the UPI Spanish wire. Chris, an old World War Two U.S. Navy pilot, was chief proof reader and translated the *classificados* into English. He came to work every evening after flying a Link Trainer around imaginary skies all day as an instructor for the Brazilian Air Force. I remember Chris best for lurching over to Pamela at an office party and telling her, in disgusted tones: "You reek of virginity."

I know that Herbert Zschech, the national affairs editor, exists because I saw him twice in the eight months I was at the *Herald*. This broad dwarf in a baggy suit came into the office every day from his farm in the country to prepare the editorial page. He was always gone when I arrived at about two p.m., but his copy was there, waiting. Zschech had been a foreign correspondent for European newspapers before the war, then an assistant to a university professor of ancient Greek language and literature. He started on the *Herald* soon after it began publishing in 1946, and is still there.

Zschech translated editorials from Rio or São Paulo newspapers into tortured prose, his sentences hundreds of words long. Translating his work into English was a major chore. He also wrote a short column, Check and Double Check, funny tidbits of news picked up from the local press or his longtime Brazilian cronies. Usually, they were funny or bizarre bits of Braziliana:

Like the item about the police chief with the unique solution to his state's homicide problem. He ordered his officers to go around the streets at night, collecting all the dead bodies and dumping them across the state line.

Or the bandits who broke into a bank at rush hour, robbed it, then ordered the staff and customers to strip and dance to a samba tune on the radio. The bandits fell over laughing, were overpowered and arrested.

Here is a sample of Zschech's unique style, from July 1, 1973 (this has been edited, but we tried to retain something of the personality). "Smuggler Rui Santos, of Guaruja, São Paulo, got red-hot with indignation on noticing that his friend Josquim kept for himself the money obtained from the sale of a large lot of contraband he had entrusted to him, instead of dividing the profits between them. In indignation, he quite forgot that smugglers are normally trying to stay out of the reach of police. He reported his unfaithful partner in the smuggling business to the police with the result that they are both now under arrest."

And here is another item that apparently amused our national affairs editor. "News item from Fortaleza, Ceara: Hugo de Paiva Bezarra, president of the Motivation Centre which is a service aimed at aiding people in trouble to gain self-confidence and optimism to lead a successful life, committed suicide on Friday."

These were the regulars, but others drifted through. Patrick was a pleasant, Irish law student at an Ivy League university, taking a year off his studies. Despite his education, he was totally incompetent, especially in proofreading, a job we all had. The computers constantly played up, feeding out gibberish like: PARIS upiO Nego$"&u ace talks . . . Patrick would find no errors in this. When I pointed it out, he would say, "Oh yeah, I must have missed that one." Firing Patrick was the toughest thing I had to do on the paper.

We never did have a full editorial staff of eight, probably because we paid $150 a month for a five day week, eight to 10 hours a day. As editor, I was rolling in cruzeiros, earning the equivalent of about $500 a month for a six-day, 60 to 80 hour week. In what was either nepotism or a vicious use of press gang techniques, I hired my wife to work in this sweat shop, thus fortuitously starting her on her own route to journalism.

All our staff members were native English-speaking except Lupi, a Guatemalan Jewish girl who spoke like a normal person but wrote like a sociologist. Our columnists, though, were an ethnic carnival. Armando, an Italian-Brazilian, contributed features about local painters. They were interesting, not badly written by our standards, and since I was trying to increase the local content of the paper, I used everything he gave me. One day, though, I rejected a story about a local boutique owner.

"But I've already accepted the gift," Armando pleaded when I stood firm. "How would *you* like a gift certificate from the boutique?" he went on. "A nice pair of those fashionable platform shoes maybe?" I finally caught on. This, Armando claimed, was the Brazilian way. Every reporter accepted little gifts; they could not live otherwise. Armando had assembled a fine collection of Brazilian original art by writing for the *Herald*. Since the boutique story never ran, I went without those platform shoes. But before I quit the paper, Armando did give me two miniature paintings. I pondered if this was retroactive graft, but before I could resolve the moral dilemma, I had left the country.

Armando wrote a story for the *Herald* about his skydiving experiences, so one Sunday afternoon, I went to a small airstrip outside Rio to take photographs. We flew in a Cessna with the back door and seats removed, me sitting on the floor at the side so that I could shoot the two divers as they left the plane. As we gained altitude, Brazilian madness took over. The pilot, a self-styled prankster, began bantering with the two nervous divers. Amidst great hilarity, he unzipped his flight suit, exposing himself and making rude gestures, finally climbing right out of his seat and crawling to the back of the plane with us, leaving the unpiloted aircraft pitching and yawing thousands of feet above the airstrip. Very funny. Only years later did it occur to me that I had been the only one in the plane without a parachute.

Soon after, Armando disappeared for a few weeks. When he returned, he confessed, sheepishly, that he had been caught in the women's section of a public toilet in the park. He had just been released from jail.

While I could communicate, if not reason, with the editorial staff, the Brazilians were something else. Pele, the country's superjock, once said: "All we are good for is Carnaval, football and making love." I cannot vouch for the love part of this hedonistic trilogy, but I know that Brazilians are better at football and Carnaval than serious labour.

Important soccer games halted all production. No pleading, threatening, coaxing or cursing could drag the staff from a big game on the radio. An announcer's shout of "Go-o-o-a-a-al" for the home town team would trigger instant celebration, laughing, singing and shouting. They would tape up crumpled copy paper for a ball, and play impromptu games, my desk and the teletype machine forming goal posts. A lost game would precipitate weeping, arguing and recriminations. Wake or party, it could last an hour, and there was nothing to do but wait until they were ready for work. In fairness, the production staff normally worked even longer hours, with less pay, than did the foreigners in the editorial department.

For months, we laboured to the background sound of a hammering, relentless samba beat. Tango is the dance of Argentina — sad, serious, the music of men in 1930s-style suits in smoke-filled night clubs. Samba is pure Brazilian — joyful, crazy, impromptu, danced in the streets in a string bikini or, during Carnaval, in expensive, million-sequinned costumes. To be in Brazil during Carnaval is to listen to upbeat cuts of the theme from *Black Orpheus* over and over. The very walls of apartments and offices vibrate to a samba beat.

As Carnaval approached, *blocos*, the neighbourhood samba bands, practised across the street from our Copacabana apartment, at first only on weekends, then for hours daily. Finally, there was no escaping samba music, which cut even through movie theater walls. For me, Liza Minelli sang *Come to the Cabaret* with a samba backing. The madness built up in our office, where an already erratic staff began to lose self-control, singing, tapping out a samba beat and breaking into dances in the middle of important jobs. During Carnaval itself, we had to close down for several days. The celebrations, which have been described as collective dementia, culminated in an all-night parade, with more than 30,000 *sambistas*, *passistas* and *ritmistas* competing for the title of Rio's top samba school. Some purists claim that Rio's Carnaval has been usurped from the black *faveladas* (slum dwellers) by the white middle class, that the true Carnaval is in Bahia to the north, but Cariocas know that theirs is *o Carnaval mais quente do mundo* (the hottest Carnaval in the world).

Even without Carnaval, Brazilians are a boisterous, childlike lot, given to adolescent practical jokes. One evening, things went well and we finished on time, before midnight. Young Cebolla ("Onion," for his wild Afro) patted me on the back as I left the office, as if to say, "Well done, boss." So I went to a local street bar, past the transvestites, for a few drinks. Then I took the long bus ride home, past Flamengo Beach, Sugar Loaf Mountain and Corcovado with the statue of Christ the Redeemer, through Botafogo and Leme to Copacabana, and walked a few blocks to the apartment. Leaning against the elevator, I noticed a rustling, and felt behind me. There, taped to my back, was a large, hand-lettered sign on copy paper. "Velha Bicha," it read: old queer.

Brazil was booming then, and the term, "The Brazilian Miracle," was heard constantly, along with the Japanese and German miracles. But, the locals claimed, theirs was by far the most remarkable economic wonder. The Japanese Miracle, they said, was built upon the resourcefulness and discipline of the Japanese people, the German Miracle on the industriousness and determination of the German people. But the Brazilian Miracle . . . now that was a *real* miracle.

Back at the *Herald*, things were rather less than miraculous. During heavy rains, the line to UPI would often be out, and sometimes the wire service would have its own mechanical troubles. They would phone that wire copy had to be collected at their office, and the beautiful, café-au-lait-coloured *telefonista* with the great legs would scream at me, "Gareeee! Oooo peeeee eeee!" Our old messenger, Teixera, Speedy, would shuffle morosely across town to pick up UPI carbons, sometimes disappearing for hours, leaving us with nothing to do.

The new computerized typesetting machines, out of place in that shabby office, were our real mechanical nemesis. They were faster and cleaner than the old linotypes, true, but no one knew how they worked. When they fed out garble, the operators would sit around for hours, puzzling over the many switches and controls. Sometimes the machines packed in totally. Then, we sent our copy across town to be set by another printer, a slow process.

Eventually, those bugs were worked out. Then, one memorable night, the machine that fed the paper through the developer and fixer packed in, and it was too late to get a technician out to fix it. Our production manager, Igor, a White Russian emigré from Manchuria, worked out a manual solution. He took the cassette into the darkened lunch room, stretched the paper out on the table and swabbed chemicals on with a sponge. It worked, but slowly.

That was a long session at the *Herald*. Early in the morning, we took one of Rio's Volkswagen Beetle taxis home as the sun rose from the Atlantic, lighting the 130-foot statue of Christ the Redeemer, standing, arms outstretched, 2,300 feet above us on Corcovado mountain. *Paulistas* (citizens of São Paulo) say that Christ is waiting to applaud the day when *Cariocas* go to work.

Although the government forbade us to use UPI Brazilian news, some drinking with their bureau chief led to us being fed their Brazilian wire. We removed the UPI credit, and ran everything we could get, usually short crime, accident or human interest stories. This way, we had stringers all over the country for the cost of a few *cachacas*, Brazil's potent national liquor, also called virgin's sweat, frigid mulatta or saint's piss. Some of the racier *cachaca* brand names were Behind the Balls, Cuckold Tamer, Ball Breaker, Super Hot, Cuckold's Consolation, In-and-Out and Masturbation. I look forward to our local LCB carrying these brands.

The deal with UPI almost got us in serious trouble with the censors one day, though, when we reported a story exclusively in Brazil. The ship *Hope*, a sort of floating Peace Corps, pulled out of a northern Brazilian port when, according to rumours, anonymous threats had been made against President Ford's daughter, who was on board. UPI reported the story to the United States (the Brazilians didn't seem to mind what was reported outside the country), and we carried it on the front page — the only paper in Brazil to report it. Secret service heavies had visited every paper in the country, squashing the story, but they forgot about us.

The incident taught me something about media workings. The next day, U.S. papers repeated the story, not as rumour, but as truth, quoting the Brazil *Herald*. If a story is repeated often enough, apparently, it becomes real.

I never ran afoul of the state censors, although they visited Eric once. But we saw them every Saturday night when the political police came down to check over *Opinião* before we could print it, thus slowing our production as well. Brazilian papers displayed characteristic élan in handling censors. When the government first censored front page stories, editors ran the paper with the space blank, letting readers know what had happened. Ordered to cease this practice, the papers would run recipes, poetry, or pictures of flowers on the front page.

The press was forbidden to speculate on a successor to President Emilio Garrastazu Medici, chosen by a military tribunal. It was known months in advance that he would be General Ernesto Geisel, so next to a story saying that a new president would be announced soon, papers would run a picture of Geisel at a ribbon-cutting ceremony or similar function.

Despite the long hours and the frustrations, life in Rio, a *cidade mais linda do mundo* (the most beautiful city in the world), was not without its rewards. On Sundays, I would cross the tesselated boulevards of Avenida Atlantica to sit on the beach drinking cans of *"cerveja, estupidamente gelada,"* beer chilled to stupidity as the hawkers said, and watching the girls from Ipanema in tangas, string bikinis so brief that their wearers must submit to a monthly *depilacao* (hair removal by hot wax).

Rio lives for the four miles of beach within the city and another 13 miles beyond the city limits. It is a centre of social life, sports (volleyball and soccer), love and spiritualism. At night, candlelit *macumba* (a benign, Brazilian form of black magic) sacrifices dot the beach. By day, it is a blatant display of young, and not-so-young, flesh.

Near-naked *Cariocas* are everywhere, on their way to and from the beaches, in the stores and restaurants. Apartments have separate entrances at the back, not for servants but for bathers, and signs on the buses advise those in bathing suits to stand so that they will not wet the seats.

From my apartment window, I looked out across Copacabana beach, jammed with weekend sunbathers. Samba bands practising in front of sidewalk cafés would suddenly move on, still playing, leading dancing beach people in a ragged parade across the busy main streets, holding up traffic. Any on-duty policeman would hold up the cars for the impromptu parade, samba being considered more important than an orderly traffic flow.

Saturday night on the *Herald* saw some heavy sessions when we resorted to the universal balm, alcohol, to help us put out our final, biggest issue of the week. During slack periods, we slipped down to one of the corner bars to stand elbow-to-perfumed-elbow with the transvestites, drinking *caipirinhas* (*cachaça*, lime and sugar) or *batidas*, a potent, *cachaça*-based fruit drink. Later, we took up large, wicker basket-encased jugs of the rough, red wine from southern Brazil, their necks sealed with plaster of Paris. As the night wore on, survivors would fall asleep on the desks, waiting for the last pages to inspect. Some Sunday mornings, I went down to the newsstand to confirm that we really had put out a paper the night before. But we never got truly ripped until we had pretty well finished, only having to check the last pages, and the paper was always there.

There was a greater feeling of being out of it in South America. While we sweated the *Herald*, Nixon was trying to wriggle himself out of Watergate and the U.S. out of Vietnam. Africa was not the dark continent; this was. The only significant Latin American news during my stint on the *Herald* was Juan Peron's return to a shoot out at Buenos Aires airport, and the bloody coup that killed Salvador Allende in Chile. Three weeks later, I was arrested in Antofagasta for taking pictures of a military installation — an empty beach — but the *Herald* was already two weeks behind me then. The *Herald* got to be easy. The machines stopped acting up. The staff, drunk or sober, football game or not, could do their jobs. Even John was learning to spell. We began to get out of the office by midnight, and the paper had fewer mistakes. People even started saying nice things about it.

So, reverting to type, I quit and hit the road again, heading East to Hong Kong and new experiences. The previous editor returned from Lebanon, and I gave the paper back to him. It was tough. Even responsibility can be habit forming.

From *Vancouver Magazine* (1974). Garry Marchant, born in Winnipeg, Manitoba, 1941, has travelled in 200 countries and writes in many magazines, including *Brides*. Before alighting in Vancouver, he knocked about the Pacific for years.

CORNWALL
by Norman Levine

There were these four gulls on the side of the roof across the street. And they kept up a continual noise. Sometimes they just opened their beaks and whined and took a few steps forward and whined again, while another would mutter a few sharp tongue things I used to do on the trumpet. Then, for some unknown reason, one of them would start to honk and let out a full-throated piercing sound, its whole body shaking. That went on for a few seconds, and back to the muttering. Two of them seemed to be muttering in a kind of conversation. Until again the piercing sound, the background mutter, and the pitiful faraway whine.

It was too hot to close the window. So I kept it open. The Back street was on the level with the front door, and the window faced a pink-painted cottage where a couple, with two small boys and a grandmother and grandfather, were down. Last week it was a honeymoon couple — this time three generations. They quarrelled outside. They scolded the children. The gulls. The cars going by a matter of inches from the window, blotting out the light. The passing visitors with their portables full on. I decided to go out and to try and work at night.

I went into Connie's Expresso and took a small blue table by the door. On the walls were blown-up black and white photographs of the harbour and the front. They were taken some time ago when the place was still full of fishing boats. A young girl in a green smock stood behind the counter. She was tall, heavy-set, and with an oval expressionless face. A portable radio beside her played uninterrupted music. I had a hamburger and gave the girl one and six. Then a cup of black coffee, and that came to another sixpence. The sign

217

behind the counter said, American Style, but there wasn't much meat
in the hamburger, and the onion was fried. Still, the coffee was strong.
I had another cup, and smoked a Gauloise, and looked out.

The water in the bay was a thick, deep blue. The sun brilliant.
It showed up the fields on top of the cliffs of the far shore; the lower
line at the bottom of dazzling sand; and the white lighthouse in the
bay, a milk bottle with a camera stuck in its throat. Two French
crabbers, anchored beside each other in the deep water, faced the
wind. But there wasn't much of a breeze. Tourists walked by the open
door. In shorts, slacks, sandals, bare feet. Holding hands. It was all
very informal. No rush.

A couple of tourists came into the restaurant. An elderly man and
a slightly-stooped woman. He had a cane and a small grey moustache.
He went to the counter and brought back some tea and wholemeal
biscuits to their table.

'Is that your radio?' he said to the girl.

'Why,' she said, 'is it too loud?'

'No,' the tourist man said.

'I bring it here for company. At home I never listen to the radio —'

'Where do you live?'

'In the Back Road.'

'You don't know how lucky you are,' the tourist man said. 'You've
got the most beautiful bay in England and the finest sand beaches
— This place is wonderful —'

'I think it's a dump,' she said. 'It's so boring. There's nothing for
us to do —'

'Have you been to Land's End?'

'No.'

'And you live here?'

'Born here and lived here all my life.'

'You'll have to be a good girl and take a look at Land's End.'

'I'm the eldest of nine,' the girl said, 'I have to look after the
others —'

'Like a mother,' the tourist woman said quietly to her husband.

They dunked the wholemeal biscuits carefully in the tea. Then ate
the biscuits. Then drank the tea.

'But I wouldn't like to live in St. Just,' the man said. 'You know
St. Just —'

'No,' she said, 'I've never been to St. Just.'

'— it's a very sinister place. We went over this morning and we met a girl there. She told us she leaves St. Just every Friday and comes into Penzance and stays in Penzance until Sunday night —'

'Penzance is a bit of a dump.'

'Would you like to go to London?'

'It's funny,' the girl said, brightening up, 'I've never wanted to go to London. The place I'd like to go is South America. Ever since I was a kid I've always wanted to go to South America.'

'That's some way from here,' the tourist man said.

The girl smiled. 'I guess I'll just have to marry someone with lots of money.'

I finished my coffee and went out.

It was very pleasant along the front. Cool air, the smell of the sea, and so much for the eyes. I walked by the stone building of the Salvation Army, Woolworths, the Shore Café. Music was leaking out of The Harbour Amusements, and at its entrance a boy, twirling a stick, gathered pink candy floss from a machine while a child rode a wooden rocking horse for sixpence. In front of Literature and Art, tourists were picking their way through the picture postcards. And others were picking their way through earthenware pots, mugs, soup-bowls, small stone lighthouses, souvenirs, at the Arts and Crafts. But there weren't many in the stores. They were lying on the dry sand of the harbour; they swam and splashed and stood in the clear shallows; they sat in striped deck chairs, green benches, along the wharf. The clock in the church, by the urinal, struck eleven. And the sun came down brutally. It caught the glass of thousands of windows facing the bay; the bright paint of the cottages and hotels; the stone of the terraces; the two piers; the blue water, and the close-cropped greens, browns, yellows, of the far shore fields. Everything appeared so vivid and sharp, as if all these colours had just been freshly washed. I walked along the harbour, by the rails. The tide was going out. It left the fine shell sand ribbed, and in the depressions bits of glistening water. Young seagulls, their feathers speckled brown and white, were foraging behind the outgoing tide. One had found a dead spider crab, and poked at its underside.

On the long granite pier a row of parked cars was being cooked and at the pier's end a small boy sat fishing, watching the water.

Seaweed clung to the granite sides — small hands severed at the wrist — below the water line they waved lazily from side to side.

I left the harbour at the slipway, walked up a narrow passage, by another car park; past a Methodist Chapel that was now an Art Gallery; past white and cream-washed cottages with Bed and Breakfast signs. And I came to the beach. Quickly, I went down the hot stone steps, and on to dry sand. At an empty stretch I took off shoes, socks, shirt, trousers — I had on swimming trunks underneath — rented a surfboard from the Beach Stores, ran across the hot dry, then damp sand, through the warm pools, until I came to the shallows. The water was cold. I waded in, ran some of the breaking water over my arms and chest, and as the next breaker came in to spend itself out, I plunged in. The shock of cold water lasted briefly. And when I stood up I no longer thought the water was cold. I went further out with the board, half-swimming, to get to the deeper water. At chest-high I stopped, my back to the incoming waves. I let two go by. They broke before they reached me, and I leaned back into them. But I took the third. I watched it gather behind me, the dark line in its upper-part advance, then, leaping on to the board and kicking my legs I was lifted and flung downward — felt the wood smack into the stomach, as I remembered from childhood jumping on a sleigh to go down a slope — and pointing downward I was carried in a glistening white cascade as the wave broke around me and water crashed into my face and eyes. When I felt the wave losing some of its momentum I twisted my body and the board from side to side so that I went through the water like a drunken driver sending patches of spray from one side then the other as I curved into the shallows, skimmed along in a few inches, until I was deposited on to the wet sand.

I went back and forward like this for about an hour. Sometimes without the board. Just arms and legs stretched fully out, and as the wave carried me forward I rotated my hands once over, and my body followed, turning round and round in the salt water until I sank. Then, pleasantly exhausted, I walked back across the sand and lay down to be dried by the sun.

It was a magnificent beach, the finest I had ever seen. An elongated C, lying on its side, facing the breakers, the Atlantic, and the horizon. Within it was a smaller C made by a line of dead seaweed and pebbles that the high tide had left. The sand within this smaller C was a light

tan colour, and damp. A few boulders were embedded in the wet
sand. The outgoing tide had made small pools around the boulders.
Children were playing happily in the pools. In a long strip that curved
the entire length of the beach, in between the two Cs, people lay on
hot, dry sand; or in the shallow crater-like holes they had scooped
out of it.

The sun was beginning to burn. I turned over on my back and
caught a light breeze. It ruffled the flags of England, Wales, Scotland,
Ireland — on top of sandcastles that a tanned boy, his hair the colour
of linen, had made not far away — and the seagulls' feathers he had
stuck in others. And brought with it the sweet smell of suntan lotion.

Just above me, on the slope of earth above the beach, was a
cemetery. Around me, scattered in clusters on the strip of hot sand,
families were stretched out. Surf boards were standing upright, stuck
in the sand, by their heads. The sun caught the boards and reflected
their white tops. They looked like the tombstones on the slopes.

I told myself, I must remember that and use it some place. But
I should have given it more thought. For the kind of images that one
finds in a particular place are not as accidental as they appear. Surf
boards around people lying on the sand getting brown — tombstones
in a cemetery. Still, at the time I wasn't interested in this place. I
was living in a book I was working on, set in winter, in Montreal.

For the next two weeks of July I did this walk and swim every
morning. I would wake up around nine-fifteen, just after the postman
went by, have a light breakfast, then make up a list, do my shopping, wander around, have a coffee at Connie's, go surfing, then sun-
bathe on the beach. And in the afternoon, on the beach again, then
more wandering around. In the evening I worked until half-past two.

By the beginning of August I felt I knew the place and it gave one
a wonderful feeling of possession and confidence. From the height
of the terraces or the bus stop it looked picture postcard but with
a 3-D view; a small bent finger flung out from the mainland into
the Atlantic with the inside of the finger, the harbour, and the outside, the beach. Then into the place — everyone walked on the road
— a kind of valley with a lot of tight little streets and condemned
cottages (with outside water taps and soapy water stagnant in the
gutter) that were bought by tourists who came here with their savings
to live out their lives, and pushed the locals into the council houses

221

on the outskirts. There were brass-piskies, brass-galleons, for knockers; and low ceilings, and narrow stairs that went straight up soon after you opened the door — the double doors like horse-stables — and outside pipes painted to look like varicose veins. Castrated cats sunned themselves in the middle of the streets. And budgerigars were kept in cages. And as you walked on various levels it appeared all angles with small turnings off, dead ends, and narrow connecting tunnels. It reminded me of a doll's house. Except for the outsize barn shapes of the Methodist and Wesleyan chapels.

Then at dusk. Watching the long sunsets on the beach. When the wet sand was flaked pink and the pastel colours of the French crabbers, going across toward the shelter of the bay, were caught by the last rays of the sun. And later. The front lit as a stage set; lit from the inside like so many pumpkins. And in the dark water of the harbour the long brilliant scratches of yellow, green, faint-red, white, from the streetlights and the cafés' neons. And still later. After midnight. Standing at the end of the pier. The moon out. The water sparkling. And I could hear the French sailors talking to the crabbers out in the bay.

When it rained the Scala (you could hear the soundtrack outside) and the Royal had line-ups. The tourists huddled in raincoats on the beach, stood by the rails or in the narrow doorways, looking miserable like a lot of wet birds. I tried the library. It was small, drab, but not gloomy. The books were so old that it became a kind of grab-bag. For the titles were rubbed out with use and neglect so that picking a book you didn't know whether it would be *The Gun Shy Kid*, or a first edition of Kirby's *Golden Dog*, printed in Montreal, with illustrations, falling to bits.

Then there was the morning exodus from the Bed and Breakfast places. Entire families came down the various slopes that led to the beaches carrying picnic lunches, plastic beach-balls, portable radios, towels, flippers, paperbacks, surf boards. And returned, tired, the same way, at dusk. Then dressing up for the night, sunburnt and tanned, they promenaded around the front, Fore Street, the two piers, the Back Roads, the Island, went into a crowded pub, a café, a restaurant. . . .

It was very pleasant for a while to just wander around and mix with people who were here for the avowed purpose of doing nothing.

I have gone into this place at some length as it is this place, as much as anything, that is responsible for what happens. It was, at first, so colourful and remote, and so un-English that I didn't think I could ever become bored with it. But I did. And it didn't take so very long.

For all its magnificent scenery, and sunshine, I began to miss people. It wasn't enough, I found, just being surrounded by tourists. I would wake up on a beautiful hot morning, a blue sky, hardly a breeze, and walk to the harbour. And watch. . . . But for all the buoyancy, the jazzed-up activity, the gaiety of the outward appearance, there was so much inertia to the place. You didn't have to do very much. The landscape did it all so brilliantly and monotonously.

And I was tired of seeing the same kind of person around me. Every two weeks a new batch would arrive. And you could trace the way their paleness and enthusiasm disappeared. It began on Monday morning buying postcards, writing them on the green benches of the front. Then soaking on the sand. By the third day their determined gaiety would have taken in an uneventful trip 'around the bay'; or 'to the lighthouse'; or 'to see the seals.' More soaking in the sun. And at night wandering through the streets all eyes and comments about the smallness, the quaint cottages, the cobblestone streets with names: *Virgin, Teetotal, Salubrious.* And in the second week buying presents from the bric-a-brac shops along the front. And then a sudden flatness when they realized that, apart from what they had already done, there was little else for them to do. So that in the last few days they were looking forward to leaving this place for 'home.' Boredom is such an essential part of a seaside town.

I began to spend a great deal of time in The Harbour Amusements playing the pin-ball machines, when I could get a free one. I enjoy the colours, the balls moving, things lighting up, the sput-sput noises. Once you get a ball going there is something inevitable about it.

Perhaps it was because my writing wasn't going. I just lost interest in the book on Montreal. I could no longer become concerned with the antics of my hero, an optimistic Irish immigrant trying to survive his first Canadian winter.

At night I sit by the desk until my eyes become watery, and I get sleepy. I listen. The surf on the beach. Just one steady noise. The car have stopped. The lights have been turned off. No sound, except the sea. I go out along the Back Road to the beach. The breaking waves, white scars in the dark. They gash the black in several places. The gashes grow wider. They join. One white line the length of the beach. Then I come back. Go up the stairs. And to bed.

I tried all sorts of devices to snap out of this lethargy. I tried waking up extra early one morning and walked along the deserted front. But all that happened was that the gulls seemed extra loud. I saw several labourers walking to work, gas-mask webbing slung over their shoulders. And the slap-slap of water against the tied boats in the harbour sounded like bacon frying. Then, tired, I watched the sunrise coming from behind the towans, over the bay. A sleepy policeman stood by the rails and watched it as well.

I tried going out with a few of the remaining Cornish fishermen. But they were old men, suspicious of my intentions. In any case the novelty of the physical act soon wore out — it was a kind of slumming.

In a moment of desperation, on a rainy morning, I went and had my ears syringed. Small, hard, purplish lumps came out with the warm water. And then to hear the resonance of one's voice. I went out, talking to myself, and listening to the sound of my voice, the different sounds the rain made on water, asphalt, wood. The wonderful sound of a car's engine, the sound of tires on the wet surface. And in Connie's hearing conversation all around me. Then back to the cottage. Hearing the clock in the room. The sound my shirt made as it crumpled. The rifle shots of my typewriter.

I found I would wake up and have to give myself small destinations in order to get through the day. And there were mornings I used to wake up with nothing to look forward to except perhaps a letter.

In the end it was this overwhelming boredom of the place and the tourists that made me seek out the people who actually live here. I don't want to sound self-righteous about this, for I owe them a great deal, but at the time I didn't realize that I was the one being used.

They needed me as much as I needed them. For they suffered from another kind of boredom. And the way the residents fought theirs was by having parties.

There was a party of a kind every night but the main ones were on Friday and Saturday. They began at the Sloop. One of the most uncomfortable pubs I know when it is crowded. You stand in the narrow passageway and people brush against you and drinks get spilled. Before closing time bottles are bought and everyone makes his way to wherever the party is given. If you were a stranger and bought a bottle, you were invited back.

There was a wonderful feeling of comradeship, a kind of fantasy of brotherhood. People came down and were what they wanted to be. If someone called himself a writer or a painter, then he was that, and accepted as such by everyone. There was no examination of credentials. The bait was the sea, the peeling off of clothes on the beach, the three hundred miles from London, the Mediterranean colours; and a lot of people, like myself, anxious for some excitement. These were the people Bill Stringer met at the round of parties in the summer of 1959. Abe and Nancy Gin — Baby Bunting — Rosalie Grass — Jimmy Stark (whom everyone called Starkie) — Hugh and Lily Wood — Albert Rivers — Carl Darch — Helen Greenway — Nat Bubis — Oscar Preston. As the professional writer he took pride in being, he had them down for characters that he would some-day use.

From *Why Do You Live So Far Away?* (1965) by Norman Levine. Born in Ottawa in 1923, he grew up there, leaving Canada as an adult to spend many years in Britain. He is widely known as the author of sensitive short stories.

MOROCCO
by Kildare Dobbs

My contact here is a Canadian I have never met, a friend of a friend. We have corresponded, but I have found it hard to get some feeling of the man from his letters. Yet I have been relying on this unknown stranger for information.

I tell the guide his address.

The man looks blank. I repeat it. Suddenly he shows his teeth in a smile of comprehension. He corrects my pronunciation, rolling the R like a kettledrum. I recall that there are no vowels in Arabic.

Then, in his careful French, the guide explains that Sandman lives in the Medina. Why had I imagined him in the French quarter, with its fountains and boulevards?

We have to drive some three kilometres. The guide thinks he knows Sandman. A tall man who always wears a Basque beret?

I have to explain that I don't know. I believe Sandman is blind, that's all I've gathered. The guide — his name is Iqbal, a dignified Moroccan in white djelaba and cap — looks blank.

He directs me into a narrow lane thronged with veiled and hooded figures, jeering children, bicyclists, donkeys. I am in fear of killing someone. Iqbal waves me on. Go ahead and kill them, he seems to be saying. When it gets too narrow, we leave the car, lock it, and plunge into the pungent alleys of the Medina. This part of Marrakesh cannot have changed much in ten centuries.

The door tells me nothing, with its iron knockers and studs. Merely another door in the blank walls that loom like ochre cliffs. A smiling Berber woman opens. We enter through a dark lobby furnished with a bicycle, a broom and a bucket, and immediately are in the courtyard with its fountain and trees, its brilliant glazed tiles and, in a shady corner, a low stone bench with dark blue cushions.

Sandman advances with his hand out, a smallish man in dark glasses, already parched in middle age like a dried apricot. He wears nondescript shirt and slacks, his left arm loosely wrapped in an elastic bandage. He greets me in an accent that's still Canadian after twenty years of exile.

As we sit down on the cushions with the guide I see behind Sandman's glasses that he is not only blind but without eyes. A war wound, he explains later. There is, of course, a small pension. I can't decide whether Sandman is intentionally bearded or whether the scattered stubble on his ruined chin is the result of neglect.

After a second Berber servant girl has brought glasses of milky coffee on a brass tray I get around to what's on my mind.

"How to find a house? Yes, I'll tell you about that in a moment. I was coming to that."

I feel a vague disquiet.

Later on he explains that he has taken the liberty of committing me to hiring a guide at three dollars a day. "Same rate the official guides get, but they're all crooks. Abdu's perfectly honest. He's one of the dancers from the Djmaa el Fna — the big square in the Medina, you know."

A dancer. I am beginning to get the picture.

On my second visit Sandman is wearing a djelaba. A young Moroccan in a straw hat is filling the tiny bowl of his pipe from a round box. The dancer. An innocent, negroid face marked with tattoos. We shake hands.

"Smoke, Wilfred," the dancer says, putting the long pipe in Sandman's hand.

The master says something in Arabic. Then to me, "You smoke *kif*?" And after the slightest pause, "Everyone else does."

"Not really."

I tell him I know very little about it.

Sandman says that Moroccan *kif* is marijuana cut with green tobacco. It is illegal to sell marijuana, but not to possess or use it. The police are tough, however, about the green tobacco, which is contraband. The marijuana, which one buys dried on the stalk, costs the equivalent of ten dollars a kilo. A Moroccan pipe holds about half a teaspoonful of the cut mixture. After two or three puffs the smoker turns the pipe over and blows out the ash. This way one can smoke all day, pleasantly high without being stoned. It is a civilized way to use marijuana.

I join civilly with my host in a pipe or two, but it makes me cough.

I am searching for a tactful way to explain that I have not come to Marrakesh for the boys and the *kif*. But Sandman is intelligent. I don't have to spell it out for him.

He is disappointed in me, I think. He senses that I don't really want to live in the Medina. I love these Arab houses but they would not suit my habits or those of my family. For one thing, there is no privacy. Not inside the house, I mean — though the life of the streets is marvellously excluded.

"I know nothing about French-town," Sandman says shortly.

I am looking for a nice bourgeois house in the boulevards.

All the same, I go with Abdu to see whatever is available in the Medina. I suppose my motive is curiosity, mingled with a desire not to offend Sandman.

Abdu, so far as I'm concerned, is a dead loss. He speaks neither French nor English — aside from a few phrases to do with *kif*-smoking — and I speak no Arabic. He leads me to the shops in the Medina where the owners of vacant houses leave their keys with agents. These are surly characters totally unimpressed by Abdu, and even less taken with me. Abdu is supposed to have run down all the clues but at the end of a hard day's trudging through the alleys and lanes, and after many a long wait while keys are hunted down, I have seen only one house — a large decaying edifice with primeval plumbing and dangerously threadbare wiring. After another day I have seen one more, pleasantly tiled and in good repair but without a quiet corner to work. On each occasion I am obliged to pay forty cents for the privilege of viewing — double the standard fee.

Meanwhile Martha, who takes a dim view of Sandman, has been shown eight houses in the French quarter by a villainous friend of Iqbal's, who calls himself Charlie.

One of these houses, a semi-ruinous bungalow in the heart of an orange grove, has seemed worth further discussion. Charlie sits down in the cool garden of our cheap hotel (just over five dollars a day for four of us) and we try to do business. He asks eighty dollars a month with the promise of repairs and certain installations. For example, we insist on a Western toilet; not romantic enough, I think, for one of these footprint jobs. I say the rent is excessive. Charlie says the owner won't discuss anything less. I answer tranquilly that in that case there's no point in further chat. Half an hour later Charlie is saying it might be arranged for seventy dollars. I dismiss this with a cynical enquiry about his commission. At which point Charlie makes the outrageous claim that he will be entitled to ten per cent from myself *and* the owner.

My lecture on conflict of interest sends Charlie away in a rage.

Iqbal appears at once. It was Iqbal who found us this hotel. No doubt he gets a cut from the management. He shows me his grey hairs.

"I am old, *m'sieur*," he tells me. "Like you."

Well, okay.

"*Restez tranquil, m'sieur*. I have a nice little place to show you — in about twenty days or a month . . ."

I visited a couple of real estate offices. A discouraging Frenchwoman, accustomed to deal with the Jet Set. A clean cut Jew, who promises to see what he can find. And I am trying to rest tranquil.

We are strolling on Mohammed V Avenue. A tall figure is approaching half a block away. His straight fair hair hangs to his shoulders.

"Doesn't that look like. . . ?" I am saying to the two little girls.

But my daughters have already recognized their big brother and are running to greet him.

He wears a white Moroccan shirt, tattered jeans, Greek sandals in need of repair. He's thin and could use a bath and shave. Otherwise he's in fine shape. Since we saw him, he has visited Ireland, England, France, Germany, Austria, Greece, Italy, Spain, Morocco. He started with $260 and is still going. He eats everything we give him.

I go with him late at night to the municipal camping. Here the ground is free. There are Germans and French with their cars and caravans. My son owns a tent — a big one he bought for five dollars from a departing traveller. At times there have been as many as six fellow occupants.

When I visit there are a number of kids sitting round the butt of a candle. An English boy, another from Vancouver, two long-locked girls from Berkeley. No one over twenty-five. They hand me the pipe of *kif* and I take a shallow puff or two.

No one is taken aback when my son introduces me.

A South African in a red blanket sits down in the entrance and is introduced. He is treated with ironic tolerance. A speed freak, one of the kids later tells me. They think he is crazy, and perhaps he is. He's a twenty-seven-year-old plumber become the compleat hippy. Right now his eyes are preternaturally bright. He's bombed out of his mind.

He tells us how marvellous it is to have a father sit down with his son and smoke *kif*. What understanding it leads to.

I disclaim any pretense at understanding.

"Why do you smoke?" the ex-plumber demands of the English boy.

"I'm escaping from the world," the boy says, calmly sarcastic.

"If that's the reason you're turning on, man, I'm sorry for you. I'm sorry for you. You want to know why I turn on, man?"

The answer is no. "You're crazy, man," one of the kids offers.

The speed freak can't sit still so long. He sees me shivering, offers his blanket, filled with disinterested love for his fellow man. I decline. He shakes hands and hurries away to shoot more speed.

There's a rumour that one of the speed freaks down in the Medina died last night. An overdose. No one is surprised.

The Berkeley girls tell me they spend their days eating.

My son confirms this. "They've got money. They smoke *kif* all day too."

Food is cheap in the Medina. A bowl of nourishing soup for less than a dime. Bread and sardines and fruit for a few cents. My son expounds some of the arts of travel and survival, reminiscing happily about hard times. A veteran and a tent-owner, he will be leaving soon for Toronto and a different kind of education.

We stroll in the Djmaa el Fna amid the tumult of dancers, storytellers, letter-writers, poets, musicians, acrobats.

"I'll miss all this in Toronto," he muses. He is already saying goodbye.

In my mind's eye I see the faces in the subway, the fruit-vendors in Kensington market, the comfortable men in offices, the wall-to-wall carpets of neutral colour, the young swingers in sports cars, the Iroquois ladies morosely drinking beer on Jarvis Street.

"I suppose so."

Sandman is scornful about the kids in the camping. Cannabis Square, he calls it. No real contact with Morocco.

He, after all, has found what he was looking for.

As for me, I have not yet unpacked my suitcases.

Shores of Africa. White town girded with white walls, scoured clean by relentless winds off the Atlantic. Dark bastions built long ago by Portuguese slavers oppose the surf. On the long white beach to the south the sands are in motion, swirling into dunes.

This is Essaouira. Here foreigners take refuge from the heat of Marrakesh — those not rich enough to jet north to the Riviera. One of the hotels looks moderately comfortable. I, however, have been lent an apartment by Sandman. A dubious favour, as it turns out.

"There's a bed," he promises, puffing *kif*. "And three good mattresses."

True, he also mutters something deprecating about the toilet. (No bathroom, of course.) But this sort of slips by me. I am eager to enjoy everything.

The toilet, which has no seat, is unbelievably filthy.

Recoiling, I hurry down into the windy street in search of Ajax, a brush, disinfectant. Africa confronts each with his own heart of darkness. Me it unmasks as the classic anal compulsive. I scrub and scrub.

Suddenly there is no water. I tug furiously at the chain without result. I even hit the cistern a blow with my brush, a frustrated Moses striking obdurate rock.

The shopkeeper on the ground floor, with his turban, striped robe and patriarch's beard, actually does resemble Moses. But all he can suggest, so far as I can make out above the roar of wind, is that maybe Sandman forgot to pay his water bill and the municipal engineer has cut him off.

In the town hall, soft-voiced functionaries explain, yawning, that at this time of day many sardine factories are using water, the supply lacks strength to mount to the first floor. At five or six or eight o'clock tonight there will be water.

Sandman, you son of a bitch.

Back in the apartment I wait at one of the windows, staring down into the street, or rather alley. It is thronged with windblown figures, the women veiled and swaddled in white bath towels, some with satin bedcovers as additional wraps, the men hooded in mattress ticking.

The gaunt figure of a hippy stalks among them, leaning into the wind, picking his way like a heron.

Around six, water begins to hiss in the cistern.

There is water in the kitchen too. It splashes with a merry sound from the tap. After we have eaten the chicken which we met, so to speak, socially in the market just before its execution, there is water to wash the pots and dishes.

The children get the bed. Lulled by the rushing air, they fall asleep at once. Martha and I lie down on mattresses.

The street is still crowded with groups of men arguing and making speeches. Gusts of their hiccuping lingo surge up with the wind. The wind blows and blows, rattling doors, banging shutters.

From the next house, a woman's cries and sobs alternate with a man's strangled tenor. Someone is beating up his wife, justifying it interminably.

The mattress feels stuffed with horseshoes, kitchen knives, used spark plugs. Luckily nothing alive.

It is true that we are saving the price of a hotel room.

How did the belief originate that cocks crow at dawn? Here, as in other countries where chickens are not yet crammed into batteries, they begin around ten p.m. and carry on through the night. But perhaps nature, even here, is dislocated by artificial light. Or it is a ghostly chanticleer we are listening to, spectre of a dinner.

Around midnight I discover that cistern and tap are dry again.

Knots of hooded figures are still gobbling like turkeys in the street, the young men holding hands. The women are locked away with the household chattels, unavailable as water.

It is no longer the voices of men and roosters that are keeping me awake. It is the belief that in the small hours there will be a brief second coming of the blessed element. If I don't jump to it and collect a supply in basin — and that plastic bucket I noticed in the kitchen — there will be none for the morning.

Slow-witted from fatigue, I go over this plan anxiously. I settle back with a sigh at last.

"What the —?"

My eyes scarred by an agonizing flare of light, I cover them. Martha has switched on the light.

Do I realize, she wonders, that the water will probably return for a short time in the small hours? That if I don't jump to it and collect a supply there will be none for the morning? She has noticed, by the way, a plastic bucket in the kitchen.

I have Sandman to thank for this.

The spectral chicken sings again. *Cook him in a stew.*

Fourteen minutes past three of a windy morning the tap starts to dribble. I crawl out and fill every receptacle in sight.

Precautionary visit to the now gurgling toilet. I am tempted to wake the children. If I had a dog with me I'd give him a terrible thrashing.

There are still men talking in the street.

On the flat roof directly opposite our window, at a distance, that is to say, of about ten feet, a surly-looking character in a fez is staring at the sky.

Nothing, I swear, can keep me awake much longer.

The wind has dropped. I am sinking into unconsciousness. It will take Gabriel's trombone to rouse me.

But that, too, vindictive Providence holds in reserve. If not the trumpeting archangel himself, the next most unwelcome sound, shaped in the brass throat of a Moroccan muezzin.

None other than the type in the fez, who has been waiting for the moment when a white thread can be distinguished from a black one. Now it has arrived, he aims his mouth straight at us. Lungs of leather expel the most resonant cries I have ever received at a range of ten feet.

"LAH U AQBAR! LAH HU AQBAR!"

God is great indeed, manifest in the greatness of his creature the Arabian voice. There is no God but this God. Never was tautology more unanswerable. The bones of my head are caving in.

From minarets all over the town voices are crying against the dark. Come to prayer, come to salvation. For the faithful the night is already over. And soon the sun, over Africa, will come forth as a bridegroom out of his chamber — that is to say pale, hollow-eyed and feeble from lack of sleep.

No wind today. Flies buzz from their hiding places to take over the town. Everyone is on the beach. Crowds watch while muscled youths in swimming-trunks twist and jerk nimbly at football. Arab ladies, fat white cocoons, waddle to changing-booths to reappear — not so much changed as metamorphosed — as slim girls in bikinis.

The ocean, smooth as milk, recedes into warm fog. Seaward, towers and battlements of the island loom vaguely. The air is hot and humid. I have a sense of hallucination.

I plod barefoot along the shore, the wet sand resisting the pressure of my feet with an equal and opposite pressure. I all but stumble over Alex, the English boy who hitched a ride with us from Marrakesh. He is basking in the sand.

He smiles up at me, blinking.

That wild look of his could be misleading. Beard, medusa locks, travel stains are hippy uniform. Quite the form, in fact. Carelessly arranged teeth are British as Enoch Powell. Alex is eighteen now. By the time he's my age, he'll rate a knighthood for services to alienation. By his own account, he has never known hardship in his young life. There's at least as much of Baden Powell as of Aldous Huxley in his quest for discomfort.

All this runs through my mind quickly and vanishes. I like Alex. He is preoccupied with the notion of a new aesthetics. It came to him in the enhanced sensibility of an acid trip.

He invites me to his camp for a cup of coffee.

We walk southward along the sea.

Alex wants to know which ideas of Marshall McLuhan's I consider valid.

Modesty, or something in the nature of table manners, forbids me to choose. One accepts the nearest. But this kind of answer, I realize will not do. Stooping slightly under the burden of imputed scholarship, I become, for a moment, the don. What, I wonder, does Alex mean by valid?

Alex is pleased with this. He smiles and, with the faintest suggestion of parody, inclines his head.

The going becomes difficult. We are crossing soft sand. The seafog, softly luminous, presses in on us. Inland a little the beach swells into low dunes marked by camel tracks. We have come about two miles. The walled town, the Moroccan crowds, far behind us, are lost in haze.

We have come to the delta of a small river, three shallow channels straying through mud flats, the farthest shore covered in dense grayish scrub.

Mud oozes between my toes. The river's three skeins, warm as blood, glide silently. Emerald-green weeds, slimy against my ankles, stream in the current. Toads flop on the gleaming flats. The heat is stifling.

Gaining stony ground, we have crossed the river.

Smoke drifts through tangled scrub from scattered campfires. Eyes stare out at us from bearded heads. Their owners lie about, bombed out of their minds, stoned speechless on *kif* or hash. Some are emaciated — victims, most likely, or erroneous dietetics. The hippy subculture is a mine of misinformation on such subjects, with a doctrinal preference for rumours and *scheisshausparollen*.

Of two girls, we see only their long straight hair, the curve of their squatting backs. American kids, Alex tells me. Picked up in Gibraltar by a Dutchman who thought it would be a gas to travel *à trois*. Now the Dutchman is in despair. The girls are such bores no one will take them off his hands.

Why do I laugh? For a'the blood that's shed on earth rins through the spring o' that country. An underworld, a limbo, the never-never land of lost children — Swedes, Germans, Americans, English, Canadians, French, South Americans. And to the eye of middle age, midway in the journey of our life, indistinguishable from hell. For I am running to Purgatory. Yet it is also not impossible Tirnanogue, land of youth, the country of blessed visions. Or it is Cockaigne, fool's paradise, where food painted by Breughel comes ready-cooked to hand. I remember the rabbi whom God commanded to leap into the flames of hell. Obeying with a cheerful heart, he found himself among angels. Heaven or hell, the mind is its own place.

I follow as Alex plunges into the undergrowth. As my own younger self, in another part of the forest, once followed a wounded rhino.

In my mind the beast at bay becomes Sandman. Old man with wrinkled dugs. Wetting his parched mouth with blood and foretelling all.

And as I sit at Alex's fireside among flies and bluebottles, sipping instant coffee with him and Russ, who comes from Hamilton, Ontario, and who is understandably shy of strangers (Hamilton, Ontario has its spies everywhere), I am perversely grateful to Sandman. The worst trips, after all, are the best.

First publication in this form. Born in Meerut, India, 1923, of Irish parents, Dobbs grew up in Ireland. In 1972 he came to Toronto, to become a Canadian, an essayist, editor and author of seven books, and to continue his travels.

GREECE
by Gwendolyn MacEwen

The island is shy and exuberant, savage and fair, bold yet self-effacing. It is a woman in heat, a man in despair, a blonde horse at sunset, a riot of fig trees, a flaking white salt bed, an arid garden of thyme and oregano, a hundred clotheslines full of octopi hung up to dry, a warm night of fireflies and tiny shrimps with burning eyes.

You know you are almost there when you can see the two huge rocks they call 'the doors' rising from the sea ahead of you. The ship stops at a large island; from there, a motorboat takes you across the transparent green water to a smaller sister island. At the dock, the fishermen are spreading out their saffron yellow nets to dry, and women carrying large loaves of bread and plastic bags full of tomatoes and eggplants are laughing at some impossibly funny joke. Bare-footed boys with nutbrown bodies run along the beach chasing something only they can see, and in the café, the old men sip their afternoon coffee, play *tavali*, or simply smoke their pipes and watch the sea.

Suddenly you know that you have been here forever.

Entry One: We are staying in the tiny house where Nikos was born. It is really one room, with a stone floor and white stucco walls; it is very, very old, and it is joined to the row of similar houses which line the 'main street' of the village. It is lit by kerosene lamps — (electricity is still a relatively new convenience on the island) — and we fetch our water from an outdoor tap down the road, in the same kind of redbrown earthenware jugs that have been used for centuries in the East. They look strange, sitting on the windowsill along with the modern blue and yellow plastic ones. Stranger still are the faded family portraits of men with sailor's caps and large mustaches and women

237

with their hair pulled back tightly into buns, who may have had their pictures taken only once in their lifetimes, and who stare in shy bewilderment from the dusty oval frames. Beside them on the wall are snappy colour photos of the younger generation all dressed up in miniskirts and tight pants smiling for the photographers in the cafés or nightclubs of Athens.

An incredibly old woman who used to be the village midwife has greeted us four times today, and asked us each time who we are and where we come from. She is more and more delighted each time we tell her, as though she can't get enough of the novelty of it all. She has an enormous wart on her chin, and she sits outside her door on a rickety old chair, her ancient body doubled over in an almost foetal position, chuckling softly to herself. 'Welcome, welcome!' she cries, each time she sees us. Perhaps tomorrow she'll remember our names, perhaps not. Her failing memory must mean that every day is utterly new to her — almost like being born again each morning.

About an hour ago she drew me close to her and said, 'If you go for *bagnio* (swim) in the sea, it is very good for your skin. It heals all your wounds. But you must take off your rings, or the sea will take them away. Yes, didn't you know? The sea *steals your gold*. . . ! I don't know why, but this is true.'

Entry two: I have met the mayor, the doctor, the school teacher, the man in charge of the post-office, telephone and telegraph system, and the chief of police of the island. I must try to remember their names and faces — (the mayor, I learned, was insulted when I failed to recognize and greet him an hour after we were introduced). The man in charge of the post-office, telephone and telegraph system, sits all day at his desk with earphones, scowling and listening to garbled messages coming from Athens or the surrounding islands, to which he responds with screams of ever-increasing frustration and even anger. He is intensely overworked. The chief of police, on the other hand, is a study in boredom. He has nothing whatever to do, due to the delightful fact that there is virtually no crime on the island, so he spends much of his time sitting in the café clicking his worry-beads, playing cards and waiting, helplessly, for something to happen. We have toyed with the idea of creating a crime for him to solve — something very Sherlockian, perhaps some sort of baffling theft. We would slip cryptic notes under his door, and plant outrageously meaningless clues all over the village. It would become known as The Case of the Six-Legged Octopus, although we still haven't figured out where the octopus comes in.

I also met a sad chap called Christos, whose melancholy, I learned, is due to the fact that he had refused to put his life savings in a bank; he kept the money, in paper, in a hole in the wall. When he went to look at it one day, it was all chewed up by mice. When he took the shreds to the banks, they refused *him*.

But most important of all, I have met Odysseus.

Odysseus has one leg, and baffling skyblue eyes, and when he smiles his shy wide smile, you can see that some of his back teeth are pure gold. He lives in a small room across the street from the church of Saint Nikolaus, and he doesn't like people very much, and that includes larger People like God and the Virgin Mary. He is the butt of a thousand jokes and rather cruel tricks, because he believes absolutely everything anyone tells him. Once someone told him that a beautiful young woman had come all the way from Tripoli to be his bride; he immediately made a journey to another island to buy fancy underwear for his betrothed. But there was no bride. Another time someone told him a queen was coming to see him; she was going to land on the northern side of the island in a helicopter. Odysseus got dressed up and waited, but there was no queen.

Sometimes he goes to the famous *spilio* — the great cave where, some say, the fabled Odysseus met the Cyclops. And there, he sells *gazoza* and orange drinks to the thirsty tourists who pour in to see the gigantic stalactites and marvel at the fabulous caverns. 'Look!' he exclaims, pointing to the boxes and boxes of empty pop bottles outside the cave. 'Look at all that work; I opened them all myself!'

His face, although lined now and weatherbeaten, still wears the clear, alarming expression of the eternal child. Someone once tried to warn him that the people were making a fool of him, but he smiled and shook his head and said that wasn't true, men couldn't be that cruel. Men were good, men didn't hurt each other. They only tried to have fun. He also tried to have fun, but he did it better alone. Sometime later he tried to hang himself on the bell-rope of the church for love of a village girl who could never be his.

'Why does he smile so much?' I asked Nikos. 'He can't have much to smile about.'

'He's just showing off his gold teeth,' Nikos said. 'He went to a dentist a few years ago and had some of his perfectly good teeth extracted so he could have them replaced with gold. The ancient Greeks, you know, used to carry coins in their mouths if they didn't have wallets, but that's beside the point. I just mean that he's literally got his life savings in his mouth. He's smarter than poor old Christos, when you come to think of it. The mice can't get at *that*!'

Odysseus, I love you.

Entry Three: The island is full of churches and shrines — some of them in the village and others nestled in the hills or higher up in the mountains, their domes like the perfect white breasts of the Mother. Each is devoted to a particular saint and the women leave *tama* — votive offerings — in the form of little metal plaques engraved with pictures of eyes or hands or feet, in the hope that the holy powers will intervene in the daily matters of health and safety. Sometimes there are sprigs of wild thyme or sweet basil hung by string or pink ribbon around the ikons. Sometimes there are lonely, dried-up flowers. Authentic Byzantine ikons hang side by side with modern plastic atrocities, and somehow it doesn't matter; holiness is holiness. When I came across boxes of detergents and dustcloths tucked in behind an ikon of the Virgin Mary, I remembered that the Greek word *katharos* means 'clean' or 'pure' both on the physical and spiritual level. Catharsis is a purification of the emotions, according to Webster, and that is holy. Every simple daily act performed with love is holy. I thought of all the women who tended these chapels through the centuries, down on their knees scrubbing the floors, the work itself an act of worship.

Today I went into the smallest and oldest chapel in the village, which dates back to the Thirteenth Century at least. It was pure white and empty, save for two ikons. Only a wooden partition, the *ikonostasis*, flanked by faded embroidered curtains separated me from the area of the Holy Altar, which is out of bounds to members of my sex. *God can get me if He wants*, I thought. *I'm going in anyway*. I proceeded to commit my act of *hubris*.

Behind the partition, in the sanctuary, the small altar was covered with a white cotton cloth. There was nothing else there — except, to my amazement, a flat wooden carving of Christ on the cross, propped up against one wall. It was so roughly done it might have been the work of a child. Curious, I turned it over. There were some letters stamped on the back. It was a piece of wood from a Coca-Cola crate.

I wanted to cry, which is nothing new because I do it all the time, and when I stepped out from the sanctuary my eyes were so watery that I didn't see the little lamp of holy oil which was hanging in front of me. I walked right into it, bashing my head against it, and winced with pain as the burning oil trickled into my hair. I thought I was dying; my scalp was seared with the heat, and I ran outside to find water, anything, to ease the agony.

My hair is still quite oily, even after several shampoos. But it's all right God was not displeased because I invaded the *Holy of Holies*. On the contrary — I have been anointed.

Entry Four: The soft porous stone at one of the beaches is like a lung. When you lie on it, you can hear the sea breathing and wheezing as the waves enter the little sea-caves and force the air up through the holes in the stone. The beach is strewn with dry seaweed like shredded paper. We dove for little black sea-urchins, and ate about a dozen of them, prying them open with a knife, squirting them with lemon juice, and scooping them out of their shells. Then Nikos went down again and came back with an incredible shell creature called a *pina*. This has to be seen to be believed. It is about ten inches long and shaped rather like a thin fan tapering to a sharp point. It never goes anywhere; that is, it gets itself firmly embedded by its tip in the sand on the seafloor and simply stays there forever, waiting for various edible creatures to pass by. It is an incredibly silly and ignorant thing and has, literally, no mind of its own. In fact it can survive only with the aid of one or two tiny shrimps which live inside its shell and act as its brain. When anything that might be food for the *pina* comes floating or swimming by, the shrimp (or shrimps) go down to the tip of the shell where the meaty blob is situated, and tickle it. The blob is thus stimulated to action; the top of the shell opens and the food is trapped inside. Thus, a *pina* without a shrimp is a dead *pina*. It will simply sit there in the sand and starve to death, having nothing that can pass for a brain to inform it to open its shell from time to time. Nikos and I have thought up a new term to describe a witless person — a *pina* without a shrimp. That's a very *in* joke; it sounds better in Greek. But in all fairness to this odd creature, I should add that it's very beautiful when pried open; the inside of the shell is a dazzling world of phosphorescence, almost like mother-of-pearl. The blob tastes good too with a dash of lemon juice and a little *ouzo*.

I was suffering from that bane which travellers the world over know by different names; here in Greece I suppose it would be 'Agamemnon's Revenge.' I looked around for a suitable place to squat; the landscape was utterly bare, and my only hope was a small prickly shrub at the top of a hill. I headed for it with the glazed stare of a person with one mission, and one mission only. A donkey, chewing thoughtfully on something in a field nearby, turned and stared at me as I relieved myself with a sigh. Indignant, I tried to outstare him; it was no use. There was only me and him, the sea and the urgent sun in all the universe.

Nikos and I went fishing off the rocks at the northwest tip of the island. The very best baits are the tiny shrimps which are found in the small pools in the hollows of the rocks, and to catch them you have to cup your hands in the water, remain perfectly still, and wait for them to come. It seems they are somehow fascinated with the colour of the human hand, and when you feel the first funny little tickle of their feet on your fingers you close your hands as quickly as possible and trap them.

Nikos caught interesting fish, but I got nothing except a large, red particularly hideous sea-caterpillar. In fact I caught it three times; I kept throwing the abominable thing back into the sea and it kept taking the bait. By the third time, I think it was too exhausted to try again.

We dove again with masks and snorkels off the rocks. Underwater is a silent, magnified world of rippling light, and waving plants with feathery tentacles, and schools of white fish which gaze at you sideways with frightened eyes, then dart away like magic. I swam out once deeper than I should have; the rocks fell away, and before me was a chasm of terrifying electric blue. I am a good swimmer and I'm not afraid of deep water, but this was another kind of depth. It was utter mystery, timeless, bottomless as the soul itself. I hovered over it for a few moments — then, trembling, turned back towards the rocks. To the left of me something silver and triangular was undulating its way towards me. I clambered up onto the rocks screaming 'Shark! Shark!' Nikos immediately dove in, and came up a moment or two later, laughing, and holding up a small bag made of aluminum foil. Maybe poets should stay away from the sea, and —

> *Perhaps we are only dim figures underwater*
> *meeting for a moment*
> *the perfect eyes of fishes*
> *which encounter us sideways*
> *in luminous surprise*
>
> *And perhaps on land we hang on*
> *to our illnesses which protect us*
> *from the full responsibility of health*
>
> *And perhaps on land we do not have*
> *to answer for our crimes*
> *while undersea we answer*
> *and the sea will answer for itself*

I had a conversation once with the underwater photographer, Ley Kenyon, who intrigued me when he said that there is really nothing to fear in the sea but oneself. Maybe then it was the self which confronted me in that bottomless blue chasm — (no other beast was lurking there.) He had laughed when I suggested that we might all meet one day at Santorini — more properly called *Thera* — where archaeologists are carrying on underwater excavations and recovering relics of a civilization which, according to the Greek scholar Marinatos, was the fabled Atlantis. 'Don't you know how *deep* you have to go to find a single thing?' he exclaimed. And I wrote sometime later:

> *Drop the sails and be silent*
> *There is something here we do not understand*
>
> *As dark as the receding tides*
> *As delicate as the tiny shrimps who*
> *Tickle their way across my hands*

There is nothing to fear in the sea
But ourselves
There is nothing to fear but man

A beautiful shell which I'd placed on a rock heaved itself over the edge in a kind of crazy suicide attempt, then began making its way back to the sea. I had forgotten that shells had live things inside of them; I had forgotten a lot of things. I was gaily swimming along close to the beach, imagining that I was Cousteau, when a shimmery, transparent jellyfish came floating along towards me. It was a bubble of living light; I had to have it. Nikos was jumping up and down and crying 'No, no!' just as I cupped my hand around the creature and received a devastating sting as it went poof and died on me, a deflated pool of slime. My hand burned for hours afterwards.

On the beach, Nikos was wrestling with the small octopus he'd just harpooned. It was coiled around his hand and wrist and halfway up his arm, hanging on for dear life. He pried it off and then proceeded to dash it many times against a flat rock. To anyone who hasn't seen this procedure it seems at first to be rather gruesome. On my first day on the island I'd seen a man far out on the rocks raising something in his hand and repeatedly smashing it on the ground; it looked almost like some sort of horrible murder. Actually, it's a very common sight on the island, and octopi are caught by the hundreds every day. The first smash against the stone ensures that the creature is dead, after which, repeated smashings force a grey-white soapy substance out of its body, in order that the meat will be tender enough to eat. If this is not done, octopus meat can be very tough indeed. After the octopi have turned from red to pale grey, they are hung up on lines to dry, and are barbecued or boiled later on. One of the things that bewilders visitors to the island is the sight of clotheslines full of dangling tentacles; it's a little disarming at first, and many people make faces and say *Ugh*. But I've come to regard it as an awfully beautiful sight.

By accident Nikos later harpooned a huge red starfish. We brought it up onto the beach, and when we removed the harpoon, one leg came off with it. I wanted to cry (which, as I have mentioned before, is nothing new) until Nikos assured me it would be all right. 'They grow new parts,' he said. 'Don't worry.' And then, to my utter amazement, the lovely creature slowly began to make its way back into the sea, leaving its leg behind it.

Just before we were packing up to leave for the day, I noticed what looked like an unusual brown speckled stone in the shallows. When I moved to touch it, it literally burst into life. It opened up two large frilled flaps, revealing tiny organs with an almost human shape, and began to swirl these flaps and rapidly propel itself away. It looked for all the world like a funny little dancer swirling her skirts around her. It left a trail of brilliant purple ink behind it, then, finding a safer place, wrapped itself up and pretended again to be a brown speckled stone. We still haven't figured out what it was, although an old sailor in the village said he thinks it might be one of the strange creatures that now and again the sea brings in from the northern coasts in Africa.

Entry Five: There's a legend among Greek seamen that if you ever see a gorgeous mermaid rising out of the water at the bow of your boat, you must take care as to how you address her, for she is the sister of Alexander the Great. She will be seeking news of her dead brother, and if you want to have fair weather, you must tell her that the great Alexander still lives and rules.

Our friend Odysseus wants above all to find himself a mermaid. Every day when we return to the village after swimming and fishing he asks us if we've found for him a real live *gorgona*. 'No,' we say, 'But maybe tomorrow.' 'Promises, promises,' he laughs, and hobbles away across the town square.

Entry Six: Today we spotted Nikos' uncle out in a rowboat looking for lobster, peering into a glass-bottomed barrel and scanning every inch of the seafloor. Behind him, manning the oars, was an extra-ordinary looking fellow who kept dropping the oars and flailing his arms around and talking to himself.

'It's Dionysus,' Nikos informed me. 'They call him *O Trellos* — the crazy one. He's all right, really. He just talks to invisible people a lot of the time.'

I learned that when Dionysus was a boy in school he was good in everything except mathematics. He had the delightful habit of carrying a non-existent 'one' over into the second line of addition. For example, if he had to add 10 and 10 and 10, he'd say: 'Zero plus zero plus zero equals zero. *Carry One.*' The answer would then be 40. That's how he dealt with the mathematics of his early years. No matter how many Nothings he added up, he always carried that positive digit into the second line of figures.

It was clear from the beginning that Dionysus had an alarming mind. His teachers tore their hair like characters in a Greek tragedy. They told him that if he didn't learn to count right, he'd end up as a lowly fisherman, et cetera. He said that his greatest aspiration in life was to end up as a lowly fisherman, et cetera, and besides, you just couldn't throw two Nothings together without ending up with a Something, and any fool could see that.

Every day when school got out, he'd go down to the pier and watch his father unravelling the tangled saffron nets that were his world, and listen to salty stories of the sea. No one is quite sure exactly when he went mad and started talking to his invisible people. But now he drinks a lot of *ouzo*, and sometimes dances in the street, but most of the time he rows the boat when Nikos' uncle goes lobster fishing.

As I watched them, the uncle, who had his head so far down in the barrel that he couldn't hear Dionysus' monologue, suddenly began pointing with one hand to a particular spot in the water. He'd obviously spotted a lobster, and didn't want to lose sight of it. Dionysus, misinterpreting the gesture somehow, began rowing around in a series of erratic circles, then for some reason, shot off in a straight southerly direction.

'Jesus Christ,' I said. 'If you uncle doesn't take his head out of that barrel, they're going to end up in Crete!'

At any rate, the lobster was lost, and Dionysus and the uncle screamed at each other all the way back to the village.

Entry Seven: There is so much to record. *Places* overpower me, especially places electric with history, or myth. There have been times in the past when I've stood in front of, say, the Great Pyramid at Giza, or in the (so-called) Room of the Last Supper in Jerusalem, feeling so stunned that my mind at the time was able only to record trivia, or worry over immediate physical concerns. *Did I bring enough cigarettes, I've lost my comb, my sandal strap's broken*, and so on.

But yesterday, a trip to the island of Delos, a kind of dream journey.

I walked down the avenue of the marble lions which line the Sacred Way leading to the main temples. Delos, where Zeus came in the form of a swan to seduce Leda. Delos, where Apollo was born, where Light was born. I moved through the ruins in an eerie fluid state of suspension in time and space. There was a time when no one was allowed to get born or die here; pregnant women and very old people could not set foot on the holy ground.

The heat and the light were dizzifying, and I thought I *must not faint, I must not stop here.* This is Delos, an island outside of human time. *Record the lions, record the stones, keep walking.* This is Delos, where you're not allowed to get born, or die. . . .

Entry Eight: Every afternoon we drink coffee with the old priest of the village. Papa Stephanos is well over eighty, and totally blind. His son, who is the official *papas* of the island, intones the morning and evening prayers in the church of Saint Nikolaus — a duty he performs with a certain lack of flair — and Papa Stephanos only presides over the ceremonies on very special holy days, two or three times a year. When he was younger, Nikos remembers, he had a voice that sent chills down your spine when he performed the ancient litanies. Nikos reminds him of this, and he smiles and sighs and says, 'Ah, I was a voice in the wilderness. . .' and goes on sipping his bitter coffee, his black-robed form casting a great shadow on the white wall of the café.

When he was young, the villagers say, he was uncommonly strong. On the joyous eve of Easter, it is customary in many Greek villages for the *papas* to pretend to hold the doors of the church closed at midnight, against the throngs of worshippers. The people then cry 'Open up, open up!' and heave their weight against the doors, which of course promptly give way. But apparently Papa Stephanos was so strong he must have had the very might of God on his side, for when he put his back to the doors, barricading them with his shoulders, the villagers had a devil of a time trying to get in!

This is no doubt a slight exaggeration, but in any case, everyone remembers that the doors always took rather longer than necessary to get opened when Papa Stephanos' weight was behind them. I find myself remembering a very pale and lacklustre young priest in Athens who had so little feeling for his calling that we once caught him trying to change a lightbulb in the middle of a particularly difficult Byzantine chant. I wonder what happens to *him* on the eve of *Paskha*? I have a vision of him spreadeagled on the floor of the church, face downward, the people gleefully marching into the church over the door, which has fallen on his back.

This afternoon Papa Stephanos' daughter Maria called to us from the porch of the little house where she lives and looks after him. She was ironing tea-towels with an enormous black iron full of red-hot coals. 'You're coming to eat with us tonight!' she cried, and the tone of her voice informed us that this was a command, not merely an invitation.

The house is situated in what is known as the *Castro*, the circular core of the village, which dates back to the Thirteenth Century and perhaps even earlier. Everything is spotlessly white, for the women paint the stairs with white lime, and even draw white lines around the stones which pave the narrow streets, as they have done for centuries in the Cyclades. The *Castro* is unbelievably small, neat, and somehow unreal — like a stage setting or a miniature model for a village, rather than, as it once was, an actual fortress.

We went to visit at nightfall. The beams on the ceiling of Papa Stephanos' house were painted a weird shade of watermelon pink, and the walls were covered with sheets of plastic with wild floral patterns. Maria cooked dinner in a kitchen the size of a cupboard, and afterwards we sat outside on the porch and listened as the sea heaved long weary sighs in the distance. We barbecued some octopi over burning coals, and some little blue crabs that we'd pried out of their crevices in the rocks by the shore, using flashlights and penknives. I was sorry, afterwards, for the way we'd blinded them and trapped them in their homes. Being a delicacy is an awful fate, really, and these creatures were very beautiful, some of them tiny as spiders in our hands. The salty smell of the smoke, combined with the scent of the countless flowers which grew all around the house, sent us all into a state of utter euphoria. When Maria passed around glasses of the local *ouzo* — which tastes rather like a combination of *pernod* and molten lava — we became witty, profound, joyful and downright silly. Papa Stephanos, the lamplight dancing in his sightless eyes, began to sing old village love songs, the kind the young men used to serenade their sweethearts with. His voice, although a little shaky, was wonderfully resonant, and he made even those sentimental old tunes sound like hymns.

Later, he started telling us hilarious stories from the old days about some of the people on the island, chuckling gleefully each time he thought of another one. It seems that Christos — the man who had his life savings chewed up by mice — had once, many years ago, borrowed a flashlight from a friend. It was the first time Christos had ever used a flashlight, the friend turned it on for him, and Christos used it for a few hours, then decided it was time to turn it out. After blowing on it a few times, he realized that was not the way to extinguish the thing. So he dunked it in water, took it out, and discovered that the hellish thing was still lit. He dunked again; still no luck. When he finally got up the courage to return the flashlight to his friend, it was two days later. It was still lit.

Maria was hanging over the side of the porch, limp with laughter, when he started telling us the story about Dionysus and the red eggs. At Easter, which is the holiest day of the year in the Greek Orthodox faith, the people bring out baskets of eggs dyed red, crack them and eat them as one of the traditional ceremonies of *Paskha*. '*Christos anesti,*' they say to one another. 'Christ is risen.' Well one year, the day *before Paskha*, Dionysus was seen standing outside the church of Saint Nikolaus defiantly holding up two red eggs in either hand. He gave them a resounding crack, peeled off the red shells, and solemnly ate the eggs. Then he stepped forward and shouted into the open door of the church, 'You see? It doesn't mean anything! This *Paskha*, it's nothing! It's all satanic propaganda!'

Then he did a little jig in the town square, and went home, talking to his invisible people all the way.

By the time Papa Stephanos got to the story of how the mother of Odysseus once tried to do away with herself, Nikos was choking with laughter, and I joined Maria and hung over the side of the porch, weakly trying to keep myself from collapsing in a heap on the ground. Odysseus' mother, a proud and rather handsome woman, had at one time been slighted or insulted by a young man in the village. She vowed in a loud voice so that all could hear, that she would do away with herself that same day. She chose death by drowning, since the sea was so close by, and she intended to walk straight into the water, never to return. Followed by a few of the village women, who screamed and moaned and tried to make her change her mind, she staunchly walked down to the beach. The women tore their hair and wept, until she did a rather strange thing. She sat down on the sand and slowly began to take off her shoes and stockings. That did it; the women broke up with laughter. 'You don't want to get your stockings wet!' they cried. 'You want to die, but you don't want to ruin your shoes!' Burning with shame, but no doubt inwardly pleased and relieved, she gathered up her things and ran back to the village, convinced that life was the best thing after all.

Papa Stephanos wiped a tear from his eye, and I realized that it wasn't there from all the laughter, but rather from a great and boundless love for the people of his island. And I suspect that he was beginning to feel — as we all did — a little ashamed of ourselves for laughing so heartily at the foibles of others. If anyone could have seen us as we were that night, it would have been evident that *we* were the village fools.

It was getting late. We'd finished the last of the octopus and the *ouzo*, and Papa Stephanos looked suddenly very weary. We said good-night. A shy, uncertain wind was feeling its way through the dry shrubs and crumbling stones of the *Castro*, as though in search of something lost centuries ago. Fireflies flitted here and there like bright particles of laughter. We went down to the harbour and leaned over the dock, shining a flashlight into the water to see the hundreds of tiny shrimps with burning golden eyes gazing up at us from the black depths.

In great laughter there is great love, I thought. And maybe being holy means being almost unbearably human. Papa Stephanos, I concluded, is a holy man.

The moon, the blind eye of night, cast silver benedictions on the water.

Entry Nine: We spent a post-rain morning climbing the drenched mountain-slopes in search of food for dinner. The electric storm of the night before had turned the village into a network of fabulous multi-coloured rivers, and the first light of dawn revealed dozens of fat grey-green snails. I had overcome my horror of these tender creatures since I first encountered them at Mystras. They were everywhere, sauntering forth from their crevices in the rocks in search of their moist and mysterious *petits déjeuners*.

The mountains were rampant with goats all sharing some secret joke, the way goats do — and we plunged upwards (if that is possible) into another world. We caught fifteen giant snails in ten minutes, and stuffed them into our knapsacks with some wild mint and thyme to keep them occupied. Then we lunched on boiled eggs and orange juice in the shadow of a small church, and tried to read an inscription in ancient Greek on a marble stone. It's terrible trying to read ancient Greek, especially when there's no space between the words. I mean: *itsterribletryingtoreadancientgreekespeciallywhentheres nospacebetweenthewords.*

Noon came darkly; more rain was afoot. We slid back down to the village and proceeded to set things up in order to cook what we believed would be a fantastic feast. So far so good. We lit the two oil-lamps in our tiny medieval home, and discussed our menu. *Escargots*, of course — (everything sounds delicious in French) — with a salad. Hollandaise sauce? Certainly! No problem — we'd whip it all up in a flash.

We had all the necessary ingredients: lettuce, tomatoes, mayonnaise, olive oil, lemons, and Whatever, all stuffed in multi-coloured plastic bags, which were lined up, row on row, in the storm-dark kitchen.

I said:

— *Okay, you do the snails, and I'll do the salad, right?*

— *Right!*

Shivering with excitement, we set about our task. It was about one-thirty in the afternoon. The village was asleep, because the villagers were wise. We were not wise; we were trapped in the strange ecstasy of French gourmet cooking on a Greek island in the Aegean Sea in the middle of what might be a typhoon.

We put one lamp in the kitchen area, and one in the centre of the room where there was a table to work on the salad.

— *Oh no, there's no water*, said Nikos.

— *Damn*, I said, *I forgot to go down to the well. I'll go now.*

So I took three plastic buckets — a red one, a blue one and a yellow one, and charged through the streets in my green plastic sandals to get water. Three different kinds of water — one for drinking, one for cooking, and one for Whatever. Five minutes later I was back, and Nikos had emptied our knapsacks of snails into a large iron pot.

They squirmed and protested a little, but it was hard to tell because the light was so dim. We lit the gas stove, poured in water from bucket A, added salt and wild thyme, and waited.

— *I think I'll start on the salad now*, I said, gathering up tomatoes, mayonnaise, lemons, etc. into a white plastic bowl. I took them to the table and realized I had no knife.

— *Bring me a knife, please . . .*

— *Well clean the other knife from the cupboard with the water in the yellow bucket . . .*

— *I can't see the yellow bucket. Bring me an extra lamp.*

— *I can't bring an extra lamp, or I can't see anything here.*

— *Well there's a hunting knife in my jacket pocket.*

— *I can't see your jacket pocket unless I have more light.*

The snails were boiling happily in the dark pot. I thought that if I could find my way to Bucket B, the blue one, I could use the fresh water from there to clean the extra knife which was in the cupboard. Of course, this meant that the water in Bucket B would become cleaning water instead of Drinking or Cooking Water. But that was OK, because then the contents of buckets B and C would be used for Whatever, while the contents of Bucket A would still be cookable. On the other hand, it was rather difficult to make out the colours in the darkness.

— *If you give me a spare candle*, I said, *I can find the other knife and clean it.*

Nikos handed me a candle from the gloom of the kitchen.

— *Take care*, he said. *I accidentally used Bucket B to clean my hands, and that means that it smells of garlic.*

I thought that would be all right, because there's nothing wrong with a bit of garlic in a normal Hollandaise sauce. However, after I had found the extra knife, I realized that the lamp in the other room needed extra fuel, and I had to return to my salad with a dripping candle in one hand and a plastic container of oil in the other. I stood there, staring at the tomatoes and mayonnaise, paralyzed.

— *Nikos*, I asked feebly, *how are the escargots coming along?*

— *Great! Just smell that fresh thyme!*

By now, the atmosphere was a grey-green cloud of lamp oil, cigarette fumes, steam, boiling spices, all lit up now and again by a dramatic flash of lightning.

— *Do you have a spoon?* I cried, in mounting despair. *I don't think I can stir the Hollandaise sauce without one.*

— *Yes, I've got a spoon, but I used it for mixing the garlic and butter, so I put it in the blue bucket. Then I realized that I had to use the red bucket because that was cleaner.*

— *What about dishes?* I cried, casually tossing the salad with a penknife and my naked forefinger.

— *Over with the salt, in the corner.*

— *You can't borrow my lamp, or I can't watch the snails!*

I thought that if I could find my way to where the napkins were, everything would be solved, because then I could clean everything with napkins, even in the dark.

— *I'm sorry,* Nikos said. *I had to use the napkins to dry the spoon which was in the red bucket so you could stir the sauce for the salad. But now that you've already done it with the penknife, I used the spoon to stuff the cooked snails in their shells with the garlic and butter. Oh, do you have a light? The stove's gone off again.*

Lightning struck, and the rain poured down. It was Eden all over again. It was funny, it was Friday, it was everything. We dined on *escargots* and salade à la Hollandaise, and as we spoke, all the other snails in the mountains wagged their damned silly silent tongues. The goats held onto their hilarious secrets. It was the end of summer.

Entry Ten: The pine groves buzz with hornets. A slim white horse stands motionless in a field fuzzy with sunlight, like a creature out of Eden. A newborn calf, all wet and scared and funny, begins to examine the world on its shaky, spindly legs. Faces of little cats peer out from among the flowers. A magnificent young bull, pure white, is being run through the village to the slaughterhouse, followed by a tractor and half of the village kids who scream and laugh. Its eyes are wild as it crashes through the narrow streets. The eyes of ancient beasts must have looked like this when they were led to the sacrificial altars of the gods. A naked, bloody young lamb hangs upside down in the window of the meat store, a sprig of parsley in its mouth.

Laughing boys race through the village square on mules; they urge them on by striking them with chains around their cheeks and eyes. I do not like this. Down the road, the man who raises rabbits chooses one for some family's dinner. The red-eyed bunny stares, the cold steel of the knife at its throat, its whole body suspended by the ears.

We take two donkeys and go out for the day into the mountains and down into a beautiful plain at the southern part of the island. We find purple grapes and give some to the donkeys who chew them thoughtfully, the sweet juice dribbling down their chins. We visit many small churches, and then head down again to the coast. The wind is rising and the waves are frilled with white froth; there was talk yesterday of a *fortuna* coming — a great storm. But it will not hit full force until evening. Meanwhile nothing is happening, everything is happening. The donkeys know their way back home.

Entry Eleven: During the war, Nikos tells me, when the Fascists occupied the island, the kids used to steal potato peels from the garbage cans behind the houses where the German soldiers stayed, and roast them over little fires by night. Nothing was real in those terrible times except death, and hunger. Papa Stephanos used to scrounge up food, moving, like God, in mysterious ways, and distribute it among the poorest families in the village. No one is quite sure how he managed this — (I must remember to ask him some time) — but he probably went around to the larger farms which would have had some extra produce, even in wartime, and convinced the farmers to consider their own immortal souls and their fellow man.

After the war, someone opened a washroom in a small café which had been closed for years, and found it full of cockroaches and useless German marks. In the end, then, the paper money of the Third Reich had served only one, fitting, scatological purpose.

Entry Twelve: This morning, three black-robed sisters, girls in their early teens, walked arm in arm down the road to the church of Saint Nikolaus to attend the funeral of their father. It seemed that half of the village was assembled in the square outside of the church. As the girls approached, the crowd parted to let them through, and all the women began to sway and moan, their voices rising and falling in eerie cadences, in the ancient, timeless music of mourning. The girls themselves looked like figures from a chorus in a Greek tragedy; their sobbing and wailing was totally unrestrained, and for a moment I felt that the scene was so pure, so perfect, it might have been rehearsed. That was my Western mind at work again; I was reared in a society which teaches children to hide their emotions, to keep a stiff upper lip, even if it means a lifetime of repressions and neuroses as a result. In the East there is no such thing as purely private sorrow. You let it all hang out — birth, life, death, everything. If necessary, you overplay emotions; you do not understate, you do not conceal. It is the only way.

In Greece, the dead are buried in the ground . . . but after a number of years, there is a ceremony in which the bones of the dead are dug up and removed to the local church, where they are placed in enclosures in the walls, and marked by stone plaques. When Nikos told me that as a young child, he was present when they took his father's bones from the ground, I was stunned to think that children were allowed to witness such a (to my mind) gruesome procedure. 'But why not?' he exclaimed. 'Death is death, bones are bones. It serves no purpose to pretend otherwise.'

What I shall always remember about this place is its purity, its innocence, its open-eyed acceptance of the absolutes of life and death, darkness and light. And in some inexplicable way, here on this tiny Aegean island, I am coming to understand that light itself is the final mystery.

Entry Thirteen: Last night two of the villagers got into an unpleasant argument in the café. One of them spoke loosely of the other's sister, and, this being tantamount to a declaration of war, the insulted party called in the mayor as witness to the slander. Plans were immediately made for court proceedings. This morning, despite very treacherous weather, the two men left the island in separate boats, keeping a wide and angry distance between one another. The mayor and his secretary accompanied the insulted party. This would be a simple story except for one thing: the island where they must take their case to court is relatively close to here. But because no boats go there directly from this island, they have to go to a neighbouring island where they'll board a large boat for Piraeus on the mainland — (a journey of some six hours) — and from *there* make their way back to where they'll appear in court. If they had a helicopter, they could be there in twenty minutes; it's a shame. But on the other hand, as someone said a short while ago, going by this huge and ridiculous circular route, any one of three things might befall them. They could die of boredom; they could make amends and play *tavali* all the way back; or they could be shipwrecked, because another big storm is on the way. In any case, a principle is a principle.

Entry Fourteen: It's *ouzo*-making time on the island. Every October, some time after the grapes have been harvested and shipped off to outside markets, and after the island has made its own wine, it's time to distill the quintessential brew which I earlier described as a combination of *pernod* and molten lava.

Whatever's left over from the grapes which were pressed for wine — skins, seeds, leaves and twigs — is stored underground for a few weeks. Then it becomes a fermented purple mass which is dug up and shovelled into huge cauldrons heated by wood fires. Through a series of ducts and pipes the potent vapour travels, is distilled, until finally the fire-water emerges, drop by drop from a faucet, and is collected in buckets. The work goes on day and night; there must be at least two men doing shifts to keep everything moving. I don't know how much *ouzo* is produced at the end of all this, but it's probably quite enough to supply the island for a year.

Tonight Nikos and I went to the little shed which is the local distillery to watch the proceedings. As we approached, the air was burning with the pungent aromas of what seemed to be the product of some medieval alchemy. Inside, the heat was overpowering, and in the glow from the fire, the faces of the workers were red and gold. The chap who was changing the buckets laughed at our bewilderment, and he handed us a small sample of the *ouzo* to taste. He is one of the few older men on the island who is minus one arm — (there was a time when the fisherman used dynamite for fishing, and there were some unfortunate accidents as a result). He laughed even harder when he saw the expressions on our faces after we'd tasted the brew. 'A little strong, eh?' he shouted over the roar of the fire. 'That's because it's the first bit to come from the tap. It's always like that.'

We learned that they do of course gauge the alcoholic content of the *ouzo*, and it's not bottled for consumption unless it is at an acceptable level. We left soon, laughing and gasping a little, our throats on fire.

We finally ended up at *Spiros' Club* which is close to the sea on the western side of the island, just behind the village. Mercifully, it being October, all but a handful of the summer tourists have left. There is a young gay Frenchman who's rented a room in the village and who's been here since June, an elderly German couple, two globe-trotting girls from South Africa, and ourselves, as the only *xeni* on the island. Spiros has made himself a mint this summer serving *retsina*, salads and fish and octopi to the tourists, and now he's a very happy man. The club is small; the tables are covered with plastic cloths in garish colours; the walls are adorned with faded reproductions of El Greco paintings; in the corner there is a huge, ancient juke-box with a repertoire which includes everything from Tom Jones to the latest Greek hits from Athens. Outside there is a garden where people can dance; it is enclosed by walls of tall swaying reeds and there is a large palm tree in the middle.

Spiros is going to close the place tomorrow, because we will be leaving. This makes him sad. He puts some coins into the juke-box, and we hear *O Sole Mio*, followed by *Lay Lady Lay*. 'Where is everybody!' he cries, and at that moment the police chief walks in with his friend Yannis. Yannis can dive deeper than anyone on the island and claims he can hold his breath underwater almost as long as a dolphin or a whale. He is also the best dancer on the island, and a superb show-off. He was always dancing, I hear — even as a child.

The Greeks have a dance called the *zembekiko*. It is normally performed by a male dancer who is either at the end or the beginning of his wits. Although one must adhere at all times to the strict and complex rhythm of the music, one is allowed all sorts of intricate variations, depending on one's ability and state of mind. The wisest time to attempt a *zembekiko* is when you are either totally sober or superbly drunk. Otherwise, the results may be disastrous, since you are likely to whirl like a dervish off the stage or swoon like a dying eagle in free fall. The dance is both a fight against gravity and a kind of flirtation with the earth. This should explain the following poem. Or perhaps the poem will explain the explanation, I'm not sure.

> *Greeks have two ways of talking*
> *— face to face or side to side —*
> *One speaks and the other watches*
> *The nearest wall*

Where the birth of other worlds
Takes place before his eyes.

The imperial and impermanent eagle
of the Byzantines
Had two heads that looked East and West
And tried to gather God
Into a single body
— the body of a bird —

I spoke before of a will that flirts
With eagles, and now I speak
Of eagles who flirt with earth
In their wide slow turning,
Their descent, their dialogue with death.

Then poised on some craggy cliff
Of mountain or of mind, they wait
For the updraft, breath of God, pure wind
To hoist them into heaven once again.

Whether with broken or unfailing wings
They fly, they rise, they fall.

So with these dancers on the broken edge of midnight
Born with the sign of the double-headed eagle,
Dancing still.

After some unnecessary prompting, Yannis gets up to dance. He puts a sprig of basil behind his ear and waits to hear the first hypnotic notes of the *bouzouki* playing the long, maddeningly seductive prologue to the *zembekiko*. He concentrates, spreads out his arms, walks around in slow figure eights, deliberately tantalizing us. He drops his cigarette on the floor, grinds it out with his foot — (never losing a single beat of the music) — and then, using the cigarette as a focal point, staring at it scornfully, he begins to dance complex, provocative circles around it.

The music quickens; Yannis crouches down and gives the floor a resounding spank with his open palm. Then suddenly he leaps up into the air, an uncoiled spring, demanding the right to fly. He drops again, touching the floor reverently with the back of his hand, brushing it, caressing it. He swivels on his heels back and forth, his head turning, addressing the four corners of the earth. His face has taken on the radiance of a child. He laughs and snaps his fingers, he whistles wildly and hisses between his teeth. His expression tells us that the world begins and ends here, that there is nothing on earth right now to compete in importance with the joyous celebration of the body, this study in fury, this mind-bending, defiant dance.

He's got it now; he's one with the dance; he *is* the dance. He's animal and bird, water and fire — he is a man free of the earth yet one with the earth, his body exploring the frightening dual nature of freedom.

'*Ellah*, Yannaki, *ellah!*' we cry. 'Come on!'

He conducts the invisible orchestra in the juke-box. He does a forward somersault, landing at the bottom of a chair which he then proceeds to pick up in his teeth, balancing the weight against his chest. His feet have not once lost the rhythm of the dance. He puts the chair down, and with a few more leaps and controlled, crashing falls, concludes the performance. We clap and pound the tables in appreciation, sending a few black olives rolling onto the floor. From here on in, the evening is made. We eat enormous amounts of fish and cheese, drink amber *retsina*, and feed the insatiable juke-box until we're down to our last few *drachmas*.

Spiros is almost in tears when we decide we must go. It has been a wonderful summer for him; it's over now. The gay young Frenchman who shyly shared our table and said little, slips out into the garden. Just as we are leaving, we see him by the palm tree with an invisible partner in his arms, waltzing to the strains of *O how we danced on the night we were wed.* . . .

The music follows us all the way down the dark path back to the village.

Entry Fifteen: I pack up the odd assortment of things that we will take away with us: a giant sponge, a crucifix made of tiny shells, eleven small beige starfish, a piece of wood which the sea caressed and then rejected, a tea-towel from Maria embroidered with Byzantine crosses, a bunch of wild mountain thyme, a rusty goat's bell, a beeswax candle from the church of Saint Nikolaus . . .

Odysseus is standing by the old gnarled eucalyptus tree in the village square, his cap tilted at a cocky angle, his blue eyes watching us. He smiles, and his smile is shot with gold. 'Good weather for sailing!' he says, 'But of course, one never knows . . . How far is Canada? Maybe I'll come one day. Is it farther than Gibraltar? I've been to Gibraltar. Goodbye, goodbye. . . .' We shake hands, and make our way down to the harbour.

Papa Stephanos is sitting in his usual chair outside the café — an eternal figure in black against the dazzling white wall. I think: *he will be here forever, he will never die.* We lean over to kiss him; there are tears in his eyes. 'Come in the spring!' he says. 'We will go to the mountains to celebrate *Paskha* . . . we will all go together. . .' We leave him sipping his bitter coffee, his hands trembling a little as he raises the cup to his lips. 'Goodbye, children, goodbye. . . .'

Farther on down the road, Nikos' aunt emerges from her house, carrying a large pink plastic bag. 'Here take this. Food. It's a long trip to Athens. There's some boiled eggs and tomatoes and cheese and bread. . . .' She bursts into tears and crushes us in her ample arms. '*Kalo taxidhi!* Have a good journey!'

By the time we reach the harbour, many laughing children have gathered behind us, their voices like little bells in the clear vibrant air. The motorboat is waiting; we jump in and wave to everyone on the dock as we speed away. The island gets smaller and smaller. It is as though we are not leaving it at all — it is leaving *us.*

Later we board the big boat for the six hour trip north to Piraeus. I sit in a deck chair and watch the waves churning as we pull away towards the open sea. I remember the old sailor's warning: '*If you see a gorgeous mermaid rising out of the water, a gorgeous mermaid seeking news of her dead brother, say to her that the Great One lives yet, lives and rules. Say this if you want fair weather. She is the sister of Alexander.*'

I want to write a letter to Odysseus, a letter which I will send from Canada, which is farther than Gibraltar, a letter which goes:

Dear Odysseus:

I will send you a golden toothbrush and a real live mermaid, if you will send me a box of fireflies and tiny shrimps with burning eyes.

Yours truly, Gwendolyn.

From *Mermaids and Ikons* (1978) by Gwendolyn MacEwen, born in Toronto 1941. Poet, playwright and novelist, MacEwen visited Greece in 1971 and 1976.

SOUTH SEAS
by George Woodcock

Because of the number of European plantations, the islands of the New Hebrides are probably better linked by air than any other of the South Sea groups with the possible exception of Fiji. Air Mélanesie was originally started as a bush pilot operation by planters and traders, and even now they have a share in the undertaking which mirrors the extent to which the New Hebrides remain a survival from the days when white interests were dominant in the South Seas.

Air Mélanesie runs a service of nine-seater Islanders, piloted by a curious combination of young apprentice flyers from Australia, getting in their hours of flight before they can qualify for the Qantas jets, and elderly Frenchmen, who are always eccentric and sometimes drunk. When we took our first trip in the airline, down to Tanna, it was an apprentice in the cockpit, and we flew uneventfully and at a low altitude over the sea and the forested edge of Eromanga until the smoking crest of volcanic Mount Yasua came into view and we descended between the lines of coconut palms on to an airstrip located in a fold of the ground so that the plane landed on the top of a slope, taxied down it and then up the opposing slope to come to a halt at a sign which announced Burton Field. There was little more than the sign, for all that was left of the airport building was a rubble of broken planks among which two white toilet pans glistened in the sunlight; it had been demolished in a recent hurricane. Some wild-looking women who had been watching the plane land from the edge of the bush retreated shyly as soon as we began to disembark. A cow lowed frenziedly among the trees. A tall young man with lovely yellow hair, piercing blue eyes and a daredevil air got down from a Land-Rover and came towards us. 'I'm Russell Paul,' he said. 'Bob Paul's my father.' He loaded our luggage into the jeep, together with that of a young German doctor working in an American institute, who had come to see the famous volcano.

Tanna has no roads — merely tracks that wind over the hills and through the groves and the jungle and turn at the slightest touch of rain into that red and slippery mud which one encounters so often on high South Sea islands. Tough vehicles with four-wheel drives are the only possible kind of transport, and Russell drove his Land-Rover with skill and an obviously intimate familiarity with the terrain. Inge complimented him on his driving. 'I should know how, ma'am, if anyone should,' he answered. 'I've been here since I was one year old. I went away for a few years to school in Australia, but that doesn't make any difference. Tanna's the only home I have, and I don't want to make my life anywhere else.' And indeed, as we got to know him, Russell Paul seemed as true a son of the islands as any white man could possibly be.

He drove us first to the big white house behind the trading store where his family lived. It was one of the wooden houses with large airy rooms and great shutters kept open with white poles, so that the breeze came in and the sunlight kept out, that are characteristic of New Hebridean traders. Shortly afterwards, Bob Paul himself came in, one of those large, loose, slightly shambling men in whom an essential toughness is combined with a great gentleness of manner. Bob Paul has been in the New Hebrides for almost thirty years, since 1946. He was one of the founders and pilots of the rough-and-ready interisland plane services that had preceded Air Mélanesie, and still served as its agent on Tanna. He was the largest trader and planter on the island. He was a member of the Advisory Council and known as a man to whom anyone, European or native, could apply for help if he felt himself the victim of injustice. He was sometimes called the King of Tanna, but it was a title he did not invite or relish, since he had learnt the inconvenience of authoritarian stances in a world as volatile as the South Seas in the 1970s, and he seemed to live at guarded peace with all men, including the militants of Jon Frum. His name throughout the Condominium was such that whenever the Advisory Council wished to put a point strongly to the two governments, its divergent groups of British, French and Mélanesian representatives always united to nominate him their spokesman. He

263

was the one man who could be relied on to reduce the passions of a situation to a fair and persuasive statement.

We were given coffee grown on the plantation, and fresh rolls baked in the Paul store; it was obvious that Bob Paul and his family had recognized that a measure of self-sufficiency was essential to the very civilized way of life they maintained on Tanna. Then we drove to the cabins, native-style huts of bamboo and palm-leaf with the necessary amenities of Coleman lamps and kerosene refrigerators, standing on the shores of a rocky cove with a few native houses on its farther shore. Beside each door a padlock hung on a hook with its key. 'There's no need to use it,' Bob Paul remarked. 'Taboo still counts on Tanna, and a padlock beside a door is now a taboo sign. You can leave everything you have without worrying. Nobody will step past that padlock.' We would have been ashamed to disregard such an assurance, and during our days on Tanna we left the cabin open with cameras and money and other usually tempting items inside it, but though the Tannese wandered freely along the shore below the cabins and through the coconut grove above, nothing was ever touched. The first night we were disturbed by noises on the veranda which sounded as if someone were about to break in, but we found it was only some of the goats which Bob Paul had introduced, before he took to cattle rearing, to keep down the weeds in his plantations.

Tanna is one of the lushest islands of the New Hebrides, so fertile that its people — unlike most South Sea islanders — live almost entirely off the land and are reputed to be poor fishermen. Nevertheless, it is by no means entirely forested, and it contains a considerable area of upland savanna. After we had decided to leave our trip to the Jon Frum village until the next day, Russell Paul suggested that we might take a trip as far as these natural pasturelands to see the herds of wild horses that now inhabited them.

The distance was comparatively slight, but travel was slow, since in this direction the tracks were particularly steep and broken down; even vehicles with four-wheel drives could travel only very slowly through the coconut-groves where the cattle and goats were grazing. There was still a good deal of devastation to be seen from the last hurricane — trees uprooted and broken off, and one palm whose trunk had been severed by a flying piece of roofing with such force that the cut reproduced the corrugations of the iron. The inhabitants were clearly fearful that the experience might be repeated; when we drove past the nondescript little European bungalows of the government station we saw that their roofs were loaded down with sandbags and blocks of cement and coral in case of another blow.

Our way took us through two native villages, and the contrast between them illustrated vividly what had happened on the island since the advent of Jon Frum. One was a Presbyterian village; we had seen nothing in the islands more dejected in its atmosphere than this shabby, rundown settlement of corrugated-roofed houses which in their pristine newness must have symbolized for some past missionary the triumph of Scottish progress and Presbyterian light. The next village was a pagan one. Its huts of cane and thatch, and its cane-walled school, all of them renewed or repaired since the hurricane, looked neat and bright, and the well-cultivated gardens around it gave the whole place an appearance of happiness and self-sufficient prosperity.

The contrast between the villages reflected the extraordinary developments by which Tanna, almost alone among the missionized islands of the South Seas, slipped back from its conversion. I remembered, from my boyhood reading of missionary narratives, how after some alarming violence and the eating of a few pious Caledonians, Tanna was brought into the Kirk by the efforts of John G. Paton and his missionary associates. It continued as a model Presbyterian island until the arrival of the American forces during World War II set going strange thoughts of material blessings, and Jon Frum arose as one of the many cargo cults of Mélanesia. Jon Frum — as we realized when we began to piece the story together — seemed to base its power largely on lingering pagan emotions which the Presbyterians had only papered over with their apparent conversions, and when the Jon Frum leaders sent kava sticks through the villages with the exhortation to abandon missionary religion, many people who never thought of joining them were willing — from fear or perhaps from a long suppressed desire to be free of a Calvinist outlook — to obey the call. The Presbyterian Church, which had commanded the loyalties of the vast majority of the islanders, suddenly found itself reduced to a small sect, and it was the least self-reliant of the Tannese who chose to remain under Christian tutelage.

Beyond the villages we turned inland into steeper country, through a forest tangled with lianas, where little canary-like birds called silver-eyes skittered among the undergrowth and we saw several of the brilliant blue and white kingfishers which migrate seasonally from Siberia to the New Hebrides and back. At last we came to a plateau where the forest sharply gave way to a low maquis which eventually became grassland. Here, at a primitive gate of barbed wire and stakes, Bob Paul's land ended and native land began, and here too Jon Frum showed its first sign. Within a little red wooden fence like the surround of a grave and about the same size, stood a tall cross, also painted red. 'It's just to show us,' Russell remarked. 'Defiance, not taboo. They wouldn't try that! After all, they still like to trade with us.'

We drove on over the trackless downs, where a few cattle and some hobbled horses belonging to the local villagers were grazing, and passed a deep gorge where a great tongue of jungle taller and thicker than the forest we had passed through came in contact with the grassland, the dense woodland sweeping down one side and the almost treeless savanna down the other, and the two meeting on the sharp line of demarcation formed by the river below. Beyond this gorge the downs, dotted with scanty groups of trees, flowed down to the sea, and it was here that we found the wild horses, whose ancestors had been left to graze freely when the Tannese had no use for them. They ran in troops varying in numbers from six to a dozen, each with its dominant stallion. Kurt, the German doctor, was anxious to take film of them, so we hid in one of the clumps of trees, and Russell careened with the Land-Rover across the savanna, driving the horses so that they raced, uncut manes and tails sweeping in the wind, towards us. As each troop swept by, the guardian stallion, mane and tail held high, ran between the mares and foals and the Land-Rover. Round they would race, and then stop on some knoll to observe us, and then, surprisingly, come sweeping down to tempt Russell to a further pursuit. At first we were inclined to pity such splendid creatures who had returned to primordial wildness and then were pursued, but soon it became evident that for them this unlethal pursuit was actually an exhilarating game. As I watched them, I seemed to be looking over an unbelievable chasm of time, for it was of the palaeolithic horses of Lascaux that I was irresistibly reminded.

We lunched back in the cabin on Paris ham and excellent Vila charcuterie we had picked up at the store, and drank Gewurztraminer wondering what John G. Paton would have said to the enjoyment of such Gallic luxuries on his savage nineteenth-century island. Russell joined us, and I said to him that I had heard there was a priest on southern Tanna who knew the history of Jon Frum better than any other white man. 'Yes, that's Father Sacco,' said Russell. 'He's a marvellous man. The sharpest man at cards I've ever seen. He knows so many of the languages of Tanna that he can make himself understood anywhere on the island. The one language he won't learn is pidgin. He says it would be a barrier between him and the natives rather than a means of communication. Come on! We'll call on him!'

So we drove through the palm groves along the coast, and eventually found Father Sacco in his parsonage that looked out over a sloping lawn towards the sea. There was something immediately puzzling about him. He looked Italian but his accent was not, and into its indefinable Europeanness there would break every now and then a mystifying twang of the English north country — somewhere pretty far north of York I decided. 'A good guess,' he laughed when I told him my impression. 'I'm a Maltese, but I spent many years in Middlesbrough before the Marist mission decided to send me here. And it's not so far from Durham miners to Tannese villagers as you'd think. They both live pretty close to the elemental. They both live close to death.'

We were standing on his veranda, and he pointed across the lawn. 'Why do you think I have such a good view of the sea? Because ten years ago the church which stood just above the beach was swept away by a tidal wave. And in the last hurricane the walls of the school building collapsed and the roof fell flat on to the ground. I was all right in my parsonage because I worked on it myself as leading carpenter, and a properly braced wooden house has the right combination of give and strength to stand any hurricane. But the night of that hurricane was terrible for the Tannese. The women and children squatted down in the centre of the houses, and the men and youths stood in a circle around them, clinging desperately to the roof timbers to prevent everything flying away. Three-quarters of the houses collapsed, and some of the roofs were blown two and a half miles before they came to the ground.'

Since the hurricane, Father Sacco had built a new school, guaranteed to stand up to any wind, and he insisted on taking us

on a tour of his compound before we settled down to talk. Like
Catholic missionaries who live for years on their own — I have met
his kind in the Canadian Arctic and the Indian jungles — he had
become something of a Robinson Crusoe, learning the skills necessary
for survival and a modicum of comfort. And after he had shown us
his special marvels — the fragment of church wall with its niched
Virgin that had survived the tidal wave, and the iron roof of the fallen
school where the sand had been blown against the windward side with
such force that it had stripped away the paint and brightly burnished
the metal — he took us into the workshop filled with a vast variety
of hand and power tools, and then showed us his never-failing pump,
drawing water from deep in the coral, water which he was giving
to the village people whose wells were still brackish as a result of the
hurricane. Then, pausing to show us a great black and white butter-
fly laying its eggs on one of his small orange trees, he took us into
his school, where the children rose and greeted us in a chorus of guttural French; half of them had blond heads of curly hair that con-
trasted disconcertingly with their charcoal black skins, but we were
not astonished, for Bob had already shown us the shelf of hydrogen
peroxide which was a fast seller in his store.

Back in the parsonage, Father Sacco talked of Jon Frum. 'It started
up when a man began to go around saying that one night he had
seen a personage on the beach who was the devil, and that by magic
he had been able to catch him, and use his powers. Whether the
original Jon Frum was the devil or the man who caught him is not
certain now even in the minds of the Tannese, but it does seem certain that Jon Frum — whoever he was — began to meet people in
the dark and pretend to inject them, which in itself is a curious thing,
since he appeared before the great campaign of penicillin which virtually eliminated yaws. There is a woman in the next village who
claims that by Jon Frum's injections she was cured of paralysis. All
this happened before the Americans came. The name of Jon Frum
survived and what we call the bush beliefs — the fragments of
paganism that lingered in the interior villages — were incorporated.
Though the interesting thing is that the bush people have a different
name for Jon Frum; they call him Kalip Apen, and I suspect that
is the name of a pagan god whose cult survived surreptitiously all
through the period of Presbyterian conversion. After the Americans

came, the idea of cargo cropped up. Whether it came from New Guinea or was generated here spontaneously I cannot say, but now Jon Frum became the being who would bring cargo, and his prophets multiplied. One man wandered around with a crazy woman whose vapourings he claimed to interpret like the priest of an oracle. Another used to put his ear to the ground, and claimed he was receiving messages from America.

'It was a situation ripe for a leader. A former teacher named Nambas appeared; he organized Jon Frum into a movement with himself as its leader, invented the bloody cross as its symbol, and turned it into an openly anti-Christian movement. He created a village at Sulphur Bay which became the Jon Frum mecca, and drilled his storm-troopers who marched up and down on special days with wooden imitation rifles and the letters USA painted on their chests in white clay. They still do it! It was he who sent the kava stick over the island to call for the abandonment of Christianity, and when the people in the villages received it, they drank kava openly — which the missionaries had forbidden — to signify that they renounced their conversion. Nambas died. Then came another leader called Milas. He went off to Vila, and came back with the story that he had been transported to America in what he called a "thing," and there he met two soldiers who told him that they were waiting for the Eagle to take off at any moment, after which the cargo would arrive in Tanna. Milas made his people clear airstrips in the jungle and build dummy planes to act as decoys for the real planes that would bring the cargo. Now Milas has gone, and his dummy planes have vanished, and all you will see in the jungle are the bloody crosses of Nambas. But the mecca is still at Sulphur Bay, and the leaders come and go. Frankly, I cannot tell you whom you will find in power when you go there.'

The next morning Mike and I, with Russell, the German Kurt, and a girl from Vila who was staying with the Pauls, set off for the Jon Frum village of Sulphur Bay, a journey that would take us close to the volcano of Mount Yasua. Inge was feeling unequal to the hard jeep journey and decided to stay at the cabin. We travelled by old horsetracks — formerly the foot-tracks of trade — that took us up over the interior spine of the island. Beside the track, every two or three miles, we passed a big trampled open space in the forest, with a single great banian tree under which rough benches had been made out of tree trunks; this was the nakamel: the meeting centre for a village whose houses were scattered in the bush; the Tannese have nothing resembling the maneabas of the Micronesians, and it is in the open, under the banian, that they gather to make their kava and discuss the affairs of men. They gather, that is, when they are at home, but in most of these upland settlements the hurricane had destroyed the crops, and the men had gone to New Caledonia to earn a little money while the women kept alive by eating coconuts. In one village Russell stopped to talk to a man with one hand; the other had been blown off fishing with dynamite. He told us that apart from himself there were only two old men and two youths in the village, though there were thirty women.

The road climbed higher, through dense woods inhabited by large black-and-bronze-winged pigeons. We went into cloud and rain, at times slithering perilously down hills that the rains had turned into slopes of red mud, and then we rose through the cloud, drove along the edges of sheer precipices which fell perpendicularly into the shifting vapours below us. Twice we met jeeps which were actually taxis, and the cars would edge round each other on the narrow road like cautious animals. As we approached the volcano the roads turned into dark grey ash, very porous and firm, and then the volcano came into sight, a great grey heap of ashes towering over the neighbouring wooded hills, with just a wisp of smoke blowing from its crest. The land around its base — the Ash Plain — was bare and black, but we turned away into the woods and went by steep roads through the dense coastal rain forest of the eastern shore of the island down to White Sands beach, where we ate our lunch in the shade of great overhanging trees, watching the boys fishing with rods in the surf and a man working with an adze on a log of yellow wood, hacking into shape a dugout canoe.

We drove back into the hills and over the Ash Plain beside the volcano towards Sulphur Bay; the Plain was as firm as the finest ocean beach, so that Russell could drive over it at top speed. It was a grim impressive scene: the black ash field with a few gaunt pandanus its only vegetation; the rusty-red field of lava that cropped out of it; the grey lake inhabited — Russell told us — with black fish imported from Africa; and the black cone of the mountain in which thunder growled and reverberated until a great columnar puff of smoke rose suddenly into the sky.

Skirting the mountain on the coastal side, we came eventually to a barrier of stakes driven into the road to prevent vehicles going any further. It was Sulphur Bay. Beyond the barrier lay a great square green of well-grazed grass, and the houses of the village were situated on two sides of the green. A young man in shorts was standing casually but observantly near the barrier. If he was a kind of sentry, he gave no obvious sign of it, and when Russell talked to him in pidgin, he waved us on over the green. As we walked there we could see that Sulphur Bay was a planned community, much larger than the other villages we had seen. The houses were arranged in orderly rows leading back from two sides of the square. Some were built in a traditional manner that has died out elsewhere on Tanna, with no walls and curved roofs like Nissen huts that came right down to the ground and were densely thatched; the wooden frames of these houses were well carpentered, so that they were sturdy and gave little purchase to the wind. All the other houses had cane walls, woven neatly into herringbone or chequered patterns, with roofs of palm or pandanus thatch. There was not an iron roof in the village, which was in accordance with the resolute traditionalism of the Jon Frum leaders that seemed to contradict their hopes of salvation through cargo from the prosperous west. Four red Jon Frum crosses within their little fences were spaced over the green, and another stood in the hollow of an old banian. A second and larger banian, with benches under it, served as a meeting place and a few women were sitting there and gossiping. The young man followed us and pointed out another rectangular fence on the edge of the green. It was the grave of Namas, the first leader of the village; some faded plastic wreaths lay on a pile of lava rubble, but there was no mark.

Most of the men, we gathered, were up on the hillsides, working in their gardens. A second young man, in a blue lavalava, was walking about with a baby in his arms, and he led us down through the rows of huts towards the beach, where a line of outrigger canoes was beached and a score of village boys were riding and tossing on the vast bounding surf that broke in the reefless bay. Seated on a log watching them was an old man with a broad greying beard who looked rather like a black Darwin. 'He's one of Nambas's successors,' said

Russell, and we went up to the old man. He shook hands and smiled very benignly, but as soon as Russell began to talk in pidgin he turned and slipped away as silently as a ghost among the huts. The young man in shorts laughed and went into a long gabble of pidgin. It turned out that the old man had been recognized as a prophet and leader until a few months ago, but then there had been disputes among the faithful, and he was forced to share his power with two of his rivals. These triumvirs were away in their gardens, and the old man did not wish to say anything to strangers out of their presence.

We strolled back over the green, and the clatter of bamboo drums sounded on the edge of the village, and then up in the hills. 'Calling pigs home,' said the young man in shorts. The clouds began to drift over the sun, and it seemed wise to begin making our way back if we did not want to be caught in a mountain storm. We walked to the row of stakes that marked the gate to the Jon Frum village. A toothless old woman in a dirty and shapeless cotton dress came up and spoke affectionately to Russell. 'This is Marguerite,' he said. 'She was my nanny!' Marguerite spoke better English than the rather difficult pidgin of Sulphur Bay, and when Russell told her we were waiting for the leaders, she laughed. 'You hear them drums?' 'Calling the pigs,' said Russell. She laughed again. 'No calling pigs. Telling big men stay away!' And though we waited for another half hour, anxiously eyeing the sky, the old man remained in hiding and the other leaders failed to appear, though some lesser men straggled down with bags of produce on their backs.

At last we gave up and left, Mount Yasua celebrating our passing by clanking its bowels and puffing up an even taller column of smoke that hung in the air and shaped itself into a miniature mushroom cloud. About half way back the rain began to fall heavily, though on the nakamels the villagers were still sitting around tiny fires over which they had rigged little awnings of banana leaves. We all felt the end of the journey had come when we reached the last of the slippery hills and the Land-Rover went out of control and slid down sideways. Luckily it did not topple over, but then there was the opposing hill, equally slippery to ascend; only after six runs at it did Russell reach the top. Ours, we learnt next day, was the last car to make the journey over the island; the others were benighted on the road and their passengers had to sleep in native huts.

When we got back Inge told us that Bob Paul and his wife had been to call and had invited us to 'tea' that evening. In fact tea was the one thing missing from the splendid meal, served with aperitifs and wine and notable Armagnac and excellent talk, that we were offered. Bob and his tall and charming wife were fine hosts, and the evening was a glimpse into the graces of planter life at its best — the life of those who refuse to let go into pseudo-native squalor and do so by holding more deliberately to the urbane aspects of life than most people nowadays in Europe or North America.

Bob Paul was not surprised by our reception — or lack of it — at Sulphur Bay. 'The movement's in flux,' he told us. 'There isn't a dynamic leader any more and the militant phase is over. The real Jon Frum people are scattered in the bush villages off the roads, and with them it's become a withdrawal. They don't want to speak pidgin or send their kids to school or have anything to do with us, and except for a few basic things they get in the barter markets up in the hills, they do very well without us. But those fellows at Sulphur Bay — they're just discontented acculturated people. Most of them hoped that when the cargo came they could turn into sham Americans, and now it hasn't come they stay on partly because it's the best run village on the island, and partly because they still hate us though they don't know what to do about it. That's why they wouldn't come to see you. You could go back a dozen times and until there's a real leader again they'll just fade away into the bush.'

From *South Sea Journey* (1976) by George Woodcock, born in Winnipeg, 1912. During his early years in England he was involved in the anarchist movement. Returning to Canada in 1949 to settle in Vancouver, he taught at the University of British Columbia, edited *Canadian Literature* magazine and achieved a literary output unrivalled in volume and range, including several travel books.

CALCUTTA
by Clark Blaise

Calcutta in December; for visitors, a perfect time. Temperatures range from the mid-seventies to the lower fifties. The street dwellers wrap themselves in double-thick scarves, in jute blankets, and sleep under whatever shelter they can afford. The middle class wear old suitcoats over their flowing *dhotis*, the women put on cardigans under their saris. The wealthier put woolen jackets on their dogs, and at the race track the super-rich can wear their imported tweeds and flannels. I still roamed the streets in a short-sleeved shirt, feeling really comfortable for the first time.

While the days are cool and generally cloudless (but for a freakish "cyclone" that struck during the wedding), the nights are dense with smoke from the millions of sidewalk braziers, the factories, the traffic, the general pollution. The nightly winter inversions, inadequate street lights, frequent power cuts, unlighted cars, street vendors with candles or kerosene lanterns set out around their mounds of fruit, popcorn, sweets, or flowers, all bring to mind a medieval village. One can walk the streets of Ballygunge on a December evening in a power cut and not be able to see his knees, the curbs and gutters, the outstretched arms, the cow patties, the broken slabs of pavement. At a quarter past five on a December evening the street lights — dim uncovered bulbs — are on, and the last orange glow of the sun is on the horizon. The toy merchants are out, the street fryers of the most tempting fritters and batterdrops in the world are shouting their prices. Popcorn is popping in battered metal pans, popped in the Indian method buried in blackened sand. Balloon vendors twist their wares, sending out a screech that attracts the children out with their parents for the nightly walk and shopping, and beggar children carrying yet-smaller babies on their hip or shoulder thread their way from open store front to open store front, hands out. Commerce, community, marriage, family; on the nights when I was feeling not Marxist but somehow Hegelian, I would drop five rupees — a good week's wages — into those hands, or others'. And I would think they were the same thing, somehow — commerce, community, marriage, family — all part of the Indian's identity, part of the world image that antedated my own.

On the side streets, any side street, the visitor would spot houses decked out in coloured lights with canopies stretching to the gutter. Clusters of cows and beggars would have already assembled outside the walls, knowing that for the next few days mounds of edible garbage will be thrown out. These are the *biyebaris*, middle-class houses rented out for the ceremony, the feasting, the housing of dozens of relatives, and for enacting, for the untold billionth time, a rite handed down, intact, from antiquity.

We entered the *biyebari* at 10 a.m. The various rooms were occupied by teams of cooks, some trimming slabs of carp into bite-sized chunks, others packing betel nut into *pan* leaves, others frying *luchis*, still more making nothing but tea. Aunts and the female cousins busied themselves arranging saris that were to be shown to the groom's party on the night of the ceremony, when they came to inspect the merchandise. Jaya's *jethoo*, Dipu's oldest brother, had already arrived from his lumber mill in Madhya Pradesh. As befitted his importance in the ceremony, he was given a room of his own to receive the *pronam* of relatives, though he rose to shake the hand of the visiting Canadian. Four straw *tolas* were brought, filled with nothing but disposable clay cups and bowls, to be destroyed after each cup of tea and each small pot of sweet yoghurt. The rest of the eating for the three days would be on the cold floor, off banana leaves. The prospect of refuse from thirty meals, twice a day for three days, had swollen the small community of beggars on the street to about eighty, some carrying sleeping rolls and braziers, others merely their bowls. A herd of milling cows, sensing activity, had made the middle of the street impassable. In one corner of the entranceway, three hired *shanai* players — Professor Mustapha Ali and what purported to be his sons — were piping away distractedly, trying to attract the *sahib's* attention for a free publicity shot. I obliged. Counting everyone imported for the work, but not counting the guests or family servants, there were about twenty cooks, carpenters, musicians, lampmen, teamakers, sweepers, and security guards.

In the next three days I suffered the full range of reactions to a ritual I could not understand: cruel, comic, absurd, moving, profound, unconscionable, scandalous. But I was to think first, in full sympathy with the tears and screaming of Jaya and her mother, that if the purpose of the ritual was to destroy the last remaining dignity of even a modestly independent girl, then it was a ceremony of genius. Bharati and I had gotten married, I couldn't help comparing, in a lawyer's office during a lunch break in Iowa City; a five-minute ceremony with a young couple who'd been having coffee at a nearby restaurant dragged in as witnesses. I'd never felt cheated or inauspiciously launched. But with this marriage ritual I was having another problem: namely, if there had to be a fuss, I expected solemn fusses. If there had to be ritual, then I wanted it on a level of high seriousness, austerity, and simplicity. Danish modern. I couldn't cope with the impurities, as I saw them, that entered Hindu worship at nearly any level.

The mixture of ritual respect and gross banality, of ritual purity and low comedy, of ancient symbolism and modern commercialism — in short, the almost unconscious blending of the high and low, respectful and profane, symbolic and literal, left me confused. I placed myself back to a wedding I'd once best-manned. What would have happened in that Connecticut suburban church if the bride's aunt had burst into the ceremony bearing some freshly fried carp and exclaimed, "What a cheap priest they (the groom's side) found! This fellow is doing it all wrong!" And if the minister had retorted, "Let us hope the bride is less of a cow than her *mami-ma*." Or if the *jethoo* — the oldest male in the ceremony and its central figure, if indeed Indian ritual has a centre, but also an uneducated man who merely owns a sawmill — were to break off every few minutes of chanting with a "Huh? I didn't get that," only to have the priest fling a few more pinches of rice into the flames with a reassuring shrug, "That's all right. Just say anything." And what if an American bride couldn't repeat, "I, Mary Smith, do solemnly swear . . . " without bursting freshly into tears, and what if her cousins never stopped giggling?

There I sat, second groom, in a cold damp corner in my Indian clothes, face made up in sandalwood paste, garlanded with white flowers that smelled of bubble gum, sneaking in an occasional shot at f/1.4 and 1/30, fearing that the slow lens noise was too prolonged and unholy, only to have the priest break the ritual and offer me a place in the centre of the room between him and the bride, or next to her *jethoo*.

The weather had turned horrible, a constant drizzle and with the temperature in the mid-fifties, like a ruined summer outing in some mountain retreat. Toes numb, nose dripping, hands in pockets, Canadian turtle neck under my *kurta*, I looked forward only to tea. I drank thirty cups a day. Carpenters struggled with the giant canopy which was to stretch over the courtyard and provide shelter for two hundred diners on the night of the ceremony, as well as for the receiving line for the arrival of the groom and his party. Like erecting tents in a hurricane, like so much in India, a problem surmounted only by the employment of the cheapest resource, human hands. The physical discomfort — I was by now swallowing back those sulphurous belches that followed inevitably from more than one Indian meal a day — merely underlined a deeper, less precise upset. I was not witnessing a ritual, I was in one; I was somehow ritualizing. I sought my customary place on the back bench and found there were no benches, no stage. The marriage ceremony was happening in a room with a priest and her *jethoo*, where Sanskrit mantras were being chanted by the hour, with flower petals being thrown on oil fires, and it was being celebrated in another room where the bride was being anointed with oils and pastes, and where the cooks were frying carp and where the aunts and cousins were chopping vegetables and exchanging gossip, and in the hallway where an Important Political Personage was dispensing favours, and in the back room where her mother was still crying loudly, and out on the street where the beggars were setting up temporary residence, already scraping the piles of banana leaves of their *jhol* and heating it in their pots while cows munched the broad, waxen leaves. All of us were celebrating a marriage. And fifty miles away in Chandranagore, the groom was at the same time repeating his mantras in his uncle's house and bathing

277

in coloured waters, and soon his bath water would be sent with a servant by train down to Calcutta so that Jaya might also bathe in it the same day.

The purpose of the ritual was not to degrade or humiliate, of course; and the genius of the ritual was to emerge unchallenged. The purpose of *jethoo's* mantras, and the cause of Jaya's tears, and the reason for her parents' sobbing in the back room was in the *meaning* of all the symbols. The purpose was to symbolize the family's relinquishment of Jaya (here symbolized as pots of fruit, rice, and flower petals) under the blessing of the marriage god, Narayan-Vishnu (the flame), and the consummation of the prayers and ceremonies was to coincide with the appearance of the groom, first through his bath water and other daily offerings sent down from his house, which were introduced into the ritual at precise moments, carried in by the bride's female relatives amid blood-curdling banshee wails (called *ooloos*), and touched to her forehead as she sat between the priest and *jethoo*. Of course there was order, even precision, to the ritual, but it was the order and precision of oriental carpetry, of intricate design endlessly repeated and varied, without a clear vanishing point or centre of attention. It was precision that demanded that the actual joining of the bridal couple could not be begun before 11:58 p.m. due to consultations with astrologers, based on the most dispassionate readings of the two horoscopes — despite the fact that a little juggling of the figures could have permitted an afternoon and not a midnight ceremony that would have permitted the two hundred guests to enjoy the feast and still get home for sleep at a decent hour. This way, fifty people had to be accommodated on various cold floors and the ceremony did not end until nearly four o'clock in the morning.

Jaya did not eat that day, and the decoration of the bride began in the early afternoon. She was powdered to a chalky grayness, her face was painted in yellow sandalwood designs. Honey was placed in her ears, so that she would hear only sweet things. On each ear she wore six sets of intertwined earrings — it being the only way of displaying all her gold at once. Her gold bangles extended nearly to her elbows, on each finger she wore three rings, on each toe, two; she wore a tiara of gold, a nose clip of gold and pearls, concentric gold necklaces, gold chains about the waist, delicate gold chains about her ankles. She stared out passively from her chair through veils of gold, while piles of silk and cotton saris lay folded at her feet. Cousins attended her sobbing with handkerchiefs, then returned to giggling and gossip. The second groom sat in his corner, fully decked out now, as isolated as the bride.

I thought of Jaya in Nagpur, the familiar little cousin who was so good with "Bert and Barnie," who used to wear a loose top and ski slacks and her hair in a braid. She was able to find cold Cokes in those dusty alleys, lead the kids to snake charmers' huts, then take them to the roof to fly paper kites. That girl had disappeared. The woman on her throne was in chrysalis. She had been sitting without moving for seven hours; her arms ached, she could not bend her head, and when the groom's party finally arrived in a caravan of cars and rented buses, she had to endure silently the inspection by his female relatives who lifted her arms to check their weight, who inspected the quality of saris, and who passed their judgments silently but unmistakably that she must be a disappointment to a good boy like Arun, so fair and handsome, but at least her father had met his obligations. She must have been thankful for the dabs of honey.

I went out under the canopy to sit with Arun, to joke with him about the hell of a fuss this whole thing was ("Ah, but it gives all these people something to do for a few days, Clark," he said), and to receive, for the first time, the *pronam* of his relatives.

The day after the ceremony, the *mamabari* relatives (but for Anju and Pritu, who had gone on to Chandranagore with Jaya and Arun the night before) packed up seven cars of relatives, filling the trunks with more gifts, and headed up to Chandranagore for a reception thrown by Arun's uncle. Chandranagore had been a French enclave, along with Pondicherry in the South, until 1952, when a plebiscite had returned both towns in India.

We arrived at night after a smoky run along fifty miles of Calcutta sprawl. If any influence of the French remained, it was in the hint of paint still on the upper porches overlooking the swirling crowds out to shop along the main road; it was seven in the evening, marketing time in Bengal. The town knew all about the marriage and of a procession from Calcutta; human signposts, spotting our strange cars, formed themselves in the middle of the road and conducted us down ever-darker alleys till a cordon of beggars raised their hands in front of a small door in a brick wall, topped with shards of glass. We parked, locked, and stepped into the garden of Arun's uncle, owner of several rice mills, *jethoo* of Arun, host, father-substitute.

Lanterns had been strung, the house was ablaze in lights, perhaps forty card tables had been set on the lawn, an orchestra was playing medleys of Hindi film, Beatles, calypso, and Doris Day songs. I found myself conversing in a corner with the uncle and other relatives; we were speaking French; it was still, after twenty years, a surer second language than English for some of the old people, and I felt for the first time, absurdly, that I had cracked an Indian language barrier. It was a different stratum of Bengal that Jaya had married into; aside from Arun, whose English was perhaps surer than his Bengali, very few spoke English at all, and those who did, didn't push it. Jaya introduced dozens of her new cousin-sisters and cousin-brothers, never faltering over a name or profession. Her eyes were as large, as happy, as I'd ever seen them.

So then, I thought: It works. Like some ponderous naturalistic novel that just happens to be unforgettable, the ritual with all its irregularities just happens to work. She knows that she will always belong to this man and to his family. All the joking and weeping, the tenderness and exploitation, the gluttony and deprivation, but mainly the moment-by-moment inventiveness *within* the rigidity, did something that no sanitized ritual ever could. It had brought me, for one thing, into the lives of Jaya and Arun and maybe three hundred others. It had brought me, of all people, fifty *pronams*. It had brought three hundred people in contact and that contact would not be severed for the rest of their lives. Jaya's remotest cousins in America will know of Arun, where he flies from, his income, his fairness and handsomeness and his retarded brother, and Arun's married sister in Madras and his copilot and his married brother in London, and the retarded one in Bangalore will know that some of Jaya's cousins have married non-Indians and non-Bengalis. All of them will know that Bharati Mukherjee, the famous novelist, who was reviewed in *Newsweek* and profiled in *Desh*, is a relative of theirs. I was beginning to understand why every Indian is so densely populated; how some of them can write five novels a year.

I ate silently, listened to music, and talked with the retarded brother, who spoke the most perfect English of his family, and who asked me more questions about Canada than I could answer. And I talked to myself as though I were my own small son: *You're seeing something incredible, kid. Remember it.*

"Everyone seems very happy," I said, after the dessert, remembering the recriminations of the week before.

The brother walked with me, his head thrust forward in the way of the feeble, but his face a more complicated and troubled version of his brother's smooth perfection. I could not help feeling that he was a proper companion for me that evening. We were walking behind the orchestra, by the wings of the house where servants were already scrubbing the giant pots.

"I wish someone had died when I was getting married," he said, "but they didn't." He entered the kitchen, dropping the empty pan of sweets in the water. I walked on alone.

There was a large garage at the end of the servants' wing. A side door was open and I went in. It was a cluttered garage, of course, more a storage room for devices I'd never seen and couldn't imagine in use. But there in the middle was a dusty reminder of Chandranagore's colonial past, and a kind of symbol of something I'd been thinking about ever since arriving in that rusting Fort-de-France of a town: a gray, classic, 1937 Citroën with boxes stored on its hood, a sagging canvas for a roof, its windows rolled down, and sudden activity from inside. From the front seat, one dark servant's head shot up, stared hard, then popped down, from the back seat two more and a woman's guttural retort.

I was back in the yard seconds later, ready to join my retarded friend who asked me where I'd gone. Through the looking glass, I thought, saying nothing. It seemed to me just then that I was standing at the end of an era, of something that went back unbroken for five thousand years but couldn't go forward even another day. I joined the two families in the main house for tea, unable to speak.

We left the *boubhat* after midnight when the town was as silent as sleep under the ubiquitous winter smoke. The cars traveled again as a caravan, for Indian highways are not safe at night — a sudden ambush by *goondas* crouched in the smog-laden gullies, a quick shoot-out, mass murder — the stuff of the daily papers. Indian roads are empty at night but for the Sikh-driven lorries carrying produce and at least two guards. In parts of central India, traffic is not safe even by day.

But I was glad to be on the road in *chhoto-mamu*'s car with its borrowed driver, and with a good assortment of the *mamabari* relatives. I was next to Anju, my favourite among the cousins, who was spinning tales about Arun's family and the goings-on in the *boubhat* after the ceremony; how rich the uncle was, how nice Arun was, how happy they would be, and yes, she suspected that despite all the practical jokes and padlocks and bells outside and hidden alarms inside, the tapping on the bedroom windows, she suspected that the marriage had actually gotten consummated on the very first night.

We pulled over sharply. "Flat tire, sir," said the borrowed chauffeur. Everyone got out. "*Chhoto-mamu*," asked Anju, "do you know this fellow? Is he reliable?" Always the fear; an unknown servant is in cahoots, his cousins are waiting in the smoke. The stuff of the papers, of Hindi films. It was the most deserted part of the road, swamps on one side, a darkened old estate behind slogan-plastered walls on the other. If he wasn't honest, we would soon find out. I remembered that first night in Calcutta; Bengalis feel unsafe in open spaces.

Chhoto-mamu assured everyone the driver was reliable. The car was unloaded. Twenty women, overdressed in Benarasi saris and gold jewelry and a like number of well-to-do urban gentlemen in their best suits stood in the middle of the Grand Trunk Highway eyeing the banks of smog like a herd of wary musk-oxen. It was a cold night, a breeze drifted over the water that felt like a drafty air conditioner. In what seemed the distance, one could hear the tinkle of bicycle bells, as empty cycle-rickshaws emerged from the smog, passed without looking, then disappeared again in the haze.

"Did a movie called *The Garden of the Finzi-Continis* ever come to Calcutta?" I asked Anju, who of course said it hadn't.

I could sense the sleepers coughing in the dark, and others walking on the gravel as they made their way to the nearby water. The night was crammed with people, all just outside our twenty feet of visibility. I kept talking of a movie Anju would never see, of a social order at the outer edge of refinement, that shatters like crystal when the mood turns suddenly brutal. I could feel brutality coming to India as surely as we heard bells and footsteps in the smoke. I mentioned the old Citroën, the servants who used it, the strange, retarded guide to the ruins.

"He makes me so sad," she said.

"Something he said to me was almost sinister," I said, aching to explain to her.

"You know what he told me?" she asked. "He told me he wished someone had died when he was getting married. Can you imagine!"

"Yes!" I could barely contain myself now; I *could* imagine it, just as Faulkner had. A desire to start over. But Anju was still talking and I held a momentary, uncharacteristic silence.

"I don't know if you know, Clark, but if someone dies during a wedding, then the whole thing is cancelled. Then there wouldn't have been a wedding, you see."

I admitted that I hadn't known.

The driver stood up, smiling, and nodded at us all.

"The flat is mended," said *chhoto-mamu. "Chalo,* let us go."

From *Days and Nights in Calcutta* (1977) by Clark Blaise and Bharati Mukherjee. Blaise was born in Fargo, North Dakota, of Canadian parents. In 1968 he accompanied his wife, the novelist Bharati Mukherjee, to her family home in Calcutta.

CALCUTTA
by Bharati Mukherjee

In January, while Clark was in Switzerland putting Bart and
Bernie in boarding school, I saw a ghost. Nothing in my adult
life had prepared me for seeing ghosts. I knew that I was prone to
miscalculation, but I had not suspected this susceptibility to the
super-natural.

My bedroom was in a pleasant-enough, split-level row house in a
colony of hierarchically arranged row houses and apartment buildings
overlooking a chemical plant. The colony itself had been hacked out
of unyielding hills and jungles. Here the vegetation was a little too
exuberant, and the monsoon sometimes washed down baby cobras
destined to be killed by house servants in someone's car porch. In
retrospect it seems the right kind of thickly curtained room in the
right kind of row house for trapping a ghost.

In a country like India where metaphor and reality continually
change places, ghosts are serious business. This ghost did not come
to me in a dream. It stood at the head of my bed and breathed warm,
sweet shafts of air on my face and pillow. The sound of its breathing
was soft, scratchy, like lizards speeding across the cement floor. It
did not speak to me; it simply stood in one spot, discomfiting me.
I recalled a childhood trick to keep away evil or frightening things:
Repeat the word "Vishnu" as quickly and as often as possible. In
Loreto House, the nuns had taught us to mix a few Hail Marys with
our apparently intractable Vishnus. So I hurled Vishnu novenas at
the ghost. After a while, it withdrew.

I do not know why the ghost disappeared. It appeared, then it was
gone; that was all. Much later in the night, because I could not con-
vince myself that nothing unusual had occurred, I slipped off my bed

— I was alone in a room that held three beds, also two metal Godrej cabinets, a desk, a chair, and a trunk that served as a coffee table — and awoke my mother who was sleeping with my father in a smaller room that housed the icons of Hindu gods.

"Whose ghost was it?" my mother wanted to know. My father snored.

I told her whose ghost I thought it was. That of an uncle who had died of gastric ulcers years before. I had rarely seen him in Calcutta in the "good old days" of which my mother and I liked to talk.

"Oh him?" she laughed. "That's all right then. You don't have to worry. He was such a quiet, mild person, I'm sure he won't give you any trouble. Even as a ghost." Then, perhaps because I still seemed nervous, she added, "You know, soon after *thakuma* (my father's mother) died, your father was off on a business trip and I slept in this house all alone. I didn't have any trouble."

That was all ghosts were to my mother: potential troublemakers to be coped with, or outwitted. Itinerant spectres, mental telepathy, and premonitions were not extraordinary. She had not been saddled as a schoolgirl with all the ethical apparatus — pocket-size books on moral science and year-long courses in religious knowledge — of the nuns of Loreto House. She and her mother and my father's mother could recount funny or chilling stories about irrational forces, often involving male ghosts and female ghosts.

I have never been excited by spiritual kinesthetics, by holy men's abilities to pull diamond rings, gold lockets, and Omega watches out of thin air. But the ghost, I had to concede, was a symptom of the frailty of my reason. Until its appearance I had approached India through the viewfinder of Clark's Nikon. What the viewfinder had framed, it had framed almost by accident, and sometimes in spite of my intentions. I had pretty shots of decently confined emotions. Then the ghost had come and shown me that there were forces present which could not be photographed at all.

After the night of the ghost I became a little too easily irascible, and found that irascibility reflected more intensely all around me. There were too many violent labour disputes, factory sieges, fire-bombings, starvation deaths, and assaults on Harijans. Then there were the minor confusions. I heard a beautician complain that she could not operate her salon because her imported equipment had

285

broken down and no one could repair it. I heard a tailor lose his temper because his assistants had gone on strike making it impossible for him to deliver my cotton hand-loom pant-suit on schedule.

My parents and I argued more than usual. My mother and I argued about the newspaper reports of clashes between the Dalit Panthers and the police. Our arguments always ended with my mother pumping angry air into her satiny cheeks and saying, "What you don't understand is that it's all political, it's not a caste battle." My father and I argued about projected trips downtown. These ended with my father citing the price of gasoline and the sacking of South Indian Udipi hotels in the city as sufficient cause to restrict us to the house.

During the month that Clark was away, my mother and I made only one trip to downtown Bombay, and that was to drop me off for a USIS seminar on contemporary American writers such as Saul Bellow and Bernard Malamud. Even that trip nearly did not come off. It was as if my father sensed that if he let go of his family again, this time the parting would be irrevocable. And so he used the threat of street violence to hold us all together under the tiled roof of the row house. Nostalgia, for the way we had once been, and for the way the entire country had been: It was nostalgia that I had to battle.

I did not go to the seminar to hear the invited Indian professors talk about American literature. I went because I had to escape crushing parental love. And I went because one of the invited Indian professors, Dr. Ranu Vanikar of Baroda University, was my younger sister, whom we had thought of as the only rebel in the family when we were growing up, and who had been the only one of us three sisters to settle in India after marriage. She had come from Baroda in spite of heavy street fighting in her neighbourhood and a city-wide curfew. We shared a hotel room, and sat up talking late into the night, every night of the conference. She was full of amusing stories about her infant son, her in-laws who lived in a separate bungalow in the family compound, her ancient but efficient part-time maids, her students and colleagues. I wished I could see her more often.

At the end of the seminar my father as well as my mother came to the hotel to take me back to Chembur. I suggested we delay the return until Ranu and the Baroda contingent had left for the railway station. But my father said that there were rumours of a serious street battle and that we had to leave at once. We quarreled in the hotel lobby. An Englishwoman in tourist clothes directed a brief and scornful stare at us for quarreling in public. My father won. We left my sister with her colleagues and drove the long and angry way home. We witnessed no riots that evening.

"But something bad might have happened," my father insisted. "You know you can't ever be too careful. You've been back long enough to see how it is."

What he said was true. Some disaster could easily have occurred. I was glad I had left India, not because I wanted to avoid disaster but because I wanted to avoid the crippling prudence that comes with living too close to imminent disasters. The year in India had forced me to view myself more as an immigrant than an exile.

Do ghosts exist, or don't they? That debate is dull and meaningless; the interesting point is that in India different perceptions of reality converge without embarrassing anyone. My year in India had showed me that I did not need to discard my Western education in order to retrieve the dim shape of my Indian one. It might have been less painful if I could have exchanged one locked trunk of ethics for another, but I had to admit that by the end of the year in India I no longer liked India in the unreal and exaggerated ways I had in Montreal. Certainly I had more friends in India, and I loved these friends more deeply. And I was glad to be racially invisible. But I believed that if I stayed on, the country would fail me more seriously than I had failed it by settling abroad. I had come carrying a childish memory of wonder and promise, unsoiled by summer visits to my parents, of the mood of Independence Day, 1947. Now, on the eve of my return to Canada, I was an irritable adult who sensed in the procession of postures at the post offices, railway stations, restaurants, races, factories, and middle-class living rooms, crushing dismay and cynicism.

Not everyone had lost faith; it is impossible to escape at least the cultural jaws of Hinduism. In a country the size of India, even minorities constitute vast populations. But those who believed, in God or government, did so out of their mammoth need to believe. Without some inviolable area of faith, daily life, even the simplest chores prove impossible to bear.

As I prepared to leave Bombay for the slow flight westward, I realized that for me there would be no more easy consolation through India. The India that I had carried as a talisman against icy Canada had not survived my accidental testings. I would return, of course, but in future visits India would become just another Asian country with too many agonies and too much passion, and I would be another knowledgeable but desolate tourist. I would never again flit inside the cool dark mansions of cultivated Bengali housewives like Anjali and thrill to teatime intimacies and tamely revolutionary ideas. I would never again share lemonade and chocolate cake with a celebrated Marxist editor and be told — with the same conviction that he heralded the socialist millennium — that my *Newsweek* photo was deceiving, and that I was not quite as pretty as his grand-daughter. Never again to be in the presence of, or under the protection of, the playfully sullen Ballygunge middle class. Next time I would probably get to know the official India better: the hotel waiters, the baggage carriers, the functionaries and smiling P.R. men of Delhi and Bombay.

It was hard to give up my faintly Chekhovian image of India. But if that was about to disappear, could I not invent a more exciting — perhaps a more psychologically accurate — a more precisely metaphoric India: many more Indias?

Writers are free to demolish and reinvent. But to be a woman writer in North America, to be a Third World woman writer in North America, is to confine oneself to a narrow airless, tightly roofed arena. In a dust-jacket photograph such a writer is usually in full dress, and appears uncommonly composed, elegant, and mysteriously forbearing. But I am not what I want my dust-jacket to suggest I am. Instead, I am anxious and querulous, convinced that every aspect of the writing profession — finding an authentic voice, an audience, a publisher, knowledgeable reviewers — weighs heavily against me because of my visibility as a stereotype. Though in my fiction I may now be ready to construct new metaphorical Indias more real to me than the literary stereotypes, I must first persuade North American readers that the stereotypes are also — if only partially — correct. Because of my readers here, I cannot take the same liberties with India, even with a private India of my imagination, that a Bellow or Malamud can take with America.

To me, the problem of voice is the most exciting one. Born in Calcutta and educated initially in Bengali, I now live in Canada and write in English about Indians living in India or in the United States. My aim, then, is to find a voice that will represent the life I know in a manner that is true to my own aesthetic. But my aesthetic has emerged during my education and stay in North America. I am of the first generation of Indian writers to be influenced by American life and fiction, to have been exposed in my impressionable years to writers such as Djuna Barnes, Flannery O'Connor, John Hawkes, John Cheever, John Updike, William Gass, and Thomas Pynchon. Even our sons are named for our friends, John Bart Gerald and Bernard Malamud. My aesthetic, then, must accommodate a decidedly Hindu imagination with an Americanized sense of the craft of fiction. To admit to possessing a Hindu imagination is to admit that my concepts of what constitutes a "story" and of narrative structure are non-causal, non-Western. A Hindu writer who believes that God can be a jolly, potbellied creature with an elephant trunk, and who accepts the Hindu elastic time scheme and reincarnation, must necessarily conceive of heroes, of plot and pacing and even paragraphing in ways distinct from those of the average American.

The works of Hindu writers writing in English about Hindu characters often read like unpolished, self-conscious translations. To avoid this ornateness, other writers opt for limpid naïveté: simply narrated stories about simple village folk. Complexities the voice cannot encompass are simply left out. But for me, an accidental immigrant, the brave and appropriate model is not R.K. Narayan, but V.S. Naipaul. In myself I detect a pale and immature reflection of Naipaul; it is he who has written most movingly about the pain and absurdity of art and exile, of "Third World art" and exile among the former colonizers; the tolerant incomprehension of hosts, the absolute impossibility of ever having a home, a *desh*. I am content that my only stability is the portable world of my imagination.

I am content. I realize, only after the return to India, that I never had the genteel sensibility of Loreto House girls, nor can I restrict myself to the conventional perimeters of Anglo-Indian fiction: romance and cultural clash if done with dignity and good humour; spiritualism, maharajahs playing cricket, village virgins clinging to their purity. Even more than other writers, I must learn to astonish, even to shock.

But I am content. Most Indian women do not give up easily. What foreigners perceive as forbearance is really a secretive love of revengeful survival. Most writers do not give up easily. What died, that year in India, was my need for easy consolation. What has survived is the stubbornness to go on.

From *Days and Nights in Calcutta* (1977). Born in Calcutta 1938, Bharati Mukherjee is a novelist and university professor. Her books include *The Tiger's Daughter* and *Wife*.

SANTA BARBARA
by Brian Moore

A graceful remembrance of things past, this California city today is an American Riviera resort, a living reproach to the era of high-rise condominiums, proliferating souvenir shops and the Gadarene host of guided tours that now deface the French Riviera from Nice to Hyères. Here, high-rise buildings have been banned for fifty years and commercial billboards since 1961. The rich remain in residence winter and summer and use "old" money in a princely way for the promotion of all manner of civic delights. Here in an extraordinarily beautiful setting between the Santa Ynez Mountains and the Pacific Ocean, Mediterranean-style architecture is the rule, and the climate (winter mean temperature average 56.8, summer, 63.04) has been designated by some authorities as the most perfect in the world. The sun shines eleven months out of twelve. Rainfall is mild.

If this makes the city sound beautiful but soporific, let me add that Santa Barbara is curiously eccentric. Its resident muse is not, as one might expect, a novelist of upper-class WASP mores, but Kenneth Millar, a mystery writer who uses the pseudonym Ross Macdonald. His private eye, Lew Archer, has mapped out its streets as his special terrain. The scholarly debates of visiting academic superstars at the financially hard-pressed Center for the Study of Democratic Institutions have been substantially funded of late by royalties from the best-selling tome *The Joy of Sex*, written by Dr. Alex Comfort. It is the city where, a few years ago, the Louds (*An American Family*) plangently acted out their divorce before a national television audience. Dame Judith Anderson and Lotte Lehmann live here, but so does Jane Russell.

The contrasts endure. John F. Kennedy came here to honeymoon with Jackie at the San Ysidro Ranch in 1953. Ironically, the same ranch was chosen seven years later by Richard Nixon when he and his aides came to Santa Barbara to sit and ponder their chances of making off with the Presidency.

And although it is a city of great private wealth, with fourteen brokerage houses downtown, a place where, one broker says, "if enough old ladies switched from IBM to Xerox, the effect on the New York market would be immediate," it is also the city to which, according to local police, "winos from all over the country come to winter in the sun."

Yet a tourist on U.S. 101, one and a half hours out of Los Angeles, driving north to San Francisco, would not guess that he is passing through California's most beautiful city. Unlike resort towns on the French Riviera, which carefully route the motorist along the seafront, past casinos, luxury hotels and beaches, Santa Barbara detours the traveler away from all that. Instead of a sight of the stately Washingtonian palms, the perfect, sandy public beaches, the fishing wharf and the teeming pleasure-boat harbour that line Cabrillo Boulevard, the passing tourist faces a slow traffic-light crawl through the business district and a trip up the freeway leading to the lonely grandeur of the Santa Ynez mountain range.

Perhaps this is because Santa Barbara is not obliged to parade its beauties as a means of livelihood. When the first astronauts landed on the moon, they navigated its surface in a small lunar golf cart that was designed here. Dozens of electronics research and development firms are located in the area, providing a prime source of income for a labour force ranging from highly skilled Ph.D.s to unskilled Chicanos.

The second most important revenue source is what the local Chamber of Commerce refers to, delicately, as "Pensions and Properties" — in other words, the retirement and other income of the many rich and middle-class old people who live here. As author Barnaby Conrad, a local resident, puts it: "This is the town to which elderly people come to visit their parents." His mother is a Santa Barbara matron of 86. Sixtyish actor John Ireland, who has just opened an elegant French restaurant in the Montecito area, says: "I like it here. It's the only place where they still call me kid."

Kids, in fact, represent the city's third largest source of income. The University of California at Santa Barbara has close to 14,000 students who live in surroundings that seem more appropriate to a Club Méditerranée vacation than the pursuit of higher learning, for this uncommon grove of academe fronts on two miles of its own sandy beach. University-owned stables and horses are available for rental, and, unlike U.C.L.A. where it sometimes seems that unless you have an on-campus parking permit you simply cannot get yourself an education, Santa Barbara bans cars to all who live within a mile of the university. Instead, 10,000 bicycles move along seven miles of bike paths in a scene resembling some futuristic Oxford. And, as one of the university's strong points is biological sciences, particularly the study of marine life, it's not uncommon to see a covey of scuba divers setting out in boats for a morning's seminar.

So tourism is only Public Revenue Number Four, but that does not mean that it has to try harder. Nature at her ugliest and private benefaction at its most munificent are the bad and good fairies that presided over the birth of the city's present beauty. Nature, in the form of an earthquake measuring 6.3 on the Richter scale, levelled the downtown part of this old California city on June 29, 1925, sparing many of the original Spanish and Mexican buildings but mercifully destroying the wasteland of Far Western schlock architecture that had overrun the former Spanish garrison town. This act of God coincided providentially with a civic movement already under way to restore the city to the look of its Spanish heritage. The city hall, the courthouse, the shopping plazas, the newspaper building, banks, a splendid hotel, a post office, all of these vital structures were built or rebuilt in a curiously harmonic potpourri of architectural styles from similar climes in the Mediterranean world: Spanish Colonial, Mission Revival, Mexican Californian, Moorish and Islamic.

Old money with the golden ring of such fortunes as Union Carbide, Morton Salt, Anaconda Copper, Hammond Organs, Arrow Shirts and Fleishmann's Yeast, rained down like a good fairy's blessings on the city. An art museum, a new harbour and breakwater, an historical museum, a bird refuge, a children's zoo, a rebuilt mission, restored old adobe structures, botanical gardens and several public parks, all came to pass. High-rise buildings were banned. An architectural board of review was formed to supervise the Mediterranean-style building. Growth was monitored and sprawl banned. The result is, today, a continual delight to the eye, a vacation spot for all seasons, and, indisputably, the most Riviera-like city in North America.

Frank Kelly, retired vice president of the Center for the Study of Democratic Institutions, recalls that when he first settled here sixteen years ago, angry letters flooded the Santa Barbara *News Press* protesting the advent of the centre and other newcomers. A plan to increase the city's water facilities was denounced in one letter with this confession of faith: "I would rather bathe only once a week than vote to bring in new water for new people."

Although the big estates of Montecito are shrinking in this era when servants come high, it was not so long ago, according to one local lady, that "the only way for a woman to make it in Santa Barbara was to be a maid, or to have a maid." New people *are* moving into the once exclusive Hope Ranch development, a sign of the times. Celebrated refugees from Los Angeles like Clifton Fadiman, Burl Ives, Eva Marie Saint, Suzy Parker and Bradford Dillman mingle with the old Barbarenos in the nearly eighty antique stores that punctuate this leisured landscape. Ross Macdonald swims daily in the pool of the Coral Casino Club, but a would-be club member was reportedly black-balled not long ago because he had made his money in the past decade. Most of the younger Santa Barbara set, their own money laundered by the generations of idleness, thought this was "much too quickly." These younger rich, incidentally, still entertain at the Santa Barbara Biltmore as though it were their own private club, but the Biltmore, a grouping of buildings in the Mediterranean style facing its own beach, is much more than that. For the tourist who can afford it, it is possibly the finest hotel in America, and certainly more pleasing to the eye than the baroque splendours of the Négresco at Nice or the Carlton at Cannes.

But, in fairness, the conservatism of the Santa Barbara rich has its strengths as well as its flaws. The Santa Barbara Art Museum, often described by rival museum curators as "a perfect small jewel," has as its principal benefactor a collector light-years distant from Norton Simon and Armand Hammer, those flashy novas of the Los Angeles art world. He is Wright Ludington (Groton, Yale, Pennsylvania Academy of Fine Arts), who used his inheritance to pursue a life of quiet connoisseurship and is proud that he bought the museum's collection of Matisses, Picassos, Derains, Vlamincks and the Greek and Roman statuary "in the twenties when prices were small. Greek and Roman sculptures were a tenth of what they are today." Recently, in the best unobtrusive Santa Barbara tradition, he sold many of his remaining paintings, built a new and smaller house and deeded his Montecito mansion to the museum. It will be sold to aid in the current plan to enlarge the painting galleries. Ludington, a reticent man, shuns interviews. Indeed, the intriguing impression that the visitor takes away from a stay in Santa Barbara is of lives, mysterious as Gatsby's, lived out in great estates, hidden from our view. Among these private worlds is that of the estate of Ganna Walska, a millionairess and opera singer, who has converted her topiary gardens and huge Montecito mansion, Lotusland, into an ashram. Few outsiders have been admitted. The late Alan Watts, Orientalist and mystic, wrote in his autobiography of the books he saw on order being shipped off to the ashram's library, comprising "everything from the esotericism of Vajrayana Buddhism, Taoism, Zen, Vedanta, Psychic Research and Magic, to New Thought, Jungianism, Hypnotism and Psychoanalysis."

And then there is the most splendid mansion facing the sea, opposite the Bird Refuge at the end of Cabrillo Boulevard. It is owned by Mrs. Huguette Clark, an Anaconda Copper heiress from Montana. There are said to be thirty-two bedrooms and thirty-two bathrooms, some of which have never been used. Its owner comes rarely to Santa Barbara and does not mingle in local society. The mansion is permanently staffed, and house, grounds and limousines are kept in readiness day and night, in case Mrs. Clark should decide to show up with a party of houseguests. A local lawyer, sent by her law firm recently to check on the readiness of the house and grounds, turned to look back as he walked down the corridors and saw a maid following him with a cloth, polishing the floor on which his shoes had trod.

Yet even the most private and powerful of these Santa Barbara millionaires must have moments when they wonder if their American Riviera can continue to escape the changes that have sullied the beauty of its European counterparts. From Mrs. Clark's mansion, looking out at the Santa Barbara channel, oil rigs can be seen, spectral on the horizon, like Martian battleships waiting to attack. And although the sands of the Coral Casino Club beach have long been cleared of the slick that fouled the shoreline and killed birds and fish a few years back, there now stands, for the use of bathers coming out of the water, a small precautionary plastic bottle and a sign no bigger than a man's hand that reads: "Kerosene for Removal of Oil Spots."

For the moment, all is luxury, calm and ease. But this city, despite its loving re-creation of the past, belongs to our world. And we cannot foretell our future.

From *Travel & Leisure* magazine (1975). Brian Moore, born in Belfast, Ireland, 1921, has been called one of the best living novelists. A Canadian citizen, he lives in California, travels widely and occasionally writes about his trips.

PORTUGAL
by Harry Bruce

Our noses were running. We were in Evora, Portugal, perhaps the most fascinating and romantic walled city in Europe, a hive of Roman ruins, convents, churches, towers, pinnacles, spires, gargoyles, Gothic arcades, ancient fountains, haunting music and explosions of flowers. And, yes, our raw, red Canadian noses were running like open hot-water faucets. Evora had inspired a writer named Miguel Torga to sing in prose, "No other town told me with such purity and beauty that I am Latin, Arabian, Christian, Peninsular and Portuguese — that I am the mixture of mystical and pagan blood which made me the miserable man I am." Evora told me, too, that I was the miserable man I was, and it told my wife that she was the miserable woman she was.

"Have you god the doilet paper?" my beloved asked. "I've goddoo blow my dose." *Honk*. We were outside the Chapel of Bones in the Church of St. Francis. The interior walls are matted with bones and skulls of long-dead monks and other folks. An inscription at the entrance told us that *those* bones were waiting for *our* bones. We didn't go in.

"I feel derrible," I said. Popping aspirins as we went and horrifying local people with violent eruptions of coughing, we sagged along narrow lanes back to our hotel for the ninth feverish afternoon nap of what we'd once dreamed would be the best two-week holiday of our lives.

We were there to celebrate the amazing fact that we'd happily survived 25 years of marriage. Surely we deserved a silver anniversary gift. Why not Portugal, land of lovers? Penny had never been there, but I had, and I told her, "God you'll love it. It's got fabulous history, fabulous food, the politest people in Europe. They're so gentle over there that when they have bullfights the bullfighters don't even kill the bulls. They just wear them out. And the scenery, the climate, the flowers, the beaches! You'll never forget it. Let's go." So we did, and we haven't forgotten it, especially the day some wretch stole our luggage and Penny's front tooth fell out, and . . . but I'm getting ahead of myself.

The dream came flawlessly true in Lisbon — for all of two days. On the third morning, we picked up a rented car, crossed the great sliding Tagus River, and plunged south to Sesimbra. It's a centre for both commercial and sports fishing, and with its Moorish castle, its bluffs, beaches, cheerful fishermen untangling their nets, and children and dogs romping in the clean surf, it looks like an enchanting place either to eat lunch or spend the rest of your life. We settled for lunch, then headed inland to a lodge called Quinta das Torres. On the way Penny began to sneeze, and then she plunged into a deep sleep. It was an omen of horrible times to come.

Quinta das Torres was the most beautiful place we've ever slept. We approached it through a long avenue of sun-filtering trees, then drove into a secret courtyard with a dead fountain in the middle. A gate slammed behind us, a small maid locked it with a gigantic key and — as we looked around at the queer pointed towers, the swans cruising beside the little temple in the pond — we knew we'd arrived in some timeless zone of tranquility and dusty elegance. An Italian architect had designed the place more than 400 years ago, and to us it symbolized everything that's still magical about European travel.

Our private living room had a 30-foot-high ceiling, a pink marble fireplace and dark furniture from various centuries. Our bedroom was worthy of royalty. The beds were massive, shapely, brass affairs with white, filmy canopies and heavily embroidered linen sheets. The entire suite cost $40 a night, breakfast included, and to celebrate our fabulous luck I zoomed into the nearest town to get a bottle of dry white port. I was back in half an hour, at five in the afternoon. Penny was already in one of the fabulous beds. She sounded as though she had whooping cough, and at 3 a.m. I awoke with a throat so sore I thought I'd end up in hospital.

As it turned out, neither of us was quite that sick, just sick enough to be thoroughly miserable. We hoped that once we reached the

Algarve — Portugal's Riviera — we'd just stretch out on a sumptuous beach and let the sun bake those colds right out of our cough-racked chests and drooling heads. After all, didn't the Algarve enjoy more than 3,000 hours of sunshine a year? That's what we'd read. But the tourist literature hadn't reckoned with our lousy luck. We reached the Algarve in driving rain. "Happy anniversary dear." "Same to you, sweetheart." It did not rain on each of the five days we were in the province of Algarve, only on two, but it was fall, and the weather was, well, brisk.

To reach the Algarve, we rolled south among trees that looked like massive green brains and then through the golden mist and towering eucalyptus trees of the Monchique Mountains. We went out to Sagres and Cape St. Vincent, the southwestern tip of mainland Europe, a breathtaking jumble of cliffs that lives up to its pre-Columbus reputation as "the end of the world." We drove among the almond, lemon and fig trees of that scented land, among thousands of dainty Moorish chimneys, and then we turned north. We buzzed through vineyard country and over the Caldeirão Mountains and, out of the Algarve, found ourselves gliding out on the cowboy plains and once-bloody battlefields of the Alentejo district. Groves of dark cork trees and high, crenellated castles punctuated the plains on their long sweep toward the Spanish border, and we sourly observed all these wonders through watery, itching eyes. To blow our noses, we carried rolls of pink and yellow toilet paper.

Meanwhile, we had so few clothes that Penny washed them each night and prayed they'd dry by morning. The loss of our luggage had been part of a day that in our memory will live in infamy. After leaving our suite at Quinta das Torres we stopped for lunch at the Pousada São Filipe, a hotel inside a mountaintop fortress just south of Sesimbra that dates back nearly 400 years. The view is among the most dramatic in all Portugal, but to see it you must leave your car outside the castle walls and mount a spooky, dripping tunnel. Once you've done that, you can't see your car. While we were washing down exquisite baby clams with good white wine, some thieving rotter (or rotters) neatly cracked a door lock on our car, grabbed the two bags on the rear floor, and made off with all our toiletries, Penny's jewelry and, except for what we were wearing, every stitch of clothing we'd brought with us.

We didn't know. We drove south all afternoon and didn't discover our plight till we checked in for the night at a fairy-tale castle in a village on the west coast. We had no fresh clothes for dinner. We also had no brush for our hair, no brush or toothpaste for our teeth, no razor for my stubble, no spirit for anything. We drifted down from our room in the tower to get a couple of predinner gin and tonics. Penny bit an olive. "That's funny," she said. "This olive has *two* pits." Wrong. One pit was an upper front tooth, or rather a 15-year old cap. She suffered no pain, but when she opened her mouth, visions of jack-o'-lanterns danced in my head. It was too much. We collapsed in fits of insane laughter, and it was then that our host and his wife entered the room.

He was over 80, courtly, a former diplomat, the uncle of a friend back home. And what did this gentleman see as he entered his living room on a Sunday night for which he'd planned a formal dinner in honour of a Canadian couple who had come to his country to mark their silver wedding anniversary? He saw a partially toothless woman in wrinkled slacks, sweater and blouse, and a grubby, unshaven man in jeans and a striped sailor's shirt. Both of them were wiping their eyes and noses with toilet paper, sputtering, coughing, choking back laughter and phlegm.

Our host and his wife, however, were the soul of Portuguese hospitality. They made us as happy as anyone possibly could have made us that evening, and in the morning we found on our breakfast tray the address of an English dentist. The dentist glued Penny's cap in place, but the next day she coughed it out again. She went back to him, and this time it held, probably because she limited her experience of Portuguese cuisine to soup, poached eggs and soft cheese.

We ended our trip in misery in the city where we'd started it in ecstasy: Lisbon. We'd decided to treat ourselves to a final night of luxury at the Hotel Ritz, which is indeed ritzy. But we simply did not look like Ritz clientele. I'd bought a couple of shirts, socks and underwear. Penny had bought one skirt. Most of our few clothes were spread out to dry on the back seat. Our luggage consisted of a plastic shopping bag. The moment we drove up to the wide steps of the Ritz, a doorman stepped forward, clicked his heels, pulled open Penny's door, surveyed the socks and underwear, and with amazing composure said, "Give me the keys, sir. The boy will take your baggage."

An assistant manager insisted on guiding us to our room. The "boy" followed with our plastic bag. He carried it as though it were a jeweled crown on a cushion, and our little parade across the polished acreage of the lobby looked like a scene from a Marx brothers movie. They left us at last in a huge room with a dizzying view of downtown Lisbon.

"I've got to go down there and find the car," Penny said. "I've got to get your clothes." In the parking lot, she carefully wrapped the laundry around a bottle of Portuguese gin we'd bought. Only Penny can make bundles so neat, but when she got back to the room she said, "I don't get it. Everyone in the lobby was staring at me. I don't look that funny."

"Of course you don't," I said. "But you do have a very fat and sensationally pink roll of toilet paper sticking out of your skirt pocket."

We blew our noses, drank the gin, and wondered where we'd be on our 50th anniversary. We knew we'd still be together. The next 25 years of marriage would be a cinch.

From *Weekend Magazine*. Harry Bruce was born in Toronto in 1934. Editor, author, columnist, essayist, he has lived and worked in Halifax for many years.

GREENLAND
by Jim Christy

It is another August just about 40 years later. After scaling these still enchanted cliffs, you stand poised just below the steel grey sky; beyond, the brown mountains unfold ridge unto ridge like the tops of a million gnarled Eskimo hands, and your vision plummets to the tide madly rolling against the sheer coast and carries out to a sea of a million stone islands, the water looking cold and dark except around the icebergs, where it is reflected in a fragile and pellucid blue.

If the cliffs and the horizon impress with Wagnerian drama, the rock below your feet as you hike along the ridges through the washes and into high mountain meadows is more like a tone poem, muted like the palette of a Debussy, with the colours of camomile and sorrel, the quartzite rock filigreed by lichen. There are certain thoughts always in the minds of travellers in the high, remote areas and they may seem predictable, almost hackneyed, in a jaded world, but they have never been as real as here, in the most rugged of countries. It is as if the land penetrated by the fjords reveals the truisms behind all these clichés of the wilderness. You really do look out across the vast stillness and feel infinitesimal, an intruder, a blink of the eye in a timeless land, but at the same time, this is all yours, you are king of an enchanted place and never before have you been so aware of your own physical presence in the world. In other countries you may see mountains stretching off as if forever but you also know that out there somewhere, maybe 50 or even 500 miles away, is a city, a town or the home of at least one lonely individual to warm the desolation; in Greenland, looking in from the sea, you understand that there is no one. The southern perimeter of land, warmed by the strange currents and made colourful for a few quick months, gives way to ice that covers the country clear to the other shore, the Denmark Strait of the Greenland Sea.

And everywhere you walk you may very well be the first. Your boots may have trampled mountain flowers elsewhere and crushed delicate arctic plants and you never gave it a thought. If such things bothered you, you'd get no peace, you'd hole up like a fanatic Tolstoy. Here, though, the green and black and yellow lichen that carpet the rock, the angelica and the mountain cotton, have never been disturbed in the seasons of their brief flourishing.

It is a Sunday in Godthaab — Nuuk in the Inuktitut language — and from the promontory above the harbour, Hans Egede, staff in hand, surveys all that his journey of 260 years ago wrought. At the old docks the Inuit fishermen are fiddling with outboard motors or handing the day's catch onto shore. One man chops deftly at his fish, filleting some and cutting the rest into strips for drying. The stainless-steel blade is a foot long and his hands are bloody and swollen. Up the hill other men are carrying baskets of fish, one woman has a string of ptarmigan over her shoulder; they are going to Braedtet, the open-air market. Two old men sit on the hillside with bottles of beer eating raw whale meat spread out on a newspaper.

As you walk the streets and muddy paths you see Inuit heading for the edges of town to hunt, .303s slung across their backs. Up on Tuapannguit, a dusty Leyland Sherpa pulls up in front of Block Q of the apartment complex that seems so incongruous in this place. Two men get out of the cab, lower the gate of the pick-up bed and begin struggling with the body of a reindeer. The head hangs limply over the edge, the velvety antlers dangle above the gravel and you see the red bullet hole in the neck. They notice me watching and bid me with smiles and waves to follow. I lend a hand and we take the body up to the building and set it down in a walkway. With a couple of sudden motions the head is off. One man slits the skin down the front. They extract the organs and begin sectioning the carcass. A few children stand around idly, watching. We could be in a residential area of Vancouver or Copenhagen but the cement is covered with blood and the faces are all broad and dark. The people are Inuit and some stare with blue eyes.

There are no Danes on the streets this day. At the church earlier there was a christening. A family of healthy, blond-haired people stood on the wooden steps of the church and as the relative with the camera crouched for a shot, the mother proudly pulled back the shawl from her baby's eyes.

In the year 887, a Norwegian colonist named Gunnbjorn Ulfsson, sailing to his new home in western Iceland, reported seeing land to the east. Ninety-five years later, Eric the Red, a chieftain from Iceland's northwest coast, was sent into exile for three years and decided to spend the time exploring the rumoured land. He found the southwestern coastal areas of Greenland to be suitable for farming, with plenty of grassland for raising sheep, and after his exile he promoted the colonization of the island. In 986 he went back to Greenland with 400 people and by 990 the first congress was in session. The government was a democracy and the small communities, whose economy was based on animal husbandry, flourished. The farms were located back in the fjords away from the chilling ocean winds. The civilization was at its peak around the twelfth century, and one of the best sources of early Greenland history is works on falconry. The sport had a fanatical hold on everyone in Europe in the Middle Ages, from emperors to peasants, and each level of society had its own species of falcon. The Greenland falcon was reserved for kings and other royalty, and books were written about expeditions to capture the birds in Greenland.

And then, soon after the apex, everything began to fall apart. In 300 years there would be no Norwegians left in the country and a myth would be born, that of the lost colonies of Greenland. For centuries, scholars drew conclusions and based careers on the various theories for the Vikings' disappearance. As is so often the case with historical mysteries, there was much theorizing. One view held that climatic changes had disastrous consequences for farming and that the Norwegians were unable to exist on a diet of fish and game, another that they were destroyed by pirates, wiped out by a Black Plague or slaughtered by Eskimos. Others believe the truth was rooted in the mistake the Greenlanders made in the year 1261, when they decided that their society would prosper even more if aligned with Europe as a province of Norway. This theory suggests that Norway imposed a monopoly on trade and, with lack of goods, the farming society of pureblooded Europeans died.

Although Eric the Red had seen the abandoned houses and kayaks of the vanished Dorset Eskimos, it had been another two generations before the Norwegians encountered their first native peoples. Later, during the decline of European trade, the Norwegians probably learned to live like Eskimos, adopting the culture and intermarrying in order to survive.

There followed 200 years during which virtually no Europeans travelled to Greenland. But all the while, debate raged on about the disappearance of the Vikings. The curiosity came down from the ivory towers and into the streets following Martin Frobisher's brief visit to the southern tip of the island in 1576. Frobisher returned to England with a genuine Eskimo. He was a spectacle and a sensation and Frobisher was credited with the rediscovery of Greenland. The Eskimo died in London of a cold.

In 1721, a Norwegian missionary, Hans Egede, in the name of the Danish crown arrived with a mandate to search for the descendants of the lost colonists. He claimed to find no trace of them: "The men and women . . . have broad faces and thick lips: they are flat-nosed and of a brown complexion. But some, however, are attractive and of a fair complexion."

Egede never did realize that he was seeing the faint reflection of his own heritage.

I am in Per Berthelsen's apartment in Block T and we are all seated in his living room watching a video cassette of a local television production that honoured the anniversary of his twenty-fifth year in the music business. Per, a full-blooded Inuit, is wearing slippers and serving refreshments. His brother, a trumpet player, and his sister, a singer, are there; so is a woman named Ernea Geisler, who comes from Disko Bay on the northwest coast, where her mother married a visiting German missionary. Per, in living colour, is telling the interviewer in Danish how 90 percent of Greenlanders seem to possess a natural ability to play music. The scene switches to the band emerging from a car stopped between deep snowbanks. They make their way, capering like arctic Beatles, into a rehearsal studio that looks like an abandoned fishing shack on the beach.

When the show is over, Per plays selections from the six albums he has recorded in Denmark with white guys who look like mid-sixties Amsterdam Provos. But the best music is on the tapes of his soon-to-be released album. It's all done by local Greenlander musicians, but they are not chanting old myths accompanied by bone rattles and skin drums. Rather, the music is a melange of sophisticated European rock with what Per calls a "funk" beat, sort of an electric Inuktitut blues.

The walls are covered with books and prints, the apartment filled with sculpture and electronic gadgets, the drinks are on a silver tray on the coffee table and out beyond the balcony, below the rock cliff, is the graveyard of early settlers in a green, grassy meadow that spills down to a sea that is dark now with only the weird white shapes of icebergs visible.

Hans-Pavia Rosing, behind a blond wooden desk, outlines the hazards of Canada's Arctic Pilot Project. One of his assistants, a young woman who looks to have no Danes in her family tree, enters the room and hands him a folder, and I note the contrast in their complexions.

"The project proposes to ship liquefied natural gas by tanker from Bridport Inlet on Melville Island to the east coast of Canada. The shipping routes run through the seal breeding area and they will be scared away by the smells and the noise. When they go, the polar bears will disappear because they live on seals. The navigation route crosses that of the whales and the narwhals and that will cause them to disappear also. And from the fall until nearly July, the ice is the means of communication in the northern areas but when the ice is broken up by the ships, of course, that communication will also be broken."

Hans-Pavia is one of those particularly handsome men not usually seen anywhere except on the screens of theatres that show old movies. There is not a line on his face, his hair is prematurely grey and his eyes pale blue. "The effects of this Arctic Pilot Project," he says, "will be devastating to our people."

You have to look closely at the tear shape of his eyes and note that his face is unusually broad to realize that he has Inuit blood and that he is indeed a Greenlander. He is the president of the Inuit Circumpolar Conference (ICC), founded in 1977. Its purpose is to unite the Inuit people of Greenland, Canada and Alaska. The thrust of the organization is the recognition that the Inuit are an indigenous people with a unique ancestry, culture and homeland, and that homeland, the arctic and subarctic areas, transcends political boundaries.

Hans-Pavia explains that the newly established air route I have used to get to Greenland, from Frobisher Bay in the Northwest Territories, was created as a result of pressure by the ICC to facilitate communication between Inuit of the three nations. "From this side it is Inuit operated, by Greenland Air. Until the route was established we would have had to fly to Iceland and on to Copenhagen and then to Montreal or Toronto. Without the route our work would be immensely difficult."

The impetus of the ICC derives from this office. The situation of the Inuit in Greenland is vastly different from that in Canada and Alaska. The group gets a grant from the Danish government, but operates independently. The Inuit basically run the country of Greenland. In Alaska some have formed corporations to promote their interests. Despite the existence in Canada of the Inuit Tapirisat, this country is the weak link. There could not be more of a contrast between towns in the Canadian Arctic and Greenland. Returning to Frobisher from Nuuk is like going back 200 years in time. Throughout the Northwest Territories you have these bleak settlements, strung out across the barrens, Inuit clustered in their homes around the newly arrived white man's hotels and government office buildings like Frobisher with its ridiculous highrise, a monument to myopia and the inflexibility of *Qallunnaaq* — white man — bureaucrats. It is all reminiscent of nothing so much as the buffalo-skin tents of Indians of the old west staked around the walls of the fort, the occupants waiting for scraps to be flung over the ramparts.

As I'm leaving Hans-Pavia Rosing's office I come out with what has been bothering me. "Look," I say, "You don't exactly resemble anyone's stereotype of an Inuit. I mean, no one outside of Greenland would dream that you belong to the same race as your assistant who was just in here. I wonder if this causes any consternation on the part of other Inuit when you go to Alaska or Canada."

"Oh, at first they might look at me curiously, but as soon as I open my mouth there is no problem. Inuktitut is my language. A

Greenlander can be defined as anyone here with Inuit blood who speaks Inuktitut."

Sunday evening and the dining room of the Hotel Greenland is beginning to fill. They are mostly Danes, couples and families, all of them handsome and healthy, all well dressed, if not fashionably dressed. The men wear neckties, the women look turned out for church. They settle down at their tables, flowers in vases at each end, the cutlery solid and heavy, yellow folded linen, everyone is square-jawed and blond and they never look around the room until the band begins to play. It is a northern European bourgeois ritual steadfastly maintained in this outpost at the edge of nowhere.

Outside, the apartment blocks command the hills overlooking the water and the streets are deserted except for cruising Datsun Cherry cabs and a straggle of teenage Inuit on the promenade by the closed shops. They loiter and goof around like bored suburban teenagers, waiting and hoping for the odd chance to score not dope, but points, the little government liquor rationing coupons. Each citizen or visitor is entitled to 72 points a month, which are exchanged for alcohol; a beer or a shot demands one point. You can sell six points for 100 kroner, which is about 17 Canadian dollars. A month's allotment or 72 will fetch 1,200 kroner.

Inside, the food keeps coming, salads and soups and aspics preceding the hearty pork chops in sauce and thick reindeer and whale steaks. There are three couples at one table and it's obviously a situation where the young lovers are bringing both sets of parents together for the first time, only she is Danish and he, an Inuit with styled hair and a grey three-piece suit. The Danish woman and the Inuit woman have the same matronly figures and that's all. The white woman looks like the archetypal movie dowager, Margaret Dumont, lacking only a lorgnette perched like a hood ornament on her breasts. Her husband is the silvery chairman of the board type with Vikings in his ancestry. The Inuit man is small, dark and craggy, wearing sport coat over sport shirt, black hair combed like Chuck Berry. He has a few white chin whiskers, slitted eyes; obviously a few years before resettlement he was harpooning whales and stalking polar bears across the floes; you can't look at him without imagining icicles on his moustache and eyebrows. He seems to be holding his own and holding the glass of white wine in some kind of toast. The tuxedoed waiter with the linen over his arm hovers about garnishing the fish with parsley.

And while this little family drama is transpiring, there is music in the background. A drummer and organist, both Danes, and everything they play is American country music. Later, during the brandy and cigars, couples get up to dance, very stiffly, it seems, discreetly shaking their shoulders to the fast ones or waltzing as the blond organist sings: "Ant thee-air runts Mare-reee, har uf guld ent leeps uf chair-rees."

Back in 1721 Hans Egede had established his base of operations on an island at the head of a fjord and he and his followers would have perished save for the charity of the native people. Egede decided to stay on after his ordeal and moved his followers farther inland to establish the town of Godthaab. Some time later, the Danish court, perhaps influenced by the ideas of Rousseau, moved to protect the Inuit culture. Greenland was closed to all outsiders, including Danes not involved with trade and the actual operation of the country. The missionaries and traders therefore intermarried with the Inuit and began what was to become the unique Greenland race.

The use of the Inuit language was encouraged by the Lutheran Church, newspapers were published in Inuktitut and by the beginning of the nineteenth century there were forms of locally elected government in operation.

When Denmark was occupied by the Nazis in 1940, Canada and the U.S. became concerned about Greenland and established consulates in the country. In 1941 the Danish ambassador in Washington reached a defence agreement with the Americans. The presence of outsiders in their country for the first time in more than 200 years would have an unpredictable effect on the postwar consciousness of the Greenlanders.

The late forties saw the development of population centres such as Godthaab and Julianehaab to serve the fishing industry, which was to be the basis of the Danish government's plans for development, plans that backfired. The people were resettled in the centres and there appeared those incongruous apartment blocks, which were filled with uprooted people suddenly cut off from their traditions. And the Danish technicians and officials were around to direct their lives. Instead of being cowed, the Greenlanders learned and they became politicized. The resettlement scheme thus inspired Greenland's nationalist politics and the experience of the war years gave them the confidence that they could exist very well without the Danes.

A home rule commission with seven elected Greenlanders and seven Danish members of Parliament was formed in 1975. In the referendum of January 1979, home rule won by a two to one margin and in the following elections the more nationalist and socialist of the two major local parties, the Siumit, won a majority.

Home rule was created by an act of the Danish Parliament and therefore cannot be revoked or amended unless by agreement. There are no Danes in elected positions in Greenland. They have reserved the powers of currency and foreign relations, but even the latter is subject to negotiation. For instance, a late February referendum on whether Greenland should remain part of the European Economic Community resulted in a 52 percent vote for withdrawal, a decision Denmark is likely to respect or at least seriously consider.

Ernea Geisler tells me she remembers a day many years ago, when she was a young girl living in the north, when a black man appeared at the rail of the monthly ship. He was the first black man she or anyone else had ever seen. They all stared at him in silence.

"He must have been a soldier or a scientist."

"No. He was all alone, travelling. A huge man. He had come all the way from Africa."

"What? What happened to him?"

"He stayed near us for awhile, then left for the north and lived there with the people."

She mentions someone in Godthaab who knew more about this mysterious visitor. We found an old man drinking beer. He had hunted and fished all his life and had come to the city to spend his last days with his family. They spoke in Inuktitut, the old man looking at me, nodding his head and smiling. "He says the black man was a very nice man and everyone loved him. He hunted polar bears and seals and when he left everybody was sad."

I was intrigued by the story of the giant black man from Africa who suddenly appeared in Greenland, and determined to find out more. . . .

His name was Teté-Michel Kpomassie and he had come from Togoland. He passed a happy childhood there in the bush until one day when he was bitten by a python. His survival was attributed to the incantations of a sorceress and Teté's father therefore vowed to dedicate the boy to the python cult. The prospect filled him with horror and during his convalescence he discovered a book about Greenland. He read everything he could find about the gigantic island of ice and pored over maps and atlases of the arctic regions. He determined to go to Greenland, which was as far away in distance and culture as he could get from his own country and the python cult.

Teté runs away and begins a journey of several years that takes him through Africa and Paris and finally to Copenhagen. All this time he makes friends everywhere and his friends help him on his way.

He takes a cargo boat through the icy waters to Greenland and indeed when he appears from below deck the crowd of Inuit is stunned. But they recover and welcome him. They at first think he is one of their own gods, the black one who lives back in the snowy mountains. When they learn that he is indeed human, the Inuit outdo each other in providing for him. Everywhere Teté goes he is offered wives and the single women throw themselves at him. He partakes of all aspects of Inuit life and keeps on the move, farther north, always on to a more remote community. Finally he is living with one old man, a crazy recluse in a shack in the snows hundreds of miles above Thule in Washington Land. Then after many months, Teté realizes he must return to Africa and tells the old man of his decision. As Teté walks toward the boat, the old Inuit man turns his back to hide his tears and refuses to watch the black man leave.

It is a storybook night out of a wild sailor's dream. There are, in fact, two sailors along in the party that moves in and out of cabs and bars all over the little town. They are a couple of boys from down east — Sydney, Nova Scotia, to be precise — who have been fishing the Davis Strait for two months. Bone-numbing 16-hour days at the end of which you flop onto the bunk, sure you'll never rise again, and before falling into a deep sleep you have time for only the briefest thought, that miracle upon miracle, somewhere along that immense Greenland coast there might perhaps be the warm and beckoning lights of a cozy port, just the lights and maybe a place to sip a beer.

It's just a thought but if you dare to dream, two months out of Sydney, you'd dream . . . of your ship tying up late at night and when you woke in the morning a dozen beautiful, dusky women stand on the dock of the bay, not looking up to deck coquettishly but demanding to come on board and when the Jacob's ladder is let down, they actually clamber up with innocent, erotic giggles like Polynesians to Bougainville's ship, or their own ancestors offering themselves to the white men on the first boats through the ice.

Donny, a 20-year-old sailor, muscular in his Greenland T-shirt, is in the back seat of the cab with a woman who doesn't speak his language; he's indulging in a little boasting about it all and concludes, "They just won't take no for an answer. You got to . . . [pay attention to them all] before they'll go away."

His buddy Arnold is twice his age, with one of those wiser Maritimer faces and eyes that can't hide emotion. He considers it all philosophically, like bounty from heaven, like a gift delivered to the wrong guy. He sits back contentedly and sighs, "I really don't believe this has happened, byes. Tonight how about we have a peaceful night, eh?"

I don't expect he thinks it's possible. As soon as we walk into a club, a woman approaches Arnold and says, "You will have a drink with me?" and he rolls his eyes heavenward.

The rest of the night is all brandy and beer and jukebox music, cab meters and flashing lights, conversations in two languages that get nowhere and don't have to. A woman stands up on a table full of bottles and begins a spontaneous strip-tease. When she has divested herself of the last garment, she empties a bottle of Faxe Fad beer over her shoulders and begins to massage herself lasciviously. Soon two compatriots are at each side solemnly pouring more beer over her. A waitress also stands by, handing them bottle after bottle, taking the money and collecting the points.

Several hours later, when it is all over, the little town is nestled in a blanket of fog. The top of Mount Sermitsiaq wears a cloud like a cotton crown all askew and from the docks comes the bass note of a ship's farewell, a deep rumbling that seems to rise from the bottom of the sea and resonate in the canyon of the fjord, as the fishermen head out to sea and home.

From *Quest* magazine (1983). Jim Christy was born in 1945. He lived in Toronto for 19 years before migrating to Vancouver. Poet and essayist, he is author of *Palatine Cat* (1978) and *Travelin Light* (1983).

JAPAN
by Loral Dean

When Noriyuki Nihei, a 34-year-old, small-time crook with 11 bungled jobs behind him, broke into a construction-camp dormitory in Chiba (near the outskirts of Tokyo), he couldn't find a thing to steal. But, like Goldilocks, he did find some steaming booty — not three bowls of porridge in Noriyuki's case, but a tub brimful of hot water. Life on the lam had robbed Noriyuki of a cherished Japanese birthright — a long, luxurious, daily soak. With 30 bathless days behind him, unspeakable in Nipponese lexicon, he could resist no longer. Ah, the ruinous weakness of the flesh! An hour later, a sleepy construction worker spotted Noriyuki snoozing blissfully in the steaming tub and delivered him, dripping and defenseless, to the police.

The Japanese are getting a lot of ink these days because of their stunning successes in the world of commerce, but it's seldom told that they've been buoyed to the crest of global trade markets on a wave of 104-degree bathwater. The Japanese are the cleanest race on the face of the earth and possibly the cleanest form of life in the entire universe. And cleanliness in Japan begins with a daily bath, ritualized beyond the ken of us shower-happy Westerners.

On a recent trip, I toured the dormitory provided for unmarried men employed in Mazda's impressively efficient, new car-assembly plant in Hofu in the southwest of Japan, 77 minutes by bullet train and bus from Hiroshima. It resembled a curious hybrid of jail and monastery. The entire concrete building, a utilitarian affair, was permeated with the odour of a fierce, ammonia-based cleanser, aptly counterpointing the scrubbed, spartan gleam of floor and wall. The superintendent escorted me through, explaining the house rules as we walked (10:30 p.m. curfew on weekdays, 11 on weekends; no visitors allowed except immediate family, to be billeted in allotted guest rooms), opening each door with one of the daunting jangle of keys at his waist.

There was a recreation room, tiny and bare except for a television set in one corner and the traditional, rush-and-straw *tatami* mats on the floor; a reading room, containing two menacing metal bookcases shelving a couple of dozen tired paperbacks; a minuscule workout area of bar-bells and assorted brawn-building machines; and a representative bedroom, furniture-free except for two narrow, single beds, some built-in, open shelves and a tiny tatami sitting area.

But the bath was something else. Only its antiseptic shine allied it with the rest of the dormitory. The bath was a thing of beauty, swimming-pool size, set in a spacious, tiled room, by far the most inviting and livable space in the building.

The words "communal bathing" bear unhygienic overtones to Western ears. The Japanese approach to group bathing (which, in the past, was coed, but is now largely segregated by sex) couldn't be less so. Indeed, the Japanese regard our method of bathing, solitary though it may be, as an unthinkably filthy practice befitting only hairy Western barbarians — soaking, as we do, in our own dirty bathwater. Japanese baths are not for washing; they're for talking, reflecting and relaxing — and the ritual soaking of a body scrubbed within millimetres of removing its epidermal layer. The dirty business of washing takes place before slipping, squeaky clean, into the pristine sanctity of the bathwater. The deck wall surrounding the Mazda dormitory bath was, like all traditional Japanese baths, ringed with evenly spaced sets of taps, each with a tiny stool and bucket in front. Armed with a bar of soap and a washcloth, each bather soaps, scrubs and rinses himself scrupulously before entering the bath.

Needless to say, the deck was equipped with drains. Their absence from a Western-style bathroom (not to mention the obscenity of a *toilet* in the same room) can prove calamitous for a Japanese on his first visit abroad. A celebrated story tells of a Japanese traveller in New York who proceeded to take a bath *à la japonaise*, oblivious to the lack of drainage in the room. His hostess, also Japanese but a longtime resident of the United States, apparently had not yet adopted the North American custom of speaking up. As the visitor doused himself with water on the bathroom floor, she silently mopped up the water streaming under the door into the hall, without a word of protest.

When we were introduced to the delights of the Japanese bath at Mazda's elegant company guest-house, we also discovered that it replaces a cherished North American custom. Lounging in one's soiled working clothes *cinq à sept* enjoying a few preprandial drinks liberally punctuated with handfuls of salted nuts does not conform to Japanese standards of cleanliness. The proper preparation for dinner in the Land of the Rising Sun is not a cocktail and hors d'oeuvres, but a leisurely bath, after which you don a freshly laundered *yukata* (cotton kimono) in which to dine.

There we were, shifting our pink, yukataed bodies from foot to foot, glassless and correspondingly speechless, while we waited what seemed an interminable length of time for dinner to be served. This is not to say that the Japanese do not drink; they do, and under certain socially acceptable conditions, they drink until they're falling-down drunk. But one of the secrets to a beginner's understanding of this most orderly and ordered of countries is comprehending that anything goes — but only if the time and place are correct. And the proper time for a few swift belts is *not* before dinner.

Hygiene in Japan may begin and end with the bath, but it certainly isn't the whole of it. I had read that Tokyo is congested, polluted, noisy and jammed with the nondescript skyscrapers of mega-cities all over the world. I was totally unprepared for its startling cleanliness and order. In Tokyo, there is no necessity for a New York-style "curb your dog" campaign; dogs are kept on very short leashes and are not often seen in public. And small boys with runny noses and scuffed running shoes don't seem to exist in Japan. School-children are seldom seen except in regimented, uniformed groups of 30 or more, preceded by a teacher often bearing a flag.

The pristine orderliness of city streets even extends to food. Everyone knows that Japanese food is as pleasing to the eye as to the palate. But outside Japan, it is not widely known that you can feast your eyes on exquisite arrangements of Japanese food while walking down any city street — not in unhygienic outdoor stalls, but hermetically sealed behind glass. Virtually every restaurant displays its wares in a glass-encased box on the street, containing beautifully painted, remarkably appetizing, plastic reproductions of the choices on the menu. Predictably, the fake food is made from a type of vinyl that is durable, dustable and won't melt. Painting plastic food is a highly specialized art not to be scoffed at: according to Isamu Majima, who runs one of Japan's largest fake-food production companies, it takes a full 10 years to become a master sardine painter.

Tokyo's subways — normally mentioned only in conjunction with the notorious "pushers" who force body against body during rush hour — are graffiti- and garbage-free marvels of wine-plush seats and immaculate, hospital-green interiors. The city's cars, well over three million of them, seem miraculously dent- and dirt-free. Not even taxis are allowed a comfortable layer of grunge. While waiting for fares, taxi drivers sweep huge feather dusters over their already shining cabs to banish the first offending speck of dust; inside, they festoon the upholstery with white lace doilies (removable for washing, of course) that match the white gloves they wear on duty. Not to be outdone, tour-bus drivers polish their hubcaps while their passengers sightsee, and heat wet, tightly rolled towels for the tourists to wipe the city grime from their hands and faces when they return. The common complaint that the Japanese have never invented anything worth a damn, but only imitate and refine others' inventions, is gainsaid by this wondrous innovation. The hot wipe that refreshes is even making welcome inroads in the New World: Air Canada offers it to weary, first-class and business-class passengers on all its flights.

Indeed, as our punctilious tour guide announced to us within seconds of landing at Tokyo's Narita airport, "everything is purified in Japan." Timid foreigners need not fear drinking the water from the taps or eating lettuce leaves or grapes in restaurants. Japanese chopsticks, called *hashi*, are not heavy and reusable like the Chinese variety, but light and disposable, therefore much more hygienic. As one set that came my way announced unequivocally on its plastic case: "Japanese Hashi Are Health, Perfection, Disinfected."

But the benchmark for hard-core tourists measuring hygiene abroad is the state of the public toilets. (I have an elderly aunt who, while touring Europe, kept a meticulous diary — not of art galleries, cathedrals or even restaurants — but a kind of Nielsen's rating of the continent's toilets.) Alas, the Japanese fall short here, if only

317

because certain bodily functions occupy the flip side of their fastidiousness about cleanliness. The Japanese regard relieving oneself as an unclean act, one which requires not only to be segregated in a room of its own (hence the obligatory separation of bath and toilet), but also to be treated, when possible, as if nonexistent.

Shoes, also unclean by definition, are left at the door of a Japanese home; inside, you wear slippers or, in rooms floored with tatami mats, go barefoot. When using the lavatory, however, one dons lavatory-only slippers, left outside the room in question and never transported to any other part of the house. Persons known to be on their way to the toilet are elaborately ignored; if, perchance, one is caught *in* the lavatory, the intrusion must be rectified at once. I discovered the latter when the sweet maid responsible for our welfare during our stay at a *ryokan* (a traditional Japanese inn) came to our door to thank us for a gift of a plastic maple-leaf button.

"My wife is in *there*," my husband told her, pointing solemnly at the closed door, by way of explaining why she couldn't thank me, too.

"Ah, ahhh," she breathed, a blush creeping up her waxen cheeks as she hastily shuffled backward out of the room. Clearly, the Mrs. must not be disturbed.

The unfeigned delight of the maid (who, we decided, was approximately 100 years old) upon receiving the plastic button from Canada seemed far out of proportion to the gift. But this ryokan was in Yamaguchi City in the extreme southwest of Japan, far from favoured Western tourist spots such as Kyoto, the ancient imperial capital city. And the sojourn of our group of eight automobile journalists and their wives, I fear, had the effect of a full frontal attack on the sensibilities of the ryokan staff.

We ate our meals in a private room furnished with tatami mats and tiny, knee-high, lacquered tables arranged in a rectangle around the room. Under these doll-sized surfaces, we were expected to sit decorously cross-legged, ensconced in the yukatas supplied in our rooms. Few of us, even the daintier females in our group, claimed full command of what one author has called the Japanese "insectlike facility" to fold one's feet in various ways without one's nether appendages going to sleep or otherwise behaving erratically. But two unusually large (even by Occidental standards) and hairy men in our group insisted on thrusting their capacious, hirsute feet straight under their doll tables, the better to greet the delicate, kimonoed waitresses as they moved, on their knees, from table to table around the room.

Perhaps my most enduring memory of the West insinuating its brute ways on the aesthetically sensitive East is the vision of a maid (who I doubt had ever been beyond the outskirts of Yamaguchi City) serving a Western-style breakfast to Claude, a charming bon vivant who tipped the scales at maybe 300 pounds. A bright green electric toaster incongruously plugged into the wall behind the lacquered tables produced slice after slice of toasted white bread for Claude. The maid, clad in a purple kimono tightly wrapped with a crimson sash, delivered the toast in shifts, pushing a tray back and forth across the tatami on her knees, while Claude, his chest hair increasingly crumb-ridden, happily put away an inordinate number of slices dripping with butter.

When we left the ryokan on our air-conditioned bus later that morning, the purple-and-crimson-clad toast-maid joined the rest of the ryokan staff to bow, smile and wave adieu in a perfectly symmetrical half-circle. If it were but mine, I would exchange all the bathwater in Japan for a drop of insight into the thoughts behind those heads bowed in an impeccably groomed and orchestrated farewell.

From the *Financial Post* magazine (1984). Born in Parry Sound, Ontario, in 1944, Loral Dean has lived in Germany, Cuba, Brazil and the United States. She is now in Toronto, Canadian correspondent for the *Dallas Morning News*.

DARJEELING
by Jerry Tutunjian

When I looked down, I noticed the little girl had emptied the contents of her stomach into my lap. Her mother apologized, but her words were drowned in thunder. We were flying towards the Himalayas through monsoon skies.

The script was all wrong: it wasn't supposed to be this way. According to my neatly-typed itinerary, I was supposed to have completed my journey and departed India a full week before the monsoons.

They hit India too soon: practically everywhere I went, heavy rains had already drenched the countryside. "Sahib, you should have come last week; the weather was so jolly good," was the line everywhere.

At Bagdogra airport, I met Chang, the Nepalese driver who was to take me to India's premier hill station, Darjeeling, fifty-six miles away. As I sank into his battered, made-in-Calcutta Ambassador, Chang explained that we couldn't take the main road through Kalimpong because bus drivers were on strike.

A day earlier, some passengers had roughed up a bus driver. In protest, the handful of drivers who provided service on the treacherous mountain road between Bagdogra and Darjeeling had not only gone on strike but had also blocked major intersections.

"Udder road is longer. Four, five, maybe six hours to Darjeeling," Chang explained as we started to climb the winding narrow road through dark green tea estates. The car wheezed, coughed and rattled as we kept climbing. Blanketed in fog, the black sedan seemed airborne. The wind whistled through window crevices, the radiator made anthropomorphic sounds and Chang took blind corners as if we were on a flat country road. His hand stiff on the steering wheel, a hand-rolled cigarette in his mouth, he looked as expressive as a cigar-store Indian.

Through the fog, I glimpsed slogans painted on the slopes — DRIVE LIKE HELL AND THERE YOU ARE; BETTER LATE THAN NEVER; DRIVE IN PEACE, NOT IN PIECES; LIFE IS PRECIOUS, LET'S PRESERVE IT. I was glad Cool Hand Chang couldn't read these Chinese-cookie gems at hairpin bends. His only concession to safe driving was to honk at every curve.

When I woke up four hours later, we were parking in front of the Oberoi Mount Everest Hotel. I had missed Bari, Ponkhabari, Kurseong, Sonada, Ghoom and several other mist-swathed villages.

Chang said good night and reminded me that we were to leave for Tiger Hill observation point at 4 a.m.

Unpacked, refreshed and hungry, I was at the dining hall within 30 minutes. A middle-aged magician called Sunil De amused the Indian guests with card tricks and sleight of hand. He beamed with pride every time the overfed children applauded and their parents shouted "bravo."

I couldn't take the show. I headed for my suite with its inviting fireplace, white Victorian furniture, flowers, heavy curtains, high ceilings, and a hot water bottle under the blanket.

Built in 1914 by an American architect who was refused hotel accommodation ("British Only"), Oberoi Mount Everest Hotel became the hub of the Raj social life. Every summer Calcutta sahibs and memsahibs fled here on horseback and on palanquin to escape the heat of the plains. The Oberoi is still the number one hotel in town.

As I was checking my next day's itinerary, the telephone rang and a male voice asked if I would care for a massage. "I will massage you in your room for 45 minutes. Only two dollars, Sahib."

I said: "Come on up." Half-way through the massage, I went to sleep and dreamed of multi-limbed Hindu gods walking all over me.

Another telephone call. "Good morning, sir. It's 3:20 a.m., sir. The driver is here for Tiger Hill, sir."

Tiger Hill is the first attraction most travel writers mention when they grow poetic about Darjeeling. It's a promontory (2,547 metres) from which tourists can view the sunrise over Mount Kanchenjunga (8,556 metres), the third highest peak in the world.

Although Tiger Hill is only six miles from Darjeeling, it took our

Land-Rover twenty-five minutes to climb the rutted road to the peak.

It is freezing and pitch dark, but the observation point is already crowded with expectant tourists wrapped in long shawls. As darkness slips away the onlookers gasp in expectation . . . sixty seconds pass but there is no sun. Thick cloud has blanketed the Himalayan peaks.

Some Indians start chanting hymns to coax the sun out of hiding. The sounds blow away in the wind. After twenty minutes of false expectations, the dejected crowd disperses. An American lady teaching in Hyderabad quips: "They should have built Kanchenjunga closer to Darjeeling."

I look at my spiral note book and read a paragraph copied from *Travel & Leisure*: "As you stand here, armed with a camera or a pair of binoculars, you see a perfectly round, sharp-edged disc rise slowly in the east in full orange radiance. The distant peaks of the Himalayas, which were shrouded in mist, first turn pink, then mauve, and finally orange as the sun emerges fully. Soon the horizon is dominated by the snowcapped peaks — firm, white, aglow." Some travel writers have all the luck.

An early monsoon, a melodramatic flight, intermittent diarrhea, a bus strike, a hair-rising mountain passage, an amateur magician, the big flop of Tiger Hill . . . I wondered what I was doing in India. At 36, was I getting too old for traipsing around the world? It was time for Lady Luck to make her move.

On the way back to the hotel, I noticed a shoeless urchin standing at the edge of the milky abyss selling tea. All he had was a kettle and three soiled cups. Enveloped in darkness and mist, the boy seemed like a ghost. The sugarless tea was the best I had ever tasted: it was also the cheapest. I decided to consider the tiny tea seller a good omen.

An hour later, the sun had burned the mist away. I could see toytown Darjeeling. I was ready for the Darjeeling of the Raj, tea plantations, private schools, crisp air and breathtaking mountain vistas.

After a hearty breakfast at the Oberoi (butter, jam, toasted bread, four eggs, cereal, orange juice and a full kettle of newly harvested tea), I stopped at the Happy Valley Tea Estate, the biggest in Darjeeling.

A labourer showed me how tea is cultivated and how it should be drunk. He explained the different parts of the tea bush and how taste varies from leaf to leaf. "The tea bush carries four grades of tea," he said. "The two leaves near the growing tip are the top grade; the growing tip is second in quality; the stem is third and the bottom is the lowest grade." Once harvested, tea processing is simple: from field to tea box takes only two days.

Like the tea, Darjeeling is four-tiered. On top is the Observatory Hill where a large Buddhist temple stands, adorned by hundreds of prayer flags. Like most other Buddhist temples, it has been abundantly overlaid with ornaments.

Below the temple is Chaurasta Square. In spite of its name, Chaurasta is triangular. Half a dozen curio stores sell Tibetan devil masks, Nepalese fur caps, jewellery from Bhutan, tapestries from Nagaland and turquoise-inlaid knives from Sikkim. At the entrance to the square, souvenir stores sell hand-painted photos of Himalayan panoramas. Craftsmen enlarge the black and white photos, then paint them with startling effect: green skies, iodine mountains, magenta trees, puce tea estates, lavender chalets.

I was haggling with a salesman for one of the photos when, in mid-sentence, he decided to turn the tables and buy my Pentax. When I told him the price, he inquired about his chances for employment in France. I told him that I was Canadian. He said I didn't look Canadian.

"What does a Canadian look like?" I inquired.

"Like an American," he said.

I persisted: "What does an American look like?"

He didn't miss a beat: "Like Jimmy Carter, John Travolta."

Eventually, I bought the picture for half its original price and we parted bosom friends.

In the broad piazza of Chaurasta, awkward honeymooners ride ponies and pose to be photographed by "instant photographers," mud-splattered Lhasa apsos run around, children lick saccharine ice creams. There is an air of permanent holiday.

A vantage point to observe life on Times Square is from the veranda of Windamere Hotel. From here — "the roof of the world" — you can also view the drama of everchanging Darjeeling weather. The scenery changes within seconds as clouds flirt with the jagged peaks, caress pine trees, swirl and pirouette up and down the terraced tea estates, which look like green Aztec pyramids.

Below Chaurasta is the third tier of Darjeeling, where most of the hotels are. It's also the residential area of the middle class — mostly Bengalis.

A Sikh shopkeeper I photographed asked if I had heard of his brother, a doctor in Ontario. When I asked him his brother's name, he told me it was Dr. Singh. I told him the name rang a bell.

At the bottom of the pyramid is the bazaar, where you can buy stone-hard yak cheese, loose tea at bargain prices, and impossibly hot red pepper.

The vegetables in the bazaar, like Darjeeling natives, are undersized. Bananas are no bigger than an adult's index finger, chicken eggs could pass for pigeon eggs, mangos are tomato sized. Horses, cats, chickens, flower-petals are all diminutive. I would like to believe this phenomenon is Darjeeling's way of bowing to the massive mountain in whose shadow it crouches. It's an acknowledgement of Kanchenjunga's supremacy.

A place where man's courage and strength are glamourized is the Himalayan Mountain Institute. You can see the complete gear — gloves, goggles, boots, ration box, oxygen cylinder, ropes, axe, ice screw piton — that Edmund Hillary and Tenzing Norkay took along during their Everest conquest on May 29, 1953. Now Tenzing is the director of the institute and if you hang around you may be lucky enough to see the middle-aged but still erect mountaineer. I saw him. He refused to be interviewed, saying he was busy. After years of interviews and the same half-dozen questions, Tenzing cannot be blamed for avoiding them. His assistant who, like most Indian bureaucrats, talked in a faintly antiquated idiom, said that Tenzing was training a batch of "new chaps."

Near the institute is a zoo where you can see rare animals such as the Himalayan peacock, red panda and snow leopard. Admission is less than ten cents.

Another interesting site is the Tibetan Refugee Self-Help Centre where 650 people live in traditional Tibetan style around their colourful temple. They make Tibetan bread, which has no salt and has the consistency of Silly Putty. Called *momo*, the rubbery bread is steamed. Tibetan beer, made from millet on the premises, tastes like buttermilk and is more potent than Canadian beer. Handicraft workshops make colourful rugs and wall hangings that fetch astronomical prices in North America. The workshop foreman said there was a three month waiting list for tapestries.

On one of the workshop walls was a poster of the Village People. When I asked the teenage craftsman about the poster, he said he wanted to see New York.

Tibetans came to Darjeeling in 1959 fleeing the invading Chinese army. Community leader Dorgee Tseten said: "We are grateful to India for welcoming us and the Dalai Lama, but we want to go back home to Tibet."

The self-sufficient community of Tibetans runs its own hospital, dairy, pig farm, nursery and school. Located at the other end of town, St. Paul's is one of India's two best private schools for boys, a transplanted Eton complete with neo-Gothic architecture, leafy walls, Penguin books, black-robed dons and students in natty uniforms. The boys, the sons of upper middle-class Indians, come from all parts of India. There are very few "townies" among them.

Rector Hari Dang talked about the school and its history. He sounded like Sidney Greenstreet. He had a framed photograph of British comedian Norman Wisdom on his desk. "Norman is a good friend," said the rector. In a rich baritone, he recited the names of some of the distinguished alumni: military strategist D.K. Polit, industrialist D.G. Aratoon, millionaire Haik Sookias — "the elite of India." At St. Paul's, it is always 1900.

Not far away is another relic of the Raj — the Darjeeling Gymkhana Club. Corridors that once echoed to the brisk footsteps of British colonels are now dusty and dank: the only sound is the shuffle of the tired Nepalese cleaning woman. The billiard room, library and lounge are forlorn. In one of the musty corridors hangs a hunting scene called *Death*.

You don't have to be a diehard British imperialist to feel nostalgia for the glorious days of the Raj. But as an Indian friend wisely pointed out later that day, "Nostalgia excuses everything."

On the way out of the club, I noticed a number of businessmen attending a reception for tea-growers in the grand hall. They seemed like people who had walked into someone else's dream.

Darjeeling is used to the juxtaposition of diverse cultures and memories; it is the downtown of Central Asia. On its streets you see

Gurkhas wearing curved knives, Sikhs in the obligatory turbans, Tibetan lamas in crimson togas, Lepcha men with long pony tails, Magars, Tawangs, Newars, Buthias and Sherpas. This is where one world ends and another begins. As Jan Morris wrote, "Darjeeling stands on the edge of mysteries." From here you can see peaks in Nepal, Bhutan, Sikkim and China. This is not Lost Horizon country, but a real place with an other-worldly air to it.

The town of 50,000 is so postcard perfect you might think it was painted by a talented eight-year-old; the mountains properly overwhelming and snow-capped, the chalets and villas perched on the green terraces. Tea gardens cascade down steep slopes, seemingly happy natives cultivate the aromatic tea, and forests stretch as far as you can see.

Darjeeling is India's cool, aloof balcony. Suspended at 2,128 metres it's far away from sweltering Calcutta. Far down, along the plain of the Ganges, life is sultry, tumultuous, often squalid. Here, you can feel and touch the sky. Here, it's forever Sunday afternoon.

Darjeeling means the Place of Thunderbolt. Few other places are so badly misnamed.

From the Toronto *Globe and Mail* (1984). Jerry Tutunjian was born in Jerusalem, 1945, and came to Canada in 1965. After working in a lumber mill he took journalism at the Ryerson Polytechnical Institute, Toronto, and worked on small town newspapers in Ontario. He is editor of *LeisureWays* magazine, distributed in Ontario.